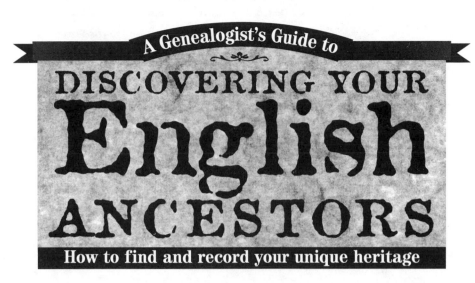

A Genealogist's Guide to

DISCOVERING YOUR
English
ANCESTORS

How to find and record your unique heritage

Paul Milner & Linda Jonas

BETTERWAY BOOKS
CINCINNATI, OHIO
www.familytreemagazine.com

DEDICATION

*To James Bertie Walter Milner, Paul's father,
whose death began Paul's quest to find his ancestors.*

*To Beverly Joyce Gibbs, Linda's mother, whose mysterious past
began Linda's quest to find her ancestors.*

*To our ancestors whose lives continue to inspire us
to find out more about our pasts.*

A Genealogist's Guide to Discovering Your English Ancestors. Copyright © 2000 by Paul Milner and Linda Jonas. Manufactured in the United States of America. All rights reserved. No part of this book may be reproduced in any form or by any electronic or mechanical means including information storage and retrieval systems without permission in writing from the publisher, except by a reviewer, who may quote brief passages in a review. Published by Betterway Books, an imprint of F&W Publications, Inc., 1507 Dana Avenue, Cincinnati, Ohio 45207. (800) 289-0963. First edition.

Other fine Betterway Books are available from your local bookstore or on our Web site at www.familytreemagazine.com.

04   03   02   01   00   5   4   3   2   1

Library of Congress Cataloging-in-Publication Data

Milner, Paul
    A genealogist's guide to discovering your English ancestors / by Paul Milner and Linda Jonas.
       p.   cm.
    Includes index.
    ISBN 1-55870-536-8 (alk. paper)
       1. England—Genealogy—Handbooks, manuals, etc. 2. British Americans—Genealogy—Handbooks, manuals, etc. I. Jonas, Linda. II Title.

CS412.M55   2000
929'.1'072041—dc21   00-036047
                                                                                          CIP

Editor: Sharon DeBartolo Carmack, CG
Production editor: Christine Doyle
Production coordinator: Mark Griffin
Interior designer: Sandy Conopeotis Kent
Cover designer: Wendy Dunning

Permissions

Some material in this publication is reprinted by permission of The Church of Jesus Christ of Latter-day Saints. In granting permission for this use of copyrighted material, the Church does not imply or express either endorsement or authorization of this publication.

Crown copyright material in the Public Record Office is reproduced by permission of the Controller of Her Majesty's Stationary Office.

The civil registration certificates and index entries are reprinted with permission of the Office for National Statistics.

The parish boundary map of Northumberland (Figure 11-1) and index listing for part of Northumberland County (Figure 10-3) are one of a series of parish maps of the counties of Great Britain appearing by kind permission of Cecil Humphery-Smith, editor of *The Atlas and Index of Parish Registers,* and the Trustees of The Institute of Heraldic and Genealogical Studies, Canterbury, England.

The Marriage Allegation and Bonds for Robert Dixon and Mary Dixon, 1805 (Figures 10-12, 10-13) and the Marriage Allegation for William Dixon and Dorothy Robson, 1798 (Figure 10-16) are reproduced by permission of Durham University Library.

Permission to reprint the Stamfordham Parish Web page provided by the author Brian Pears.

Acknowledgments

Paul and Linda, although thousands of miles apart, have been excited by the process of learning from one another while writing this book. Finding our English ancestors is a subject about which we are both passionate.

Of course, without the assistance of many others nothing could have been done to create this book. We first wish to thank the many students, clients, workshop participants, and library patrons who over the years have asked questions forcing us to learn and to become better teachers.

We are indebted to the board members of the British Isles Family History Society–U.S.A. and the board members of the British Interest Group of Wisconsin and Illinois for their continual support and for taking over many of our presidential duties as we were writing this book.

We gratefully acknowledge the following researchers who read our book and gave us valuable input: Nancy Lee Bier, Nancy Ellen Carlberg, Janice Gibson Cloud, Joan Georgick, Frederick A. Hill, Mark D. Howells, Sandra Luebking, Mary D. McKinnon, and Darris Williams.

We thank the staff and volunteers of the Family History Library of the Church of Jesus Christ of Latter-day Saints for their continuing efforts to make accessible the original records and tools needed by family historians all over the world. Family history would not be as popular today as it is without their ongoing efforts.

Finally, we want to thank Paul's wife, Carol Becker; his children Heather and Eric Milner; Linda's husband, Bill Jonas; and her children John, Stephen, Robert, Katie, Annie, Betsie, and Julie Jonas for their ongoing patience, support, and interest.

About the Authors

Paul Milner is a native of northern England. He is a professional genealogical researcher who has specialized in British Isles research for the past twenty years. For the past six years he has been the president of the British Interest Group of Wisconsin and Illinois (BIGWILL). During the same time period he has written and edited the society's newsletter. He writes book reviews for the Federation of Genealogical Societies's quarterly journal, *Forum*.

Paul is a nationally known and popular speaker at genealogical conferences and seminars. His speciality is the British Isles, and his lectures typically draw audiences of several hundred genealogists.

Linda Jonas, a U.S. native, is the president of the British Isles Family History Society–U.S.A. During her presidency, the society has become a well-respected international organization. The society hosts a prestigious annual three-day seminar on British Isles research; it is consistently sold out. Linda has acted as seminar chair for the past three years, and under her guidance the event has offered up-to-date information by the most respected and experienced speakers from around the world. She has also designed the highly acclaimed society Web site and writes the *BIFHS-USA Guide to British Isles Research* found there.

Linda Jonas has been a full-time professional family historian for the past twenty years and has focused on helping Americans find their British Isles ancestry. She is a popular lecturer and writer on all aspects of U.S. and British Isles research. Linda has been supervisor, staff trainer, and instructor at the Los Angeles Family History Center, which holds the largest British Isles resource collection outside of Salt Lake City. She recently moved to McLean, Virginia.

Icons Used in This Book

Case Study

Examples of this book's advice at work

Printed Source

Directories, books, pamphlets and other paper archives

CD Source

Databases and other information available on CD-ROM

Reminder

"Don't-Forget" items to keep in mind

\di'fin\ *vb*

Definitions

Terminology and jargon explained

Research Tip

Ways to make research more efficient

For More Info

Where to turn for more in-depth coverage

See Also

Where in this book to find related information

Idea Generator

Techniques and prods for further thinking

Sources

Where to go for information, supplies, etc.

Important

Information and tips you can't overlook

Step By Step

Walkthroughs of important procedures

Internet Source

Where on the web to find what you need

Technique

How to conduct research, solve problems, and get answers

Library/Archive Source

Repositories that might have the information you need

Timesaver

Shaving minutes and hours off the clock

Money Saver

Getting the most out of research dollars

Tip

Ways to make research more efficient

Notes

Thoughts, ideas and related insights

Warning

Stop before you make a mistake

Table of Contents At a Glance

1   Getting Started, *1*

2   Research Process Guidelines, *5*

3   Uniqueness of English Research, *13*

4   Accessing the Resources of the Internet, *27*

5   Accessing the Resources of Libraries and Family History Centers, *35*

6   Civil Registration and Its Indexes, *50*

7   Analyzing Civil Registration Certificates, *69*

8   Census, *85*

9   Post-1857 Probate Records, *118*

10 Parish Registers, *131*

11 Pre-1858 Probate Records, *160*

12 What's Next?, *175*

Index, *180*

Table of Contents

1   Getting Started, 1

Find out how to get started in genealogical research and specifically in English research. We discuss the joys of seeking our English ancestry. We encourage researchers to go beyond merely assembling pedigree charts and to seek an understanding of the historical context in which their ancestors lived. We explain the book's organization and its focus on the tools and records that make research easier in the United States than in England.

2   Research Process Guidelines, 5

We summarize how to search for one's English ancestors, describing where to start and emphasizing the need to clearly identify the goal of the research. The modern research process consists of four steps: using the Internet, visiting local libraries, researching at Family History Centers, and climaxing with taking a trip to England.

3   Uniqueness of English Research, 13

English research is different from U.S. research. We examine the major differences, including geographic and political terms, English record keeping, the importance of place, family history societies, money, religion, class, and special problems.

4   Accessing the Resources of the Internet, 27

The resources of the Internet can be overwhelming to the beginner. We show how to commence genealogical research using the Web site of the Family History Library, then how to use the most important sites for English genealogy.

5   Accessing the Resources of Libraries and Family History Centers, 35

See what to look for in a public library. Learn about the Family History Library and how the majority of its records can be accessed anywhere in the world through the Family History Centers. We give the beginner a good overview of what general resources are available and how to access them before delving into records designed to find their particular ancestors. We show the researcher how to conduct preliminary English searches by using the International Genealogical Index (IGI), the Ancestral File, and the Family History Library Catalog.

NOTE FOR READERS: The following chapters deal with individual record types. We will trace one family through the records, showing how we accumulate more information with each document. For each major record group we provide background on what the record is and when and why it was created. We explain the actual recording process. We give step-by-step guidelines and illustrations for searching the records without going to England. We highlight available tools to make the process easier, tell you what to do if you can't find your ancestor in the records, provide bibliographies for further research, and give suggestions for steps to follow next.

6   Civil Registration and Its Indexes, *50*

Civil Registration began in England and Wales on 1 July 1837. All births, marriages, and deaths are recorded in one national system. We describe the system, why it was set up, and how to use the indexes.

7   Analyzing Civil Registration Certificates, *69*

We now have our first English documents. Here is where we will learn to analyze records in depth. We provide illustrations of each certificate and show how to evaluate the accuracy of the information found.

8   Census, *85*

Genealogically useful census returns began in England in 1841 and continued every ten years (except 1941) to the present. The records are geographically organized. We illustrate the process for finding people and places in census records. We show how to use census records in conjunction with civil registration records to reconstruct entire families and find places of origin needed to advance into probate records and parish registers.

9   Post-1857 Probate Records, *118*

Since 1858 all probate records in England and Wales have been processed in one central court system, so only one set of indexes needs to be examined. We describe the probate process, illustrate the probate calendar and provide instructions for its use, and show how to get copies of the full will or letter of administration.

10   Parish Registers, *131*

The parish registers of the Established Church (Church of England) include records of baptisms, marriages, and burials. They are the principal records used to work backward from the mid-nineteenth century. We describe the indexes and tools that are available to help you find your ancestors in the parish registers. We examine each record and show what to expect.

11   Pre-1858 Probate Records, *160*

We summarize the pre-1858 probate process. We present the ecclesiastical probate jurisdictions, the probate records, and how to access them.

12   What's Next?, *175*

We make suggestions on the next steps for more advanced research and discuss what tools are available to guide you. We encourage readers to visit their ancestral homeland and to write their family history.

Index, *180*

ONE

Getting Started

Whether you are new to genealogy or have been researching for years, you are now ready to trace your English ancestors. You are in for a real treat. No matter who you are and no matter where you live, you can find your English ancestors! *A Genealogist's Guide to Discovering Your English Ancestors* will give you step-by-step instructions for tracing your English ancestry without traveling to England. You will learn about the most important records for English research and see the latest techniques for using them anywhere in the world.

WHO ARE YOU?

1. You were born in England or are a child of a recent immigrant. You are new to genealogy. You live outside of England and want to know how to find your English ancestors.
2. Your ancestors left England many generations ago. You are an experienced researcher and have traced your ancestors in the country where you are now living. You know that your ancestors came from England, and you want to know how to start your English research.
3. You've done some English research but are now looking for ideas.

No matter what your circumstances, we can help you. Linda Jonas specializes in tracing immigrant ancestry. All of her English ancestors came to America before the Revolutionary War. Paul Milner is an immigrant. He and his ancestors were born in England, but Paul has done his research since moving to the United States. Each of us has more than twenty years experience doing English research from outside of England. We can assure you that a trip to England is not a necessity for doing English research. If you are looking for a reason to go to England, though, don't worry. We will give you one, but it may not be what you expect.

If you are new to genealogy, you will soon find that tracing your family is challenging and exciting. Most genealogists believe that once you start looking for your family, you will be "hooked for life." It can be one of the most interesting and enjoyable things you've ever done. If you are an experienced researcher, you already know the joys of finding your family. But you are in for an even bigger thrill now! As exciting as tracing your American ancestors can be, there is not much that can compare to finding the origins of your immigrant ancestors.

WHO ARE YOUR IMMIGRANT ANCESTORS?

Some people begin their genealogy looking for famous ancestors or hoping to find royal lines. A few people are even disappointed when they think that their immigrant ancestor was just an "average guy." Be assured that your immigrant was not average. Your immigrants never led "normal" lives. These are people who did something extraordinary; they left their homes, possessions, families, friends, and homeland forever to try to find a better life.

Most immigrants left England for economic reasons. A few of your ancestors left for religious reasons, like the Puritans who came to New England from 1629 to 1640. Sometimes there were both religious and economic motives. Some of your immigrants did not come by choice. For example, English prisons were cleared and convicts were shipped to the American colonies. There were even some women and children kidnapped from the countryside or from the streets of cities such as London to provide needed colonial laborers. But whatever the reason for leaving England, all immigrants left the only life they had known and came to their new country with hope for a brighter future.

When your ancestors arrived in the new land, they may have been disappointed. Your ancestors did not find the American streets to be "paved with gold." No matter when or where they arrived, whether they came to the wilderness or came to a large city already settled with people they knew from their homeland, your immigrants were pioneers. They all have incredible stories to tell.

WHAT DO YOU KNOW ABOUT YOUR ENGLISH ANCESTORS?

Notes

How did your ancestors live in England? Of what social class were they? What religion did they practice? How did social class and religion influence their lives? What were your ancestors' occupations, and how did they practice them? What kind of work did the women do? Did your ancestors stay in one place, or did they move around? Did your ancestors receive poor relief (welfare)? Where did your ancestors meet, fall in love, and get married? Where did the women have their babies? How many children did they have? Did all of the children survive to adulthood? Did your ancestors go to school? Did any of them attend universities?

You are not expected to know the answers to these questions yet, but you will soon learn how to find out about your ancestors' lives in England.

Why did your immigrant ancestor leave England? What was happening in England at that time? Where did he live, and how was his life there? What were the circumstances when he left? Whom did he leave behind? Did your ancestor travel alone? How difficult was the farewell? Did he have property to sell? Did he distribute goods to family or friends? What did he decide to take with him? How much money did he have? Were there people he loved that were left behind and never seen again? Did he find a better life? Was it worth it?

You are not expected to know the answers to these questions either. Throughout the book, we will examine various sources that will help you to discover why your immigrant ancestor left England.

HOW CAN YOU FIND OUT MORE ABOUT YOUR ENGLISH ANCESTORS?

Finding more about your English ancestors is the focus of this book, so just follow the examples. *A Genealogist's Guide to Discovering Your English Ancestors* is unlike any other book on genealogical research. It is a personal conversation between you and the authors. Together, we will research a real family. We will search for this family in civil registration, census returns, parish registers, and probate records to see what we can find out about the family members and the places where they lived. You will learn what each record is and why it was created. Then we'll see who actually recorded the information and examine the reliability of the evidence it contains. We'll look at each document in detail and discuss how to weave the bare facts into a story about our ancestors. As we search for "our" family, you will see how you can find the same kind of information for your own ancestors. Together we will get onto the Internet, walk into a Family History Center, see how to find the sources you need, and talk about how to read and interpret them. You'll discover why the documents may not tell what you expect. You'll find suggestions to solve problems you may encounter and learn where to go next.

IT'S EASIER TO TRACE ANCESTORS OUTSIDE OF ENGLAND THAN IN ENGLAND!

That may be hard to believe, but it's true. The English records that you will use to begin your English research are civil registration, census returns, parish registers, and probate records. Because of the way records are organized and stored in England, it is actually easier to do research from this side of the ocean than in England. Research in England involves traveling to many record offices. You will not have to do that.

Important

The field of family history is experiencing some very exciting changes. Because of these, your ability to conduct effective research from your hometown is far greater today than it ever has been. It is easier today than it was even a few months ago, and it keeps getting better and better!

Because of the microfilming efforts of the Genealogical Society of Utah, almost all of the original records you need to begin your research are available from the Family History Library through its Family History Centers worldwide. That means that you can do the majority of your research in one building. Furthermore, because of the indexing efforts of family history societies throughout the world, there are many new indexes to make your research easier. Several indexes are available on compact discs containing vast amounts of information never before available. Indexes for home use can also be purchased in other formats. Many background materials are easily available over the Internet or by loan through a public library. This book will give specific step-by-step instructions for accessing and using the information available from the Internet, libraries, and especially Family History Centers.

You can start your research in the comfort of your own home. You will then use the services of libraries and Family History Centers in your area. Therefore, **this book focuses on these three basic search procedures:**

- the Internet
- local public and university libraries
- Family History Centers

We will examine each of these approaches in the next chapter.

The last search procedure is a trip to England. You won't need us for that. Your trip will be a celebration of your ancestral past and the culmination of your efforts.

YOU CAN FIND OUT HOW YOUR ANCESTORS LIVED

Your ancestors had more than three events (birth, marriage, and death) in their lives. The fascinating stories of how they lived will not fit on a pedigree chart and family group sheet—the standard genealogical forms. Discovering the stories of your ancestors will bring real meaning to your research. There are clues to your ancestors' lives in England in public documents. This book will point you to English documents that will allow you to retrace your ancestors' steps and reconstruct their stories. But it is up to you to go beyond compiling the names, dates, and places that fit on a pedigree chart and begin to find out how your ancestors really lived. Once you have discovered the stories about your family members, you will understand more about them, your country, their country, and yourself. Your English ancestors have beautiful and often heart-wrenching stories to tell. It is up to you to tell them.

So let's go find our English ancestors!

TWO

Research Process Guidelines

WHERE SHOULD I START?

If you are completely new to genealogy, start with a trip to your local library or bookstore to find books on general family history research. You can also borrow books for beginners from any of your friends who are doing family research. Read any and all books you can obtain on how to get started. Use the guidelines and ideas presented in these books to help you collect what you have available in your own house and among your relatives. Then organize your genealogy collection so you know what you have and what you need.

Good books to get you started are

Allen, Desmond Walls. *First Steps in Genealogy: A Beginner's Guide to Researching Your Family History*. Cincinnati: Betterway Books, 1998.

Carmack, Sharon DeBartolo. *Organizing Your Family History Search: Efficient & Effective Ways to Gather and Protect Your Genealogical Research*. Cincinnati: Betterway Books, 1999.

Croom, Emily Anne. *Unpuzzling Your Past: A Basic Guide to Genealogy*. (3rd ed.). Cincinnati: Betterway Books, 1995.

Greenwood, Val D. *The Researcher's Guide to American Genealogy*. (3rd ed.). Baltimore, Md.: Genealogical Publishing Company, 2000.

Printed Source

A brief introduction to family history research called *Discovering Your Family Tree* is one of the guides from the Family History Library. You can read it online at <http://www.familysearch.org/sg/> where you can also view and print the basic forms that are necessary for doing genealogy: a pedigree chart, family group record, and a research log.

IDENTIFYING YOUR IMMIGRANT ANCESTOR

Many genealogists have made the mistake of finding that their immigrant was born in England, finding someone by the same name there, and assuming that

Warning

Technique

they have found their ancestor. **In the excitement of finding out that an immigrant ancestor is from England, you, too, will want to immediately start researching in English records. Don't!** A mistake like this can lead to years of tracing an incorrect family line. It is essential that you have enough information about your immigrant to distinguish him from the many others of the same name in England. Find out everything that you can about your ancestor. It is helpful to know your ancestor's full name; place of origin; dates of birth, marriage, and death; spouse's name; children's names; parent's names; date of immigration; occupation; religion; and cousins', friends', and associates' names. Of course, you don't have to know all of that before commencing English research, but the more information you have, the easier it will be to identify your ancestor in English records.

Clues to the origin of your ancestor will be found in the country to which he immigrated. Therefore, if your ancestor came to the United States, look for his origins in U.S. records. It is beyond the scope of this book to show you how to find records in North America, but the following suggestions will provide a brief reminder of records to check.

Start looking for information that may be available in your home or in the homes of other family members. Some of your ancestors may have left diaries or verbally passed down their stories to their children. Search for diaries, letters, photos, and family bibles, as well as personal items, such as tools, clothing, and sewing implements. The more you can find, the more you will know about your ancestors' lives. Do not give up after asking your immediate family. Contact aunts, cousins, and even family friends.

Once you have examined sources at home, look for documents in the country where your ancestor settled. As with any ancestor, it is always best to start your immigrant's life story at the end. Genealogy is done in reverse, working backward through time. Therefore, you will begin to reconstruct your immigrant's story by searching for books and documents that were generated after his death. Look for family histories or genealogies that have been written about your immigrant ancestor or his descendants. Search the Internet to see if someone else has information on your family. A distant relative may have already done much of the work for you. Look for local histories that may contain details about your ancestor or his community.

After searching the Internet, looking through books, and contacting relatives, you are ready to look at original records. Often the most revealing records are those written after your ancestor's death. Start first with your ancestor's probate record, then look for his obituaries. There is often more than one obituary, and these can be found in church, ethnic, society, and town newspapers. An immigrant ancestor's entire family needs to be traced, and often his friends and associates as well. When looking for documents for your ancestor, look for the same documents for each of his children, brothers, sisters, spouses, etc. Search for passenger lists and naturalization records of all family members. Look through land records, court records, christenings and marriages, military records, death records, etc. Each of these records will tell you more about your ancestor, and one of these records may tell you his hometown. Each document will lead you to others until you have enough to compile your ancestor's life story.

There are many published immigrant indexes that will help you find your ancestor's origins. The best for North American researchers is

Filby, P. William, with Mary K. Meyer, eds. *Passenger and Immigration Lists Index.* 3 vols. plus annual supplement. Detroit: Gale Research Co., 1981–.

Printed Source

The title of the book is misleading. It is not just an index to passenger lists; it is an index to all records that allude to immigrant status. These can include census records, land records, naturalization records, and many others. You will find the name of the immigrant, a date in which he appeared in the records, the place where the record was found, and the book or article from which the index was taken. Note that the date is not necessarily the date that your ancestor immigrated. It just means that your ancestor was in that place in the year mentioned. The series originally contained three volumes and has annual supplements. The title changes with each volume as the number of indexed passengers increases. You must check every volume of Filby's indexes. Better yet, you can search them on compact disc, Family Tree Maker's Family Archive CD 354, *Passenger and Immigration Lists Index, 1538–1940* (1999 Edition). If you do not find your immigrant indexed in the above source, then check this reference for a list of additional sources:

Filby, P. William, ed. *Passenger and Immigration Lists Bibliography 1538–1900: Being a Guide to Published Lists of Arrivals in the United States and Canada.* 2nd ed. Detroit: Gale Research Co., 1988.

After you have read a basic genealogical guidebook and have assembled clues to the origins of your immigrant ancestor, you will be ready to begin your English research. Now is when the fun really starts!

THE MODERN RESEARCH PROCESS FOR FINDING YOUR ENGLISH ANCESTORS

Technology is changing the research process. **So let's outline a modern four-step research process,** with more details in later chapters:

1. Internet Search
2. Library Search
3. Visits to Family History Centers
4. Trip to England

Step By Step

1. Internet Search

An Internet search should be your first step. If you do not have access to the Internet at home, you can often learn to use it at a public or university library. Let's divide the Internet search into a two-stage process.

The first stage is the surname search to identify what research has been done on your name. Some people will have entire Web sites devoted to a particular

Warning

family. Others may post queries about families they are researching. Contact the individuals who put the information onto the Internet and find out what documentation they will share with you. This way you will avoid the struggle of searching for solutions to problems already solved. Do get the documentation you need. **Be skeptical of all research you find on the Internet (or in print) until you have personally verified the material and obtained copies of the original records.**

The second stage is to use the Internet to find out about your ancestor's environment. Look for information about the area in which your ancestor lived, his occupation, or his military service. Many family history societies now have online information about the individual parishes within their county. This may include photographs or histories of the church or village, information about the records that have survived for the community, and even lists of people. You can go to other sites to find out about specific occupations. Check out what resources, guides, or indexes have been published. You may be able to purchase many from the county family history society. Many society members will also look up information for you in specific resources they own or can access.

You will find specific Internet sites to search in chapter four: Accessing the Resources of the Internet.

2. Library Search

This step complements and expands upon what you have found on the Internet.

Visit your local public library and ask if any libraries in the area have genealogy collections. If not, you will still be able to borrow books through inter-library loan. Don't forget the university libraries in your area; many have good collections on English history and geography. See if anyone is researching your surname, and check for materials about how your ancestors lived.

Suggestions appear in chapter five: Accessing the Resources of Libraries and Family History Centers.

For More Info

3. Family History Centers: Source for Original Records and Indexes

After you have searched the Internet and local libraries, your next step is to search the original records. This is the most exciting part of genealogy. For anyone outside of England, the place to start looking for copies of original records is the Family History Library (FHL) and its network of Family History Centers (FHCs). Most of the indexes and records that we will discuss are available through your nearest Family History Center. Read about the Family History Library in chapter five.

4. Trip to England: The Final Step in the Research Process

Of course, you want an excuse to go to England, don't you? Well, it is not to do research, at least not on the first trip. Yes, you may need to go to a County Record Office or to the Public Record Office to get a document that was not available on microfilm, but do not spend a lot of time in record offices. You can usually hire someone to get a copy for you.

The reasons for your trip are to sightsee and visit the villages and towns where your ancestors lived. You can easily find out what life was like for your ancestors. Go see the churches, the village hall, the market square, the factories, the farms, and the local pubs. You may be able to walk streets that your ancestor once walked or to stand in front of the font where your ancestor was baptized. Talk to the local people, listen to how they speak, and learn what is important to people in that part of the country. Some of the people may know stories of those who emigrated long ago. You may even find that you have relatives living there. Get a sense of the culture of the area. It is different from other parts of England.

Visiting England may be a once-in-a-lifetime trip. Don't waste it by spending all your time in record offices. Experience life in England and explore your ancestral roots.

VERIFY ALL EVIDENCE

No matter where you obtain your information, everything you find needs to be verified by examining the original source. It is tempting, for example, to accept the word of relatives living in England because "they should know." Never take anybody's word for anything! Memories fade, and people make mistakes. Furthermore, just because something is in print doesn't make it true. Indexes, books, or online databases are no substitute for the original record. The original record may give more information that is not recorded in the index, and it will often contain further clues.

Reminder

We will now look at an example from the 1881 census of England to show why you must always examine the original records, if possible.

Let's say that your ancestor is Henry Goddard. You know that there was a census taken in England in 1881, and you want to see if Henry was still alive then. In this case, there is a marvelous new index that can make your search easy. We will use this index in chapter eight, Census. But for now, all you need to know is that you will be able to find a complete transcript of the census. Look at Figure 2-1. Henry Goddard is in the 1881 census transcript for St. Pancras, London. His name appears in the ninth entry from the bottom of the page. Henry was eighty years old, and his occupation was "Door Keeper H +." The "+" means that the occupation stated on the census record was too long to fit in this field. We know that if we look at the census on microfilm we will see his occupation more completely spelled out, but a more complete description of "Door Keeper H +" may not sound too important. Henry was living with his wife, "Kis J.," and a servant, Elizabeth Cox. We also want to examine entries for his neighbors to find out who they were. He was living next to a man named Karl Wass whose occupation was "Author Politi +." We don't recognize this man as a famous author. Now look at Figure 2-2, which is a copy of the census return on microfilm. Henry Goddard is on the fifth line from the bottom of the page. Here his occupation is given in full: "Door Keeper House of Lords." Wow! Wouldn't you want to know that your ancestor was not just any doorkeeper, but a doorkeeper at the House of Lords? Look at the neighbor above him. His

1881 CENSUS—AS ENUMERATED, COUNTY: MIDDLESEX											

Lndn St Pancras , 0211 59 47 PAGE: 20337

CENSUS DATA © BRITISH CROWN COPYRIGHT 1982.
MICROFICHE EDITION OF THE INDEXES © COPYRIGHT 1990, BY CORPORATION OF THE PRESIDENT OF THE CHURCH OF JESUS CHRIST OF LATTER-DAY SAINTS.

CENSUS PLACE	HOUSEHOLD ADDRESS	SURNAME FORENAME	RELATIONSHIP TO HEAD		AGE	SEX	OCCUPATION	CO	WHERE BORN PARISH	NOTE	PIECE RG11/	FOLIO NO	PAGE NO	FILM NUMBER
Lndn St Pancras	35 Maitland Pk+	TARLETON	Anne B.	Wife	M	40	F	---	WOR	Astwood Bank		0211	59	47	1341046
Lndn St Pancras	35 Maitland Pk+	TARLETON	James R.	Son	-	14	M	Scholar	WAR	Birmingham		0211	59	47	1341046
Lndn St Pancras	35 Maitland Pk+ /	PLAYER	Ann	Lodg	M	56	F	Annuitant	HAM	Portsmouth		0211	59	47	1341046
Lndn St Pancras	35 Maitland Pk+	PLAYER	Caroline	Daur	U	25	F	---	HAM	Southsea		0211	59	47	1341046
Lndn St Pancras	35 Maitland Pk+ /	HUSS	Irina J.	Lodg	U	34	F	Teacher Of	GER			0211	59	47	1341046
Lndn St Pancras	36 Maitland Pk+ //	PETTIFANT	Victoria M.	Head	W	43	F	Annuitant				0211	59	47	1341046
Lndn St Pancras	36 Maitland Pk+	PETTIFANT	Bertha F.	Daur	U	27	F	---				0211	59	47	1341046
Lndn St Pancras	36 Maitland Pk+	PETTIFANT	Alice M.	Daur	U	23	F	---				0211	59	47	1341046
Lndn St Pancras	36 Maitland Pk+	PETTIFANT	Carria J.	Daur	U	19	F	---				0211	59	47	1341046
Lndn St Pancras	36 Maitland Pk+	PETTIFANT	Alfred G.	Son	U	17	M	Assist Libra+	WSI	W Vincent		0211	59	47	1341046
Lndn St Pancras	36 Maitland Pk+	PETTIFANT	Fanny Y.	Daur	U	13	F	Scholar	WSI	W Vincent		0211	59	47	1341046
Lndn St Pancras	36 Maitland Pk+	MAISON	John H.	Neph	U	10	M	Scholar	WSI	Barbadoes		0211	59	47	1341046
Lndn St Pancras	36 Maitland Pk+	HIND	Clarena	SisL	W	64	F	Annuitant	WOR	Fordington		0211	59	47	1341046
Lndn St Pancras	36 Maitland Pk+	BORNSHOOK	Charles	Vist	M	48	M	Annuitant	CON	Launceston		0211	59	47	1341046
Lndn St Pancras	36 Maitland Pk+	BORNSHOOK	Eliza M.	Vist	M	43	F	---	CON	Launceston		0211	59	47	1341046
Lndn St Pancras	36 Maitland Pk+	JONES	Sarah A.	Serv	U	25	F	Gen Serv	GLA	Pontypool		0211	59	47	1341046
Lndn St Pancras	37 Maitland Pk+ //	CARPENTER	Elizabeth	Head	U	42	F	Annuitant	MID	St Johns Wood		0211	59	47	1341046
Lndn St Pancras	37 Maitland Pk+ /	SHORT	Elizabeth	Lodg	U	40	F	Governess P	SCT	Glasgow		0211	59	47	1341046
Lndn St Pancras	37 Maitland Pk+	BATNALL	Newman W.	Lodg	U	25	M	Clerk Commerc+	LAN	Warrington		0211	59	47	1341046
Lndn St Pancras	37 Maitland Pk+	BATNALL	Edward F.	Lodg	U	34	M	Artist In O				0211	59	47	1341046
Lndn St Pancras	37 Maitland Pk+ /	MORGAN	Charles H.	Lodg	U	37	M	Artist In O				0211	59	47	1341046
Lndn St Pancras	38 Maitland Pk+	EVANS	Alfred	Lodg	U	56	M	Journalist				0211	59	47	1341046
Lndn St Pancras	38 Maitland Pk+ //	KELLY	Mary F.	Head	M	32	F	---				0211	59	48	1341046
Lndn St Pancras	38 Maitland Pk+	KELLY	Martha D.	Daur	-	10	F	Scholar				0211	59	48	1341046
Lndn St Pancras	38 Maitland Pk+	THORN	James A.	Vist	U	25	M	Annuitant				0211	59	48	1341046
Lndn St Pancras	38 Maitland Pk+	THORN	Helen	Vist	U	20	F	Annuitant	USA	--- (F)		0211	59	48	1341046
Lndn St Pancras	38 Maitland Pk+	GREEN	Rose	Serv	U	22	F	Gen Serv	OXF	--- (F)		0211	59	48	1341046
Lndn St Pancras	Maitland Pk+	KILLENBOCK	Annie	Serv	U	20	F	Gen Serv	NTH	Kings bury		0211	59	48	1341046
Lndn S	Maitland Pk+ //	KAST	Gustav	Head	M	34	M	Ivory Wker Em+	GER	--- (F)		0211	59	48	1341046
Lndn S	Maitland Pk+	KAST	Fanny	Wife	M	33	F	---	GER	--- (F)		0211	59	48	1341046
Lndn S	Maitland Pk+	KAST	Ella	Daur	-	5	F	---	MID	St Pancras		0211	59	48	1341046
Lndn S	Maitland Pk+	KAST	Hilda	Daur	-	3	F	---	MID	St Pancras		0211	59	48	1341046
Lndn S	Maitland Pk+	TAYLOR	James	Bord	U	27	M	Commercial Cl+	FOI	--- (B S)		0211	59	48	1341046
Lndn S	Maitland Pk+	SCHMTZ	Rudolf	Bord	U	27	M	Commercial Cl+	GER	--- (F)		0211	59	48	1341046
Lndn S	Maitland Pk+ /	GAVELY	Frank	Head	U	24	M	Medical Stude+	SUR	Nenrick		0211	59	48	1341046
Lndn S	Maitland Pk+	GAVELY	Harry	Bro	U	21	M	Medical Stude+	SUR	Nenrick		0211	59	48	1341046
Lndn St Pancras	40 Maitland Pk+ //	WILLIS	Edwin	Head	M	58	M	Organ Builder	MID	Christchurch		0211	59	48	1341046
Lndn St Pancras	41 Maitland Pk+	WILLIS	Mary	Wife	M	58	F	---	MID	St Pancras		0211	59	48	1341046
Lndn St Pancras	41 Maitland Pk+ //	WASS	Karl	Head	M	63	M	Author Politi+	GER	--- (F)		0211	59	48	1341046
Lndn St Pancras	41 Maitland Pk+	WASS	Jenny	Wife	M	66	F	---	GER	---		0211	59	48	1341046
Lndn St Pancras	41 Maitland Pk+	WASS	Elain	Daur	U	26	F	---	MID	St Pancras		0211	59	48	1341046
Lndn St Pancras	41 Maitland Pk+	DENNICH	Helen	Serv	U	57	F	General Serv+	GER	--- (F)		0211	59	48	1341046
Lndn St Pancras	42 Maitland Pk+ //	GODDARD	Henry	Head	M	80	M	Door Keeper H+	SUR	---		0211	59	48	1341046
Lndn St Pancras	42 Maitland Pk+	GODDARD	Kis J.	Wife	M	60	F	---	ESS	Herongate		0211	59	48	1341046
Lndn St Pancras	42 Maitland Pk+	COX	Elizabeth	Serv	U	13	F	Gen Serv	ESS	Herongate		0211	59	48	1341046
Lndn S	Pk+ //	SCOTT	Robert	Head	M	24	M	Shipping & Pa+	MID	Hampstead		0211	59	48	1341046
Lndn S	Pk+	SCOTT	Alice	Wife	M	25	F	---	MID	St Pancras		0211	59	48	1341046
Lndn S	Pk+	SCOTT	Alice E.	Daur	-	1	F	---	MID	Acton		0211	60	49	1341046
Lndn S	Pk+	SCOTT	Herbert G.	Son	-	5m	M	---	MID	Acton		0211	60	49	1341046
Lndn S	Pk+	GILLETT	Mary A.	Serv	U	21	F	Gen Serv	SOM	Somerton		0211	60	49	1341046
Lndn St Pancras	43 Maitland Pk+	MILES	Sarah A.	Serv	U	18	F	Gen Serv	HRT	West Hythe		0211	60	49	1341046

Boxed annotations on figure: **References to original source** — **Occupation contractions** — **Karl Marx incorrectly indexed as Karl Wass** — **Henry Goddard, Door Keeper H+**

+ = SEE ORIGINAL CENSUS FOR FULL DATA
M = MARRIED U = UNMARRIED W = WIDOW(ER)
D = DIVORCED O = OTHER
m = MONTHS w = WEEKS d = DAYS
> = GREATER THAN < = LESS THAN
N = SEE MISCELLANEOUS NOTES

Figure 2-1

Microfiche version of 1881 census index for part of St. Pancras, London, in the county of Middlesex, extracting all information from the original census. Indexing errors do occur, so all entries need to be compared with the original. Note entries for Henry Goddard and Karl Wass (Marx). See Figure 2-2 for original census page. Copyright © 1999 by Intellectual Reserve, Inc. Census data © British Crown copyright 1999. All rights reserved.

name is Karl Marx—not Karl Wass—born in Germany. His daughter's name is Eleanor, not Elain as indicated in the census transcript. His occupation was Author, Political Economy. Again, wow! Wouldn't you want to know that your ancestor was living next to Karl Marx? Henry Goddard's life is now far more interesting! The moral of this story is *always go to the source.*

EVALUATE THE EVIDENCE

Even original records contain errors. You cannot copy information from any record onto your family group sheet and automatically assume that the information is correct. You will need to look at all information on the record and determine what it is really telling you. Who was the informant? How good was his knowledge of the facts? Did anyone have reason to lie about the facts?

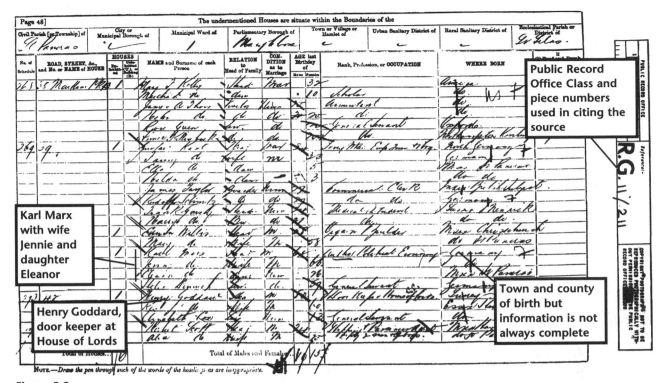

The annotations on the figure read:

Public Record Office Class and piece numbers used in citing the source

Karl Marx with wife Jennie and daughter Eleanor

Henry Goddard, door keeper at House of Lords

Town and county of birth but information is not always complete

Figure 2-2
Actual page from 1881 census for part of St. Pancras, London, in the county of Middlesex. Observe entries for Karl Marx and Henry Goddard, noting the indexing errors and contractions as shown in Figure 2-1.

We will discuss how to decide the accuracy of information when we examine civil registration certificates, census records, parish registers, and wills. We will go through the contents of the records and find out what to look for. You will see what to do when you don't find what you expect.

DETERMINE THE NEXT PROJECT

After you have examined any record in detail and recorded the information, always ask, Where do I go from here? What has this record told me? Has it given me more information about the life of my ancestor? Do I notice changes from previous records? Try to use any new information to lead you to other records that will tell you more about this ancestor and more about others.

First, how can you find out more about this particular ancestor? If your ancestor was a miner, a cheesemonger, a parlor maid, etc., then how did he or she practice the occupation in that time period? Under no circumstances assume that a person doing a job today is doing the same work as someone having the same occupation in the past. Find out more about the occupation. If you find that your ancestor lived in a small rural cottage, was a servant in the manor house, or was a member of one family among many in a tenement house in the city, try to learn how he lived his daily life. You may be able to find some firsthand accounts written by a person in a similar situation.

Second, does this record provide clues so that you can find out more about

Tip

other people in the family? Where is this information leading you? For example, do you now have a street address, so that you can get into the census returns of the entire family; or do you know the mother's maiden name, so that you can start looking for the marriage of the parents; or do you know the daughter's married name, so that you can start locating her descendants?

Make a list of all clues and how you want to follow up on them. Be creative. One document may provide you with a number of leads.

After creating the list, prioritize your options. For example, in one record you may find your ancestor's occupation and a street address. Where you go first will depend upon what records are easily accessible or what you most want to know. If your ancestor was a nurse during the Crimean War and you want to find out more about what she may have done, you may head off to the nearest library. On the other hand, if you already have a particular census return at your local Family History Center, you may want to use the address you have just obtained to find your family in the census. There are no rules to help you decide what to do first. That's one thing that makes family history research so much fun. You decide what you want to do by asking yourself, What will get me excited? What interests me?

Every time you find a new ancestor or another place where your ancestors lived, remember to go back through the first three steps of the research process. Look for people who are currently researching the new ancestor's surname, look for what has already been written about this name, and look for original records. Revisit the Internet, your local library, and a Family History Center. Do the same to find out about the place where your ancestor lived: Check sources on the Internet, look for history and geography books in the library, and find original records in a Family History Center.

WHERE DO I GO FROM HERE?

For More Info

Before you start the research process, **find out more about what makes English research different from research in other countries. See chapter three.** The rest of the book will take you through the research process, examining the tools you will use in detail. Enjoy the journey.

THREE

Uniqueness of English Research

E nglish research is not the same as U.S. research, and that's what makes it so interesting. This chapter will outline some of the major differences and explain some terms.

THE COUNTRY

England, of course, is a country of its own. But it can also be described as part of Great Britain, the United Kingdom, and the British Isles. For many North Americans, these words can be confusing. Let's define them.

In 1536, King Henry VIII united England and Wales under the same system of laws and government. In 1707, Great Britain was formed when the Parliaments of the Kingdom of England and Wales and of the Kingdom of Scotland passed the Act of Union. In 1801, Ireland was united politically with Great Britain to form the United Kingdom of Great Britain and Ireland. In 1921, most of Ireland separated from the United Kingdom. Since that time, the full name of the United Kingdom is the United Kingdom of Great Britain and Northern Ireland. It is abbreviated as the U.K. The term *British Isles* has traditionally described the two major islands of Great Britain (England, Scotland, and Wales) and Ireland (Republic of Ireland and Northern Ireland) plus the Channel Islands, the Isle of Man, and all the other islands surrounding the coast.

To summarize:

Great Britain includes England, Wales, and Scotland.

The **United Kingdom** has different meanings depending on time period. From 1801 to 1920 it included England, Ireland, Scotland, and Wales. Since 1921 it includes England, Scotland, Wales, and Northern Ireland.

British Isles includes England, Ireland, Scotland, Wales, the Channel Islands, and the Isle of Man.

Until recently, all countries of the United Kingdom have been controlled by a single Parliament based in London.

\di'fin\ *vb*

Definitions

The Isle of Man and the Channel Islands are dependencies of the British Crown but have their own Parliaments.

Size

Comparing the size of the United Kingdom to the size of the United States, you can see that England, which is only a part of the United Kingdom, is a relatively small area. But it contains a large population in that area!

Geographic Area (in Square Miles)	
United Kingdom of Great Britain and Northern Ireland 94,251	United States 3,679,192 Oregon 98,386 Utah 84,904 Wyoming 97,818
1996 Population	
Population	United Kingdom 58,295,119 United States 263,814,032
Population density	United Kingdom 619 per square mile United States 72 per square mile

Population Figures Comparing England and Wales to the United States		
Year	England and Wales	United States*
1551	3,011,000	
1601	4,109,000	
1651	5,228,000	50,400
1701	5,057,000	250,900
1751	5,772,000	1,170,800
1801	8,893,000	5,308,000
1851	17,928,000	23,191,876
1901	35,528,000	76,212,168
1951	43,758,000	151,325,798
1991	48,968,000	248,709,873

*The United States did not exist until the American Revolution. Figures quoted for the United States are based on the previous year's census figures. Population figures are estimates prior to 1801.

THE IMPORTANCE OF PLACE

As in all genealogical research, it is important to locate the places where events occurred in the life of your ancestor. However, in England, it is not enough to know the name of the county where your ancestor lived. **The parish is the fundamental unit of the Church of England, so you will need to know the name of your ancestor's parish.** You should also know where it is in relation to other parishes, who had responsibility for its records, and a little about the surrounding land formations. You will, therefore, need to become very familiar with maps and gazetteers.

Important

Begin by locating the county. Figure 3-1 shows all pre-1974 counties and is used to see where the county boundaries were located when your ancestors lived there. Modern maps are needed when you are going beyond the basic resources and need to know where records will be stored now. For family historians, all pre-1974 counties have been given standardized three-letter codes known as the Chapman County Codes. These codes are easy to use when recording the name of the county and entering information into a computer.

Next, you will want to see where your ancestor's parish is located in the county. **The best outline maps showing the relationship between Church of England parishes are found in** *The Phillimore Atlas and Index of Parish Registers* (see page 25). Here you can see the proximity of your ancestor's parish to surrounding parishes.

Printed Source

You will also want to see where the various towns and other local features are located. The best maps are the detailed Ordnance Survey maps. The most readily available maps of these are the modern Landranger (1:50,000 = 1¼ inches to 1 mile) and Pathfinder (1:25,000 = 2½ inches to 1 mile). Every location on the Landranger Map Series is identified in *The Ordnance Survey Gazetteer of Great Britain* (see page 26). **You can also search the Ordnance Survey Gazetteer at <http://www.ordsvy.gov.uk/products/landranger/lrmsearch.cfm>.** Older nineteenth-century Ordnance Survey maps (1 inch to 1 mile) have been reproduced by David & Charles, Brunel House, Newton Abbot, Devon.

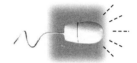

Internet Source

If you are looking for ancestors in major urban areas, the best maps are popularly known as the Godfrey maps. The maps are generally late nineteenth century and early twentieth century and are detailed enough for you to be able to identify individual houses. The reverse of each map often lists local city directories for the same time period. Contact the publisher at **Alan Godfrey Maps, 12 The Off Quay Building, Foundry Lane, Newcastle-upon-Tyne, NE6 1LH, England, or at <http://www.alangodfreymaps.co.uk/>.**

Internet Source

In addition to locating your place on a map, it is essential that you consult gazetteers. A gazetteer is a dictionary of place names, often with descriptions

---

Chapman County Codes for England

BDF	Bedfordshire	HRT	Hertfordshire	SOM	Somerset
BRK	Berkshire	HUN	Huntingdonshire	STS	Staffordshire
BKM	Buckinghamshire	KEN	Kent	SFK	Suffolk
CAM	Cambridgeshire	LAN	Lancashire	SRY	Surrey
CHS	Cheshire	LEI	Leicestershire	SSX	Sussex
CON	Cornwall	LIN	Lincolnshire	WAR	Warwickshire
CUL	Cumberland	LND	London (city only)	WES	Westmorland
DBY	Derbyshire	MDX	Middlesex	WIL	Wiltshire
DEV	Devon	NFK	Norfolk	WOR	Worcestershire
DOR	Dorset	NTH	Northamptonshire	YKS	Yorkshire
DUR	Durham	NBL	Northumberland	ERY	Yorkshire (East Riding)
ESS	Essex	NTT	Nottinghamshire	NRY	Yorkshire
GLS	Gloucestershire	OXF	Oxfordshire		(North Riding)
HAM	Hampshire	RUT	Rutland	WRY	Yorkshire
HEF	Herefordshire	SAL	Shropshire (Salop)		(West Riding)

Figure 3-1
Map of England showing
pre-1974 county boundaries.

Printed Source

providing additional information. Depending upon the gazetteer, this information will include the name of the parish or chapelry, the relationship of the place to other major localities, population figures, topographical and historical features, the ecclesiastical jurisdictions in which they lie, and details about nonconformist chapels in the area. You will want to use several gazetteers whenever possible because they give different information.

The most accessible gazetteers in print are *A Topographical Dictionary of England* (see page 25) and the abridged version, ***A Genealogical Gazetteer of England*** (see page 26). See the sample entry for Stamfordham for the wealth of detail to be found in Lewis. We will learn more about the people of Stamfordham later in the book.

For those really hard-to-find places, try *Cassell's Gazetteer of Great Britain and Ireland* (six volumes, 1893–98), which is now available on CD-ROM from Quintin Publications, 22 Delta Drive, Pawtucket, Rhode Island 02860-4555 or at <http://www.quintinpublications.com>. Or try Wilson's *Imperial Gazetteer*

ENTRY FROM *TOPOGRAPHICAL DICTIONARY OF ENGLAND* BY SAMUEL LEWIS, 1831

STAMFORDHAM, A parish (formerly a market town) in the north-eastern division of Tindale ward, county of Northumberland, 12½ miles (W.N.W.) from Newcastle upon Tyne, comprising the chapelry of Ryall, and the townships of Bitchfield, Blackheddon, Cheeseburn-Grange, Fenwick, Hawkwell, Heugh, Ingoe, Kearsley, East Matfen, West Matfen, Nesbit, Ouston, and Walridge, and containing 1827 inhabitants. The living is a vicarage, in the archdeaconry of Northumberland, and diocese of Durham, rated in the king's books at £14. 18. 1½., and in the patronage of the Crown. The church is dedicated to St. Mary. There is a place of worship for Presbyterians. Lime and coal abounds within the parish. The market has fallen into disuse, but the market cross, erected by Sir John Swinburne, Bart., in 1735, is still standing. Fairs, for the sale of cattle, pigs, &c., are held on the second Thursday in April, and on the 14th of August, if on Thursday, if not on the Thursday following; there are also statute fairs for hiring servants, on the Thursdays before Old May-day and November 14th, and on the last Thursday in February. A free school was founded in 1663, by Sir Thomas Widdrington, Knt., who endowed it with property now producing about £220 per annum.

of England and Wales (six volumes, 1870–72). One or both of these sets should be available in nearby large public or university libraries.

FAMILY HISTORY SOCIETIES

When you have identified where your ancestor originated, join the family history society for that area. Local societies open many doors for further research.

The services will vary with each society, but you can expect many things:

1. Most societies produce a high-quality quarterly journal with articles that illustrate family history in that area. The journal will include articles describing the local records, information about local indexes, historical articles about life in the area, and information about what is new.

2. You will have access to books and indexes made available through the society. Many will be of a very local nature and may only be available through the society.

3. Many societies provide research services on behalf of their members. You'll have access to expert assistance with your personal research. The locals know the records and what is available.

4. You'll be able to make contact with others with similar interests. Most societies publish queries that will help you find others who are researching your surname. You may discover a cousin. Even at a distance, many friendships develop as members cooperate on research projects and share their love of tracing families in a given locality in England.

Definitions

JURISDICTIONAL TERMS FOUND IN GAZETTEERS

Borough Town possessing a local government by royal charter.

Chapel (1) Small Church of England church without parish status or rights of burial and dependent upon a parish. (2) Religious meeting house of a nonconformist group.

Chapelry A division of a large parish having its own chapel.

Church The religious meeting house for the Church of England used for all ceremonies.

City A town which has a Cathedral and a seat of a Bishop of a diocese.

County or Shire Civil division of country. Forty counties until 1974.

Diocese Consists of several ecclesiastical parishes, overseen by a bishop.

Extra-Parochial Land exempt from church and poor rates. Often issued marriage licenses and probated wills.

Hamlet Group of houses, usually without a church.

Hide Administrative unit originally considered to be the amount of land necessary to support a peasant household (40 to 120 acres).

Hundred Subdivision of a county. Contained 100 hides of land.

Liberty District within a county exempt from the jurisdiction of a sheriff.

Parish (1) Civil subdivision of county. (2) Ecclesiastical unit having a parish church.

Province (Canterbury and York) Collection of dioceses overseen by an archbishop.

Registration District Post-1837 division of country. Contains several civil parishes, liberties, precincts, and wards.

Town Larger collection of houses, often with a regular fair or market, but smaller than a city.

Tything Consisted of ten hides: a rural division originally of ten householders.

Village Collection of houses, larger than a hamlet, but smaller than a town.

Wapentake Subdivision of a county in Northern England corresponding with a hundred in the south.

Ward Civil administrative division of a city or borough.

Every county has a society that is a member of the Federation of Family History Societies (FFHS). This organization is the coordinating body for all the societies. To find out how to join a local society, visit the FFHS Web site and see the list of FFHS member societies in England. There you will be able to link directly to each society's Web site or obtain a mailing address for those societies without Web sites. **The address is <http://www.ffhs.org.uk/members/England.htm>.**

Internet Source

You can also write to the FFHS at the address given below and request a current listing of societies and their addresses. You can specify which parts of the country you are interested in. You might also want to list the specific area of your ancestor's county, especially for those counties, such as Yorkshire, with multiple societies. Please send with your request two International Reply Coupons, available from your post office, to cover the cost of the return postage.

> Federation of Family History Societies
> The Benson Room
> Birmingham and Midland Institute
> Margaret Street
> Birmingham B3 3BS
> United Kingdom

MONEY

You will find references to money as you do your research. For example, a parish history may tell you the average daily wages of a farm laborer.

Prior to 1974, England used a monetary system of pounds, shillings, and

British Coins in Use During the Nineteenth Century	
1 farthing	= ¼ penny
1 ha'penny	= ½ penny
1 penny	= 1 penny
1 three-ha'penny	= 1½ pence
1 threppence	= 3 pence
1 groat	= 4 pence
1 sixpence	= 6 pence
1 shilling	= 12 pence
1 florin	= 2 shillings
1 half-crown	= 2 shillings & 6 pence
1 three-shillings	= 3 shillings
1 double-florin	= 4 shillings
1 dollar	= 5 shillings
1 crown	= 5 shillings
1 quarter-guinea	= 5 shillings & 3 pence
1 third-guinea	= 7 shillings
1 half-sovereign	= 10 shillings
1 sovereign	= 1 pound
	= 20 shillings
	= 240 pence
1 guinea	= 21 shillings
1 double-sovereign	= 2 pounds
1 five-pounds	= 5 pounds

pence. The plural of *penny* is *pence*. Two pennies were called "tuppence." (Remember the song from *Mary Poppins*? "Feed the birds, tuppence a bag. . . .") There were twelve pence in a shilling and twenty shillings in a pound. Therefore, 1 pound = 20 shillings = 240 pence. They were written using the Latin forms of the words, so pounds are represented as L or £, shillings by s, and pence by d. For example, you may find a fee recorded as 2s. 6d. (two shillings, sixpence). A more complete list of coins in use during the nineteenth century is found in the table on page 19.

THE IMPORTANCE OF RELIGION

There is no separation of church and state in England. The Church of England is the official church of the country. The Church of England is also called the Anglican Church and the Established Church. Common abbreviations are C of E (Church of England) and EC (Established Church). England is divided into ecclesiastical units known as provinces, dioceses, archdeaconries, rural deaneries and parishes. Because of the importance of the Church of England you will find many records of your ancestors in the Church of England parish records.

Your ancestors may have been Catholic or other nonconformists, that is they did not follow the beliefs of the Church of England. They are still likely to have baptisms, marriages, and burials of family members recorded in the Church of England. This was important so that they could prove their right to inheritance, hold local office or be assured of poor relief (local welfare system). In fact, between 1754 and 1812 everyone (except Jews and Quakers) was required by law to be married in the Church of England to have a valid marriage.

Sources

Before the nineteenth century, the parish church was the center of both religion and civil administration in the parish. The parish was responsible for such things as relief of the poor, administration of justice, collection of taxes, fixing the roads, licensing, and raising men for the militia. Therefore, **the parish kept many types of records relating to your ancestors.** Civil government increasingly assumed many of the responsibilities of the Church of England. A major change occurred with the Poor Law Reform Acts of 1834 when the Poor Law Unions were formed to build workhouses and administer aid to the poor. Even though the Church of England no longer has the all-encompassing responsibilities that it once did, in many small rural communities the local church is still the central meeting and activity center.

THE IMPORTANCE OF SOCIAL CLASS

Social class was extremely important to your English ancestors. English society was highly stratified; all men were not "created equal." Class determined the way a person lived: what he did, what he wore, where he sat in church. In many cases, it even determined his religion. For example, the wealthy tended to stay in the Church of England in order to go to the universities, enter the professions, or hold public office. The poor needed to be in the Church in order to be assured of poor relief. The majority of nonconformists came from the lower middle class.

The aristocracy consisted of titled families and their relatives. **The best source for relevant biographies is *The Complete Peerage* (see page 25). Pedigrees of the peerage are available in *Burke's Genealogical and Heraldic History of the Peerage, Baronetage, and Knightage* (see page 25).** The ranks of peerage from highest to lowest were duke, marquess, earl, viscount, and baron.

The gentry were next on the social scale. You can find pedigrees of many gentry families in *Landed Gentry* (see page 25). The descending ranks of gentry were baronet, knight, esquire, and gentleman.

The middle class were master tradesmen, professionals (e.g., clergy, physicians, and solicitors), and yeomen farmers.

The lower middle class were craftsmen, shopkeepers, and husbandmen.

The working class consisted of journeymen, agricultural laborers, and servants. Those who were not working, such as paupers, were still "working class." These people were usually illiterate.

Most of us are tracing ancestors from the final two groups.

Printed Source

ENGLISH RECORD KEEPING

English records are different from North American records in the types of records created, where they were created, and who created them. In most U.S. states, the county courthouse is the primary place for locating records. What is recorded is often dependent upon local laws. In England, almost no records used early in the family history research process were created by the county government. The first records we will discuss were created by the national government. The earlier records were created by the Church of England in its parishes and dioceses.

Records Created by the National Government

In the United States, vital statistics are recorded by the various states, and in many of them compulsory registration of births and deaths was not introduced until the twentieth century. In England, the national government has provided a coordinating structure, known as civil registration, for registering all births, marriages, and deaths in the country since 1837. The government also compiles nationwide indexes to births, marriages, and deaths! See chapters six and seven on civil registration to find out what these records contain and how to use them.

Since 1801, the British government has taken a national census. There have been federal censuses in the United States since 1790. **The British census is more difficult to search than the U.S. census, but the results are well worth the effort. See chapter eight on census records for more details.**

For More Info

There has been a central probate system in England and Wales since 1858. There are even nationwide indexes. This is a major difference from North American research. Can you imagine checking a nationwide index for any probate record that occurred in the United States in the year 1859? Dream on. But you can do that in English research! See chapter nine on post-1857 probate records for more details.

The majority of nationally produced records are stored at the Public Record Office (PRO) in Kew, Surrey. The PRO is the approximate equivalent of the National Archives in the United States.

Records Created by the Church of England

In the United States, church records can be difficult to find and may even be nonexistent. In Canada, church records are used more in family research. But in England, church records will be among your most important resources. You will use the records of baptisms, marriages, and burials created by the Church of England. See chapter ten on parish records for further details.

Prior to 1858, probate records were the responsibility of the Church of England. We will explain them in chapter eleven on pre-1858 probate records.

SPECIAL PROBLEMS WITH ENGLISH RECORDS

Names

Research Tip

The popularity of different Christian names has changed through the years. **As you search the records, understand that some names are regularly abbreviated (William to Wm.), some can be interchangeable (Elizabeth and Isobel, Edward and Edmond), and some have nicknames (Will, Dick, Bess, Betty and Molly).** The best reference book is *The Oxford Dictionary of English Christian Names* (see page 26). It is currently out of print, but you can access it through interlibrary loan. An inexpensive book is *First Name Variants* (see page 25). Also try a good book of baby names showing name variations; any bookstore should have one. It will help immensely to know that your great-grandfather Henry can also be listed as Harry. You will miss female ancestors entirely if you don't know that Ann, Hannah, and Nancy are variations of the same name and that Margaret, Daisy, and Peggy can be the same person. You can obtain a concise given names explanation for family historians under the category "Christian Names" in *The Dictionary of Genealogy* (see page 25).

Names can also be found in Latin, especially before 1733. There is an excellent listing of Latin forms of English names in *Genealogical Research in England and Wales* (see page 25). The list includes ancient and unusual names found in records of England.

Handwriting

Several styles of handwriting were used in the past. By 1700 the secretary style of the prior sixteenth and seventeenth centuries had been replaced by the italic style that is very similar to current handwriting. These two handwriting styles cover the vast majority of documents that family historians will encounter.

At first glance, they may appear to be impossible to read. But you can do it! A little practice will produce results. Copybooks exist showing how the letters were to be formed. If you practice reading these books, you will soon become adept at reading the original records.

Tip

When you first meet a document in either italic or secretary style, try to transcribe it in full—word for word. Leave a gap for any word or part of a word that you cannot transcribe. By the time you reach the end of the document, you will be able to go back and fill in some of the gaps. Words omitted earlier may be easier to read in a different context. In transcribing, you need to remember that any given word might not have been spelled the same as it is today, and might not have even been spelled the same as elsewhere in the document.

Although reading a new document may at first seem formidable, you can accomplish it with practice and patience. Try it, you'll like it!

For an inexpensive basic guide to reading old handwriting, see *Reading Old Handwriting* (see page 26).

Latin

If you thought reading the old handwriting was fun, you're really going to love this. Before 1733 (except for 1651–60), Latin was the language used in all legal documents. Latin terms and abbreviations can sometimes be found in documents normally written in English, especially if the writer wanted to highlight a part of the document as being special or different. Latin terms are even found on tombstones.

You will be able to do a lot of English research without ever worrying about Latin. In fact, the records we will be discussing are all written in English. However, a basic familiarity with Latin will be useful. For most genealogists, **the following three resources will cover the subject quite well:**

Sources

1. Family History Library's, *Genealogical Word List: Latin*

This contains the most common words found in genealogical documents. The SourceGuide contains this word list (click on "Latin Genealogical Word List"). You can use the SourceGuide free on the Internet at <http://www.familys earch.org/sg/>. You can also purchase it on compact disc from the Salt Lake Distribution Center. *Genealogical Word List: Latin* is also available in a very inexpensive printed booklet that can be ordered from the Salt Lake Distribution Center (see chapter five for the address). It may also be available for purchase at your nearest Family History Center.

2. Denis Stuart, *Latin for Local and Family Historians*

You can learn from this book to read most of the Latin you will ever need. It takes you step-by-step though the language and gives you lots of practice.

3. Charles Trice Martin, *The Record Interpreter: A Collection of Abbreviations, Latin Words and Names Used in English Historical Manuscripts and Records.*

This is the standard reference work. The book is divided into sections that include Latin abbreviations, French abbreviations, a Latin words glossary, Latin names of places, Latin forms of English surnames, and Latin Christian names.

Calendar

Dates in old English documents were recorded differently than in modern English ones. Many dates were unique to the country. **You will need to be aware of**

Warning

- **Julian and Gregorian Calendars**
- **Ecclesiastical dates**
- **Regnal dates**

1. **Julian Calendar:** Prior to 1752, England used the Julian calendar, which had been introduced in Rome in 46 B.C. The year ran from 25 March to 24 March. The Church of England had declared 25 March (Lady Day) to be New Year's Day because it was believed to be the day that Christ was conceived.

Gregorian Calendar: The Julian calendar year of 365¼ days was eleven minutes and fourteen seconds longer than the solar year. By 1580, the difference amounted to ten days. Pope Gregory commissioned the more accurate Gregorian calendar to correct this. The Gregorian calendar was adopted at various times throughout the world. Scotland adopted the Gregorian calendar in the year 1600. England did not do so until 1752. The American colonies were under English law and adopted the calendar at the same time. By then, the calendar difference was eleven days, so 2 September 1752 was followed by 14 September 1752. This caused rioting because some people thought that the government had stolen eleven days from their lives! In addition, New Year's Day was moved from 25 March to 1 January. January, February, and March became the first three months of the year (New Style) instead of the last three months of the year (Old Style).

The calendar change from Julian to Gregorian can present difficulties if you are not careful. The months September, October, November, and December used to be the seventh to the tenth months of the year. *Septem* is Latin for "seven," *Octo* for "eight," etc. They were abbreviated 7ber, 8ber, 9ber, and 10ber (or Xber), and the abbreviations continued to be used after the calendar change. These month abbreviations are not to be confused with July to October, which are now the seventh to the tenth months. When finding the English parent's marriage date of 14 April 1605 and the child's birth date of 4 March 1605, you could make an incorrect conclusion if you forget the calendar change. The child was born after his parents were married. The proper method for transcribing dates prior to 1752 is to use both Old Style and New Style for any date occurring between January 1 and March 24. Thus, a document dated in England as 15 February 1716 should be transcribed as 15 February 1716/7.

2. **Ecclesiastical dates:** Most documents before the nineteenth century that you will use were recorded by officials of the Church of England, or even earlier by the Roman Catholic Church. You will see dates recorded by a holiday name such as Candlemas (2 February), Lammas (1 August), Michaelmas (29 September), or Martinmas (11 November). Dates may be recorded in terms of their relationship to a moveable feast or fast in the church calendar, for example the third Sunday in Trinity. A good source to help convert these references is *Dates and Calendars for the Genealogist* (see page 27).

3. **Regnal dates:** Up to the nineteenth century, many official documents were dated using regnal years. This means that dates were based upon when the monarch came to the throne. For example, King Henry VII came to the throne 22 August 1485. The first year of his reign is written as 1 Henry VII, and it

ran from 22 August 1485 to 21 August 1486. The regnal year 16 Henry VII corresponds with the year 1500–1501. You will rarely encounter regnal years in the documents you will be using for basic genealogy (especially after the Restoration of the Monarchy in 1660), but you need to be aware of what they mean. The use of regnal years decreased with time, and they are now rarely used.

THE UNIQUENESS OF ENGLISH RESEARCH

Records in England are different from those in North America. There are similarities in some, such as census records, but the specifics vary. The English geography is different, customs are different, and even though we speak the same language, the words have different meanings. Our ancestors' lifestyles were very different from our own. The more in-depth research you do in English records, the more you will realize that you are traveling through a whole new world. In fact, you might be tempted to say, "Toto, I have a feeling we're not in Kansas anymore." Be aware of the differences, look for them, and enjoy them. We'll lay the yellow brick road for you, and if you follow it, you're going to have a wonderful adventure into the past.

WHERE CAN I FIND MORE INFORMATION?

Bardsley, Alan. *First Name Variants*. 2nd ed. Birmingham, England: Federation of Family History Societies, 1996.

Burke, John. *Burke's Genealogical and Heraldic History of the Peerage, Baronetage, and Knightage*. London: Burke, 1826–.

Burke, Sir John Bernard. *A Genealogical History of the Dormant, Abeyant, Forfeited, and Extinct Peerages of the British Empire*. 1843. Reprint, Baltimore, Md.: Baltimore Publishing Co., 1996.

Burke, Sir John Bernard. *A Genealogical and Heraldic Dictionary of the Landed Gentry of Great Britain and Ireland*. London: Burke. 1846–.

Burke's Family Index. London: Burke's Peerage Ltd., 1976.

Chapman, Colin. *Weights, Money and Other Measures Used by Our Ancestors*. Baltimore, Md.: Genealogical Publishing Company, 1996.

Cokayne, G.E. *The Complete Peerage*. 2nd ed. London: The St. Catherine Press, 1940.

FitzHugh, Terrick V.H. *The Dictionary of Genealogy*. 5th ed. London: A & C Black, 1998.

Gardiner, Juliet, and Neil Wenborn, eds. *The History Today Companion to British History*. London: Collins & Brown Ltd., 1995.

Gardner, David E., and Frank Smith. *Genealogical Research in England and Wales*. 3 vols. Salt Lake City, Utah: Bookcraft, 1964.

Humphery-Smith, Cecil R., *The Phillimore Atlas and Index of Parish Registers*. 2nd ed. Chichester, West Sussex: Phillimore & Co. Ltd., 1995.

Lewis, Samuel. *A Topographical Dictionary of England*. 2 vols. Originally

Sources

published 1831. Reprint, Baltimore, Md.: Genealogical Publishing Company, 1996.

Martin, Charles Trice, comp. *The Record Interpreter: A Collection of Abbreviations, Latin Words and Names Used in English Historical Manuscripts and Records*. Chichester, West Sussex: Phillimore & Co. Ltd., 1994.

McLaughlin, Eve. *Reading Old Handwriting*. 2nd ed. Birmingham, England: Federation of Family History Societies, 1987.

The Ordnance Survey Gazetteer of Great Britain. 3rd ed. London: Macmillan, 1992. Reprint, Southampton: Ordnance Survey, 1995.

Richardson, John. *The Local Historian's Encyclopedia*. New Barnet, Hertfordshire: Historical Publications Ltd., 1974.

Smith, Frank. *A Genealogical Gazetteer of England*. Baltimore, Md.: Genealogical Publishing Company, 1982. Reprint, 1995.

Stuart, Denis. *Latin for Local and Family Historians*. Chichester, West Sussex: Phillimore & Co. Ltd., 1995.

Webb, Clifford. *Dates and Calendars for the Genealogist*. London: Society of Genealogists, 1998.

Withycombe, E.G., comp. *The Oxford Dictionary of English Christian Names*. London: Oxford University Press, 1947.

For More Info

WHERE DO I GO FROM HERE?

You're ready to find your family. **Step one of the research process is an Internet search. See chapter four.**

FOUR

Accessing the Resources of the Internet

Y ou can start your English research from the comfort of your home by using the Internet. First look to see what information already exists about your family, then find out about the places where your ancestors lived.

You don't need to know all about the Internet to use it effectively. **We will examine the four most important sites for finding information about your English ancestors:**

- FamilySearch, the Web site of the Family History Library
- GENUKI, historical and genealogical information provided by the Federation of Family History Societies and its members
- British Isles Family History Society-U.S.A., designed to help Americans trace their British Isles ancestry
- Cyndi's List, the ideal place to find out what else exists

Internet Source

Please note that the Internet changes rapidly. The exercises suggested in this chapter may cease to work because information on a Web site has changed. However, these four sites are here to stay, so you should be able to find them and do your own surveys. You will have a great time!

FAMILYSEARCH

The Web site of the Family History Library, <http://www.familysearch.org>, is a great place to begin family history research. It includes many of the FHL's computerized research programs and guides. The site made international news when it was introduced in 1999. Here you will find out about your family surnames, more about the places where your ancestors lived, and about family history in general. You can even download a free computer program to record your genealogy. You will want to be familiar with all aspects of this site.

The International Genealogical Index, the Ancestral File, and the Family History

Step By Step

Library Catalog are all accessible from the FamilySearch Web site. If you have never used these programs, you can read a description of them in the next chapter.

Start by connecting to the FamilySearch home page at <http://www.familysea rch.org>. You will see a screen that allows you to conduct an "Ancestor Search." You can enter as much or as little as you know about your ancestor. If all you know is his or her surname, enter it in the "Last Name" box and click "Search." The program will automatically look for all occurrences of your surname in the Ancestral File, selected countries of the International Genealogical Index (including British Isles!), and selected Web sites. You can instantly get a good overview about what has been done on your family.

The page you will use the most is the "Custom Search" page. Click on the tab for "Custom Search" near the top of the home page to go to this section. From here you can connect to a page that will list the Family History Centers near you. You can also access the SourceGuide, the Ancestral File, the International Genealogical Index, the Family History Library Catalog, and you can search selected Web sites and mailing lists.

The first thing you will want to see is the SourceGuide. This contains various guides written by the Family History Library, including Research Outlines, foreign language word lists, and much more. From the "Custom Search" page, go to "SourceGuide" and add it to your list of bookmarks or favorites. It is located at <http://www.familysearch.org/sg/>. From the SourceGuide screen, click on "How-to Guides." The guides are organized by place, title of guide, and description. The first guides listed do not relate to any particular place. Go down the list of places until you get to "England." Here you will see several important guides, maps, and forms, including

- England Research Outline
- England and Wales Map (Boundaries Before 1974)
- Using the 1881 British Census Indexes
- British Census Worksheet

Sources

Click on "England Research Outline." The guide describes all of the major record sources for English research, tells you where to find a record, and describes how to find it in the Family History Library Catalog if it is available there. There is also a printed version available for purchase, but the online Research Outline is far superior. For example, when you read about a particular record in the online version of the England Research Outline, you can often click on the title of the record and bring up a list of the associated Family History Library film numbers. This is one of the finest resources in genealogy, and it is available free on the Internet!

The SourceGuide has many other resources that you will want to investigate. For example, you can look at the *Latin Genealogical Word List* if you encounter any Latin words in English documents. If you do not have access to the Internet at home, you can purchase the SourceGuide on compact disc. It is available from the Salt Lake Distribution Center; see chapter five for the address.

In addition to the SourceGuide, be sure to search the online versions of the International Genealogical Index, the Ancestral File, and the Family History

Library Catalog. At the present time, the online versions do not have the same search capabilities as the ones that are available in Family History Centers, so we will describe these programs in chapter five when we go into the Family History Center. However, you will also want to use them online so that you can continue your research at home.

The FamilySearch Web site is regularly updated and expanded. Once you see how much easier it can make your research, you will wonder how we ever did family history without it.

GENUKI

After you have searched the FamilySearch Web site, **the GENUKI Web site, <http://www.genuki.org.uk>, can help you learn more about the places your ancestors lived.** The historical and genealogical information on GENUKI is provided with the cooperation of the Federation of Family History Societies, its member societies, and a large group of volunteers. The site's stated aim is to serve as a "virtual reference library" of genealogical information.

Internet Source

The GENUKI Web site is organized with the same structure as the Family History Library Catalog. Places are organized into four levels: British Isles, Country, County, and Parish or Town. Therefore, you should look for materials that relate to the British Isles as a whole, then for materials relating to all of England. After you have found these general sources, you will want to find out more about the county where your ancestor lived, then the individual parish or town. The information for each place is organized with the same subject categories used by the Family History Library Catalog. These subject categories are listed in chapter five.

Let's navigate through the GENUKI site to find information about the British Isles, England, the County of Northumberland, and the parish of Stamfordham in that county. **Start at the GENUKI home page at <http://www.genuki.org.uk>.** The home page discusses the site in general and leads you to further information about how the site is organized. You will want to read this the first time you use the site. The information for the British Isles is contained in the section called "United Kingdom and Ireland." Click on this link. When the "United Kingdom and Ireland" page appears, add it to your list of bookmarks or favorites. You will return to it again and again. From here you can find out about the major archives and libraries, study some occupations, etc. Explore the various categories at your leisure.

Step By Step

Now click on the map for the "Regions." England is the country colored red. You will now be able to find out about gazetteers for England, schools, and many other subjects. Look through the categories, then go to the section that contains a list of counties. Click on "Northumberland." You will find a general description of the county and its location and information about Northumberland archives and libraries, societies, history, and much more.

After the county search, we will read information about the specific place where our ancestors lived. At the top of the Northumberland page, there is a link to "Northumberland Towns & Parishes." Click on this link for a large list of towns and parishes. There is information about all of these places on the Internet! Click on "Stamfordham." You will see a map of the area and text similar to the following:

Stamfordham

"STAMFORDHAM parish comprises the townships of Bitchfield, Black-Heddon, Cheeseburn Grange, Fenwick, Hawkwell, Heugh, Ingoe, Kearsley, Matfen (East), Matfen (West), Nesbit, Ouston, Ryal, and Wallridge. It is bounded on the north by Bolam, on the west by St. John Lee and Halton, on the south by Corbridge and Ovingham, and on the east by Heddon-on-the-Wall and Newburn. It is about five and a half miles long, by four and a half broad, and contains an area of 18,089 acres. Population in 1801, 1,652; in 1811, 1,813; in 1821, 1,827; in 1831, 1,736; in 1841, 1,777; and in 1851, 1,781 souls. This parish comprises the finest part of Tindale Ward; it is well wooded, and some of the lands are occasionally enriched by the overflowing of the river Pont, which rises a little to the south of St. Oswald's, in the parish of St. John Lee, and after passing through Ponteland, to the west of the marshy lake called Prestwick Carr, it empties itself into the Cat-raw, which proceeds in a north-easterly direction to Stannington Vale, and then assumes the name of the 'Blyth' river, under which name the united streams flow to the sea at Blyth." [From *History, Topography, and Directory of Northumberland,* Whellan, 1855].

- Census
- Church History
- Church Records
- Civil Registration
- History
- Military Records
- Poorhouses, Poor Law, Etc.

Census

The 1851 Census Index (microfiche CN14) published by the Northumberland and Durham Family History Society may be of value to researchers interested in this parish.

Return to top of page

Church History

The Original Indexes website provides information about *Matfen, Holy Trinity*; and also information about *Ryal, All Saints* under the headings *Church* and *Monumental Inscriptions.*

Return to top of page

Church Records

[Click on the "Church Records" link for this fact.]

Stamfordham, St Mary the Virgin; Records of baptisms 1662–1978, marriages 1662–1962 and burials 1662–1865 are available at Morpeth Records Centre. Bishops' Transcripts for the period 1769–1836 are deposited at Durham University Library Archives and Special Collections, 5 The College, Durham City. The International Genealogical Index (I.G.I.) includes baptism 1662–1812 and marriages 1727–1812 for this parish, and Boyd's Marriage Index includes marriages 1662–1812 and banns 1754–1812. Transcripts of baptisms 1662–1812, marriages 1662–1704 and 1727–1812 and burials 1662–1812 for Stamfordham are available at Newcastle Central Library, Local Studies Dept.

A photograph of <u>Stamfordham, St Mary the Virgin</u> supplied by <u>George Bell.</u>

Matfen, Holy Trinity: Records of baptisms 1844–1974, marriages 1846–1979 and burials 1845–1972 are available at <u>Morpeth Records Centre.</u>

A listing of <u>Matfen marriages 1846–1901</u> provided by <u>George Bell</u>.

A transcript of monumental inscriptions at Stamfordham, Ryal and Matfen (microfiche TN87) is published by <u>Northumberland and Durham Family History Society</u> and these records are also available in book form at <u>Newcastle Central Library</u>, Local Studies Department.

A photograph of <u>Matfen, Holy Trinity</u> supplied by <u>George Bell.</u>

A photograph of <u>Ryal, All Saints</u> supplied by <u>George Bell</u>.

Nonconformist Records

Cheeseburn Grange, St Francis Xavier (Roman Catholic): Records of baptisms 1775–1863, marriages 1787–1906 and deaths 1783–1797 are available at <u>Morpeth Records Centre</u>. Baptisms 1775–1840 can also be seen at <u>Melton Park</u>. The International Genealogical Index (I.G.I.) includes births/baptisms 1775–1840 and some marriages. Transcripts of baptisms 1775–1840 and deaths 1786–1797 are available at <u>Newcastle Central Library</u>, Local Studies Dept.

Stamfordham (Presbyterian): Records of births/baptisms 1754–1896 are available at <u>Morpeth Records Centre.</u> The International Genealogical Index (I.G.I.) includes births/baptisms 1754–1875.

Adjacent Parishes

The following parishes are adjacent to Stamfordham: <u>Bolam</u>, <u>Bywell St Peter</u>, <u>Corbridge</u>, <u>Halton</u>, <u>Heddon on the Wall</u>, <u>Kirkheaton</u>, <u>Newburn</u>, <u>Ovingham</u>, <u>St John Lee</u>, <u>Whalton.</u>

Return to top of page

Civil Registration

[Click your browser's "back" button from the "Church Records" link.]

This area is now within Northumberland Central Registration District. Certificates of birth, death and marriage can be obtained from: *Superintendent Registrar, Register Office, 94 Newgate Street, Morpeth, Northumberland, NE61 1BU*. Please read <u>the notes on the county page</u> before ordering from a District Office.

Return to top of page

History

The history of Stamfordham Parish is included in: Northumberland County History Committee, *History of Northumberland*, Volume 12. Newcastle, A. Reid, 1926.

Return to top of page

Military Records

A transcript of <u>Matfen War Memorial</u> provided by <u>Original Indexes</u>.

Return to top of page

Poorhouses, Poor Law, etc.

Stamfordham Parish was part of Castle Ward Poor Law Union. The Union Workhouse was located near the village of Ponteland. Some records are held at <u>Morpeth Records Centre</u>, but these are of limited genealogical value.

Return to top of page

[*Last updated: Saturday, 2nd October 1999, 14:27—Brian Pears*]

All of the underlined words are links to even more information. For example, you can see a photograph of the church at "Ryal, All Saints" by clicking on the link.

The GENUKI Web site is continually growing and updating. This will be one of your most important resources for information about places in England.

BRITISH ISLES FAMILY HISTORY SOCIETY—U.S.A.

The purpose of the British Isles Family History Society–U.S.A. (BIFHS-USA) is to help Americans trace their British Isles ancestry. The British Isles Family History Society–U.S.A will make your research easier by helping you find the most important books, Web sites, and resources for English genealogy. The BIFHS-USA Web site has been rated by Cyndi Howells (owner of Cyndi's List; see below) as one of the best genealogy sites on the Web.

Start by connecting to the home page at <http://www.rootsweb.com/~bifhsusa>. Put this page on your list of bookmarks or favorites. The home page has three very important links:

Internet Source

- Guide to British Isles Research
- Publications for Sale
- List of Links to Other British Isles Resources

Click on "Guide to British Isles Research." The *BIFHS-USA Guide to British Isles Research* tells how to use the massive BIFHS-USA collection at the Los Angeles Family History Center, but it can be used to help you find and order materials for any other Family History Center. There is a table of contents to this guide. The "Where to Begin" section tells you how to begin research in a Family History Center. There is a more comprehensive guide in this book, so you can skip that section. There are also guides to family history resources for the General British Isles, England and Wales, and other areas of the British Isles. Click on "General British Isles." This section contains records that apply to more than one country. The guide is organized in the approximate order that most people should search the records. You can see that the guide starts with the section "How to Do British Isles Research." It then has a list of "Finding Aids" which are catalogs, indexes, and other guides that will help you find records. There are also important reference books, gazetteers and maps, and biographical sources. The Family History Library call numbers are given for each item. The end of the "General British Isles" page includes the link "England and Wales." Click on that now.

The "England and Wales" page does not repeat any of the sources from the "General British Isles" page. You will find a brief description of English civil registration, census records, church records, probate records, and other resources. FHL call numbers are given for all items. You may want to print the guide and take it with you to a Family History Center.

Many of the best books for English research are available through BIFHS-USA at discounted prices. They are listed on the Web site in "Publications for Sale" or "List of Publications for Sale." You can view the book list sorted by author, title, publisher, or country. When you use the list sorted by country, be sure to look for the books coded with "E" for England and "G" for General British Isles.

Now let's go to "List of links to other British Isles resources." The most important Web sites for English family history are listed. These include the Federation of Family History Societies, the Public Record Office, and the Society of Genealogists. Each entry has a brief description that tells you about the organization, its Web site, and why you want to visit it. You should visit all of the sites listed in the "General British Isles" and "England" sections.

There are many other valuable pages on this site. The BIFHS-USA Web site is one of your best resources for researching England from abroad.

CYNDI'S LIST

After you have been to the Web sites recommended by the British Isles Family History Society–U.S.A., you may wonder, What else exists? You can answer this question by visiting Cyndi's List, <http://www.cyndislist.com>. Cyndi Howells has compiled links to genealogy sites of all kinds and organized them by country and by category. The full title of the site is "Cyndi's List of Genealogy Sites on the Internet," but everyone calls it "Cyndi's List." This site is incredible.

Connect to <http://www.cyndislist.com>. You will find general information about the site first, then "Cyndi's List Category Index." Scroll down the list to see how much is available for Internet genealogy. Near the bottom of the list is the link "United Kingdom & Ireland Index." Click on that link. You will now have a page that contains only links to the United Kingdom and Ireland. It is located at <http://www.cyndislist.com/uksites.htm>. Add this page to your list of bookmarks or favorites. You will need to use the links "General UK sites" and "England." Click on the link "England." When the page appears, look through the various categories. You will see "General Resource Sites," "History & Culture," and several other categories. Each subject category contains links to Web sites. Some of the links contain brief descriptions. You will find many things that interest you. Go to the section "Queries, Message Boards & Surname Lists." You can search the RootsWeb Surname List by typing your surname in the box labeled, "Type in your surname from England." Before you do, see the surname lists index from GENUKI. Click on the link "Northumberland and Durham, England—Surnames List." The page that appears should contain the sentence, "Here is a list of surnames in Northumberland and Durham being researched by people with E-mail addresses." Click on "list of surnames" in that sentence and you will obtain an alphabetical list. We want to see if anyone has information about the Telford families in Northumberland. Click on the letter "T" to see. Is anyone researching that name?

You can spend countless hours looking at links from Cyndi's List, but try to come up for air every once in a while so you can finish reading this book! You should also let people know about your research by creating your own Web sites and queries. You will find many opportunities to do this as you explore Cyndi's links. Genealogical research has never been this easy or this much fun.

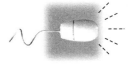

Internet Source

For More Info

WHERE DO I GO FROM HERE?

You should now know something about your English ancestors. Perhaps you know the name of the place where your immigrant originated. Maybe you know your ancestor's religion or occupation. You will want background information about how your ancestors lived. Armed with that, you will begin to search original records that contain your ancestors' names. Step two of the research process is to go to public and university libraries in your area. Continue your research at your nearest Family History Center for step three. **See chapter five to get started on both.**

FIVE

Accessing the Resources of Libraries and Family History Centers

LIBRARIES

L ibraries house many resources that can help you find more about your English ancestors. In fact, English historical materials are some of the richest in the world, so you should be able to find plenty of books about how your ancestors lived. You have probably been using school and public libraries all of your life. However, you may still need assistance, especially with using computerized catalog systems or with ordering materials by interlibrary loan. Most libraries will have trained staff to assist you. Printed library guides will also be available to help you find resources.

The first thing you should do is find a pamphlet or other guide that describes the library's cataloging system. Use the catalog to locate the books recommended below.

You will seek answers to the following two questions:
1. Has someone else researched your family?
2. What happened where your ancestors lived?

Tip

Has Someone Else Researched Your Family?

To find out if someone else has begun research on your family, examine all four of the following books which index published British family pedigrees:

Marshall, George W. *The Genealogist's Guide.* 1903. Reprint, Baltimore, Md.: Genealogical Publishing Co., 1998. This book indexes pedigrees that include at least three generations in the male line. All were published before 1903. Marshall's work was continued by John B. Whitmore.

Whitmore, John B., comp. *A Genealogical Guide: An Index to British Pedigrees: In Continuation of Marshall's Genealogist's Guide, 1903.* London: Society of Genealogists, 1953. Also published by Harleian Society as volumes 99, 101, 102, 104. Whitmore continued the work of Marshall. This book covers pedigrees published between 1900 and 1950. The work was continued by Geoffrey Barrow.

Research Tip

Barrow, Geoffrey B., comp. *The Genealogist's Guide: an Index to Printed British Pedigrees and Family Histories, 1950–1975*. London: Research Publishing Company, 1977. Continuing the work of Marshall and Whitmore, Barrow's book indexes pedigrees published between 1950 and 1975.

Thomson, Theodore R., comp. *A Catalogue of British Family Histories*. 3rd ed., with addenda. London: Society of Genealogists, 1980. This book indexes British family histories published before 1980.

You will also want to consult sources that list family histories in general. The following is one of the best:

Kaminkow, M.J., ed. *Genealogies in the Library of Congress: A Bibliography*. Baltimore, Md.: Magna Carta Book Co., 1972. This source indexes several thousand genealogies, not just British ones. It contains two volumes and two supplements, so you will want to check them all. If you find a book that interests you, you can usually obtain it by interlibrary loan.

After you have looked for printed pedigrees and family histories, look for published biographies, such as:

Dictionary of National Biography. London: Oxford University Press, 1995. This was originally published in sixty-three volumes and later updated with supplements. It is now available on CD-ROM which allows you to search for any name or place. This source is particularly valuable if your ancestor was famous, did anything noteworthy, or held a major office.

Next look for people who are currently researching your surname. Consult the following:

Johnson, Keith A., and Malcolm R. Sainty. *Genealogical Research Directory*. North Sydney, N.S.W.: Genealogical Research Directory (published annually since 1980). Look through every volume.

The British Isles Genealogical Register. Published on microfiche by the Federation of Family History Societies. 1st ed., 1994. 2nd ed., 1997. These are two separate editions and are not revisions of one another.

If you do not find some of the above books, ask the librarian whether they are available by interlibrary loan.

What Happened Where Your Ancestors Lived?

In this search you are trying to find out what happened in the area where your ancestor lived. What were the major events in the area? What were the primary occupations? When did major changes occur?

For example, did the population of the village move into a large town because the Jacobite army was approaching? Was there a large flood in the area that destroyed the bridges or crops and killed many people? When were the major explosions in the mines? When were the labor strikes and from where did the replacement workers come? Did the parish have emigration schemes, paying for the poor people to leave the country? Who were the major landowners?

University libraries should have many books that can help you find more about your ancestor's place. Look in the English history section of the library. Small public libraries will usually not have a large English history collection, but the librarian can help you order such books through interlibrary loan.

Library/Archive Source

The *Victoria History of the Counties of England* series, published by the Institute of Historical Research at the University of London, is an especially useful source for local history. These volumes will give great detail about localities. Each county consists of two parts, often in multiple volumes. The first part is a general description of the history and geography of the county. The second part is a detailed history and topographical description of smaller geographic units, often parishes, with information on the major landowners, manors, schools, charities and hospitals. Not all English counties are included in this series, but volumes are still being written and published.

Also see if there is a guide for your county in the Genealogical Bibliography Series. Stuart Raymond has edited these bibliographic guides for more than twenty English counties. Some are now out of print, but the librarian should be able to help you locate them. You can purchase the current ones through the Web site of the Federation of Family History Societies, <http://www.ffhs.org.uk/pubs/pubs.htm>.

For current information on new indexes or resources, revised research on family names, and geographical or occupation-specific articles, you will need to examine the English genealogical periodical literature. Start with PERSI (*Periodical Source Index***).** This index, covering many English society journals, is produced by the Allen County Public Library in Ft. Wayne, Indiana. The index is available in some libraries as a multivolume print collection, but is also available on CD-ROM for purchase from Ancestry Publishing Company. It can also be searched online at <http://www.ancestry.com/ancestry/search/persiadvsearch.asp>.

Sources

You may also want to browse the library shelves in a few important areas. If your library uses the Dewey decimal cataloging system, you will certainly want to look in the 929 Genealogy section and 942 English History section of the library. If the library uses the Library of Congress system, genealogy will be in the CS section and English history materials will be located in the DA area. Do not, however, restrict yourself to history and genealogy! Use the catalog to look for travel and tourism books for England. Search for books about your ancestor's occupation. Look for biographies and diaries of other people so that you can find out more about life in England when your ancestors were there. See what magazines and journals are available. If you want a general overview of a subject, you might try to find materials in the children's or young adult's department. For example, books written for young people can be valuable for beginning research on old occupations because the books will usually give a good overview and also show illustrations of tools and of people practicing their trades. Walk through the entire library. Be creative!

If there is more than one library in your area, visit as many as possible. You will soon become very adept at finding materials you need. When you have completed your library searches, it's time to go to the Family History Center.

ACCESSING THE RESOURCES OF THE FAMILY HISTORY LIBRARY

Can you imagine a giant library entirely devoted to helping you trace your family history? The Family History Library is your dream come true.

Library/Archive Source

What Is the Family History Library?

The Genealogical Society of Utah (GSU) was founded in 1894 to gather genealogical records. It started a library to house these records. The collection eventually became so large that a new building was needed. The library is now called the Family History Library and is located directly west of Temple Square in downtown Salt Lake City at

> 35 North West Temple Street
> Salt Lake City, Utah 84150
> Telephone: (801) 240-2331

The Family History Library is the largest genealogical library in the world. It is a private library operated by the Church of Jesus Christ of Latter-day Saints, but it is open free of charge to the general public, and you will not be proselytized.

What Does the FHL Have?

In 1938 the Genealogical Society of Utah began microfilming records all over the world. These microfilms form the bulk of the collection of the Family History Library. **The FHL now has more than two million rolls of film. It also has a massive collection of books, periodicals, microfiche, compact discs, maps, resource guides, and many other materials to help you find your ancestors.**

Important

The FHL has two types of records:
- Previous research: family history research already done by others.
- Original documents: records created at the time of an event in your ancestor's life. Most of the records date from 1550 to 1920.

The Family History Library's largest collections are for the United States and for the British Isles. The main building of the FHL has five floors: The top floor is administrative offices, and the other four floors are public research areas. Two floors are dedicated to U.S. research, one floor to British Isles research, and one floor to international research. There are even more resources in the FHL's nearby Joseph Smith Building. Staff is always available to assist you. Library staff also answer brief questions by telephone. For help with your English research questions, call (801) 240-2367.

If you have an opportunity to travel to the Family History Library, by all means do so. You will find so many records there that it will be hard to tear yourself away.

Do I Have to Travel to Salt Lake City to Do My Genealogy?

No! In 1964 a system of Family History Centers was established to help people living outside the Salt Lake City area. There are currently more than three thousand Family History Centers. Family History Centers are usually located in local Latter-day Saint churches. The FHCs are open to all researchers, regardless of religious affiliation.

Many of the resources of the Family History Library are available through Family History Centers. What you want most, of course, are the microfilmed copies of original records, many of which are not available anywhere else. For a small fee, you can borrow almost all of them through your local Family History Center. The FHL does not lend other materials and is not a part of the interlibrary loan system. So if the FHL has a book you want that has not been microfilmed, first see if other libraries have copies. Your local librarian will assist you in locating and borrowing the books you need. If you cannot locate the materials elsewhere, you may want to use the photocopying service of the Family History Library. You should be able to obtain a "Request for Photocopies" form at any Family History Center.

Reminder

A list of Family History Center locations and telephone numbers is available from the Family History Library at the address and phone number listed on page 38. **You can also obtain a list of addresses, telephone numbers, and operating hours of Family History Centers worldwide from <http://www.familysearch. org/Browse/BrowseLibrary.asp>.** Contact the individual centers to verify their hours of operation before you visit. If there is more than one FHC in your area, be sure to visit them all. All Family History Centers have the same access to the resources of the Family History Library, but each FHC has different resources of its own.

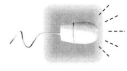

Internet Source

All Family History Centers are staffed by volunteers. Some are quite knowledgeable, and some are beginners. However, the Family History Library publishes a large number of useful research guides to help you use its resources. It also produces blank pedigree charts, family group record forms, and research logs to record your family information. All forms and research guides are available at minimal cost; many are free. They are listed in the *Family History Publications List* (item number 34083000). You can get this free publication from the FHL, the Family History Centers, and the Salt Lake Distribution Center. You can also obtain this and most of the guides from the SourceGuide on the Internet at <http://www.familysearch.org/sg/>.

Several free research guides are mentioned in this chapter. You will find them at Family History Centers and on the FamilySearch Web site. All of them can be ordered from

Salt Lake Distribution Center
1999 West 1700 South
Salt Lake City, Utah 84104
Telephone: (801) 240-2504

Timesaver

GETTING STARTED AT A FAMILY HISTORY CENTER

When you walk into any Family History Center, the first thing you should do is find out what information is already available about your family. Go to a computer in the Family History Center and use the FamilySearch program. FamilySearch is used to access several databases including the three that we discuss here: the International Genealogical Index, Ancestral File, and the Family History Library Catalog. These databases will get you started.

The International Genealogical Index (IGI)

One of the most valuable resources at any Family History Center is the International Genealogical Index. The IGI is a large database containing more than 300 million names. About nine million additional names are added yearly. The IGI is available in the FamilySearch program on computer. It is also available on microfiche, but the microfiche version is out of date. A third choice is to access the International Genealogical Index on the Internet at <http://www.familysearch.org>. At the time of this writing, the FamilySearch program at the Family History Centers is your best choice. There is a free four-page printed guide available online and in most Family History Centers that will help you learn to use the IGI. It is called *Using the International Genealogical Index (on compact disc).*

Step By Step

Even without instructions, the IGI is easy to use. Each screen provides instructions, so just follow the directions given. **Let's use the International Genealogical Index** to see if we can find a child named Dorothy Jane Dixon who may be the sister of Mary Isabella Dixon, whom we will meet later. Dorothy Jane and Mary Isabella were listed in the 1851 census together, and both were born in the parish of Stamfordham.

If you conduct an "Individual Search" in the IGI, you will find an entry for Dorothy Jane Dixon (see Figure 5-1). If you press the Enter key when her name is selected, you will get details about her baptism. Baptisms are called "Christenings" and are abbreviated "C" or "chr" in the IGI (see Figure 5-2).

Figure 5-1
Results of search in International Genealogical Index for Dorothy Jane Dixon, born about 1809 in Northumberland.

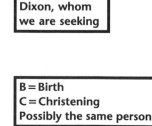

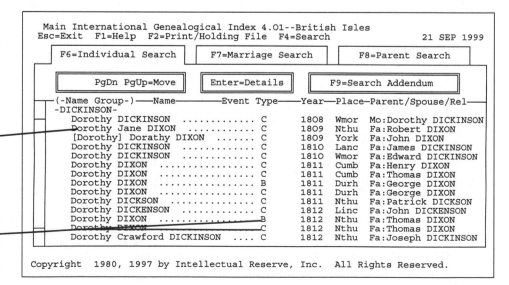

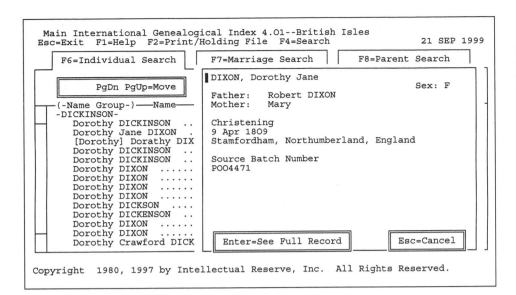

```
Main International Genealogical Index 4.01--British Isles
Esc=Exit  F1=Help  F2=Print/Holding File  F4=Search        21 SEP 1999

 ┌── F6=Individual Search ──┐  ┌── F7=Marriage Search ──┐  ┌── F8=Parent Search ──┐
┌─────────────────────────┐  │DIXON, Dorothy Jane                    Sex: F
│    PgDn PgUp=Move        │  │
└─────────────────────────┘  │ Father:   Robert DIXON
 ┌(-Name Group-)──Name──   │  │ Mother:   Mary
  -DICKINSON-              │  │
    Dorothy DICKINSON  .. │  │ Christening
    Dorothy Jane DIXON  . │  │ 9 Apr 1809
    [Dorothy] Dorothy DIX │  │ Stamfordham, Northumberland, England
    Dorothy DICKINSON  .. │  │
    Dorothy DICKINSON  .. │  │ Source Batch Number
    Dorothy DIXON  ...... │  │ P004471
    Dorothy DIXON  ...... │  │
    Dorothy DIXON  ...... │  │
    Dorothy DICKSON  .... │  │
    Dorothy DICKENSON  .. │  │
    Dorothy DIXON  ...... │  │
    Dorothy DIXON  ...... │  ┌───────────────────────┐   ┌────────────┐
    Dorothy Crawford DICK │  │ Enter=See Full Record │   │ Esc=Cancel │
                             └───────────────────────┘   └────────────┘

Copyright  1980, 1997 by Intellectual Reserve, Inc.  All Rights Reserved.
```

Figure 5-2
Pressing the Enter key gives you the details on the source for any entry in the International Genealogical Index. In this case, Dorothy Jane is the daughter of Robert Dixon and wife Mary. She was christened 9 April 1809 in Stamfordham, Northumberland.

Dorothy was baptized 9 April 1809 in the parish of Stamfordham, Northumberland. Her parents are Robert and Mary Dixon. We cannot tell from this entry if she is Mary Isabella's sister, but we will see later in Mary's marriage record that her father's name was Robert Dixon. We seem to be on the right track, but we need to do further research to be sure.

We want to know about other children born to Robert and Mary Dixon. We can move directly from the Individual Search screen of the IGI to conduct a powerful search called the "Parent Search." This can show us all children on the IGI who have the same parents. Press the F8 key to obtain a screen where you input the names of the parents (see Figure 5-3). Here we type in the father's name, "Robert Dixon." We do not yet know his wife's surname, so we just type "Mary" as the spouses's name. Because Robert Dixon is a common name, we will filter the search to include only Robert and Mary Dixons in the county of Northumberland. Press the F10 key to filter the search. Once done, the computer will search for all children born in the county of Northumberland to any

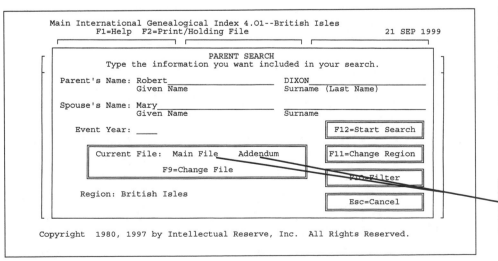

```
Main International Genealogical Index 4.01--British Isles
        F1=Help  F2=Print/Holding File                21 SEP 1999

 ┌─────────────────┐   ┌─────────────────┐   ┌─────────────────┐
┌──────────────────────────────────────────────────────────────┐
│              PARENT SEARCH
│    Type the information you want included in your search.
│
│ Parent's Name: Robert_____    DIXON_____
│                Given Name         Surname (Last Name)
│
│ Spouse's Name: Mary_____    _____
│                Given Name         Surname
│
│   Event Year: ____              ┌────────────────────┐
│                                 │ F12=Start Search   │
│      ┌─────────────────────────────────┐
│      │ Current File:  Main File  Addendum │  ┌──────────────────┐
│      │       F9=Change File               │  │ F11=Change Region│
│                                           │  ┌──────────────────┐
│   Region: British Isles                   │  │ F10=Filter       │
│                                 ┌────────────────────┐
│                                 │     Esc=Cancel     │
└──────────────────────────────────────────────────────────────┘

Copyright  1980, 1997 by Intellectual Reserve, Inc.  All Rights Reserved.
```

Figure 5-3
Pressing the F8 key will automatically select the parents of Dorothy Jane, who are Robert Dixon and his wife Mary. You need to search both the Main File and the Addendum.

Both the main file and the addendum need to be searched

Figure 5-4
The results of the Parent Search for Robert Dixon and wife Mary. It shows a list of potential children. You have to figure out which, if any, are your relatives.

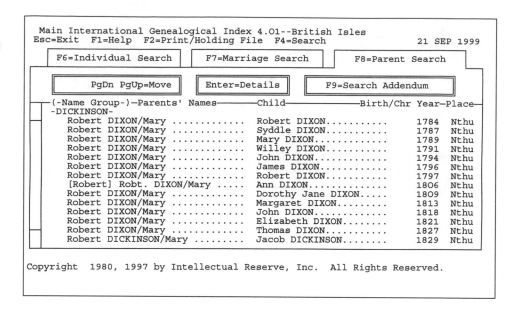

```
Main International Genealogical Index 4.01--British Isles
Esc=Exit  F1=Help  F2=Print/Holding File  F4=Search        21 SEP 1999

   ┌─ F6=Individual Search ─┐ ┌─ F7=Marriage Search ─┐ ┌─ F8=Parent Search ─┐

   ┌─── PgDn PgUp=Move ────┐ ┌── Enter=Details ──┐ ┌── F9=Search Addendum ──┐

─(-Name Group-)─Parents' Names──────────Child──────────Birth/Chr Year─Place─
-DICKINSON-
    Robert DIXON/Mary ............  Robert DIXON...........   1784   Nthu
    Robert DIXON/Mary ............  Syddle DIXON...........   1787   Nthu
    Robert DIXON/Mary ............  Mary DIXON.............   1789   Nthu
    Robert DIXON/Mary ............  Willey DIXON...........   1791   Nthu
    Robert DIXON/Mary ............  John DIXON.............   1794   Nthu
    Robert DIXON/Mary ............  James DIXON............   1796   Nthu
    Robert DIXON/Mary ............  Robert DIXON...........   1797   Nthu
    [Robert] Robt. DIXON/Mary .....  Ann DIXON.............   1806   Nthu
    Robert DIXON/Mary ............  Dorothy Jane DIXON.....   1809   Nthu
    Robert DIXON/Mary ............  Margaret DIXON.........   1813   Nthu
    Robert DIXON/Mary ............  John DIXON.............   1818   Nthu
    Robert DIXON/Mary ............  Elizabeth DIXON........   1821   Nthu
    Robert DIXON/Mary ............  Thomas DIXON...........   1827   Nthu
    Robert DICKINSON/Mary ........  Jacob DICKINSON........   1829   Nthu

Copyright  1980, 1997 by Intellectual Reserve, Inc.  All Rights Reserved.
```

Robert and Mary Dixon. The search returned several pages of results. The page that contains Dorothy Jane is shown in Figure 5-4.

Because Dorothy was christened in 1809, we will want to see the details of the children born to Robert Dixon and Mary who have christening dates from 1806 to 1827. They could all be part of the same family. You can press the Enter key for each child to see the details for each baptism, but there is a way to see the details of all children at once. You can create your own file, a "holding file," that contains only the names you want. Press the F2 key to create a holding file. It will include the details for each child you select. You can then either save the holding file to a disk or you can print it. Figure 5-5 contains the printed holding file of these names. You see that Ann Dixon and Dorothy Jane Dixon were both baptized in Stamfordham. The information in the index was extracted from FHL film number 095028 (indicated in the Batch and Source column). The other children were born in the parishes of Lucker, Widdrington, Longframlington, and Long Horsley. Are they all children of the same Robert and Mary Dixon, or is there more than one Robert and Mary Dixon having children in Northumberland at the time? Why is Mary Isabella not listed among the children? We will not know until we search the parish registers. We will save this printout of the holding file to begin our parish register search. **We will discuss parish registers further in chapter ten.**

One parent search will usually not be sufficient. You will also want to do a search including the maiden name of the wife, because sometimes the original records give the wife's maiden name and sometimes they do not. The parent search will produce different results with and without the maiden name. As you will see later, Robert Dixon married a woman whose maiden surname was also Dixon. So we should conduct another parent search for all of the children born to Robert Dixon and Mary Dixon. We generate a completely different list of children when we do this (Figure 5-6). You can see that there is an Ann Dixon, born or baptized in 1805 to a Robert Dixon and Mary Dixo*. The

For More Info

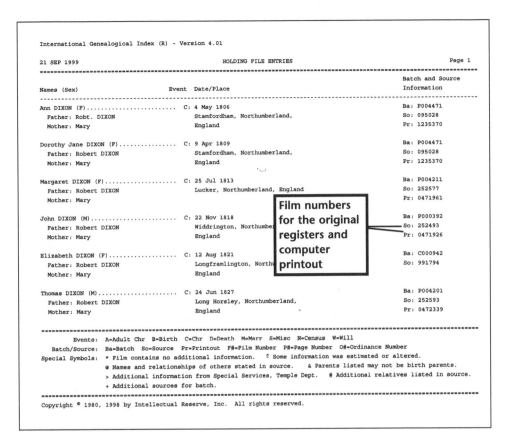

Figure 5-5
From the results of the parent search, you can examine the details of each entry. If any children look like possibilities, you can add them to a holding file and then print. In this holding file, only Ann and Dorothy Jane were later proved to be children of our Robert Dixon and wife Mary. There are other children in our Dixon family that are not included in the International Genealogical Index.

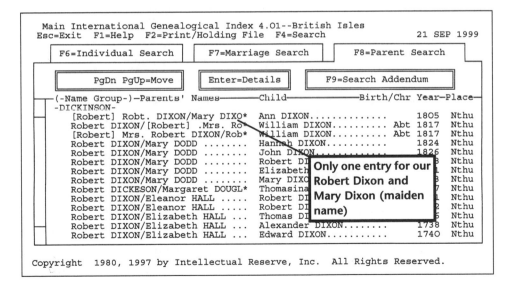

Figure 5-6
A second parent search should be done if the wife's maiden name is known. Here a search was done for Robert Dixon and Mary Dixon (her maiden surname, not married name). This results in one potential child—Ann Dixon.

asterisk (*) means that the name is too long to fit in this field. We must press Enter to see the details of this christening (Figure 5-7).

The parent search is only one of the search capabilities of the IGI on compact disc. Explore the International Genealogical Index for each of your English ancestors. If your ancestor's names are included in the IGI it can help you find dates and places of baptisms and marriages, names of spouses, and names of parents. It is the fastest and most efficient way to begin your research.

Figure 5-7
The details for Ann Dixon show that her parents were Robert Dixon and Mary Dixon and that she was christened on 6 December 1805 in Haltwhistle, Northumberland.

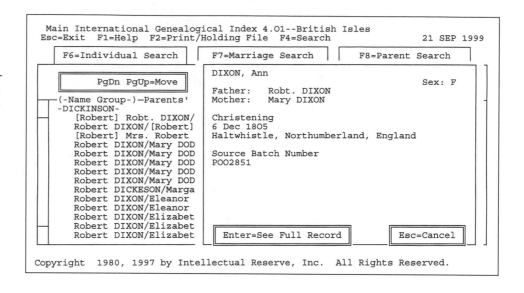

```
Main International Genealogical Index 4.01--British Isles
Esc=Exit   F1=Help   F2=Print/Holding File   F4=Search          21 SEP 1999

   ┌─ F6=Individual Search ─┐  ┌─ F7=Marriage Search ─┐  ┌─ F8=Parent Search ─┐

                                 DIXON, Ann
        ┌─ PgDn PgUp=Move ─┐                              Sex: F
                                 Father:    Robt. DIXON
   (-Name Group-)—Parents'       Mother:    Mary DIXON
   -DICKINSON-
      [Robert] Robt. DIXON/       Christening
      Robert DIXON/ [Robert]      6 Dec 1805
      [Robert] Mrs. Robert        Haltwhistle, Northumberland, England
      Robert DIXON/Mary DOD
      Robert DIXON/Mary DOD       Source Batch Number
      Robert DIXON/Mary DOD       POO2851
      Robert DIXON/Mary DOD
      Robert DIXON/Mary DOD
      Robert DICKESON/Marga
      Robert DIXON/Eleanor
      Robert DIXON/Eleanor
      Robert DIXON/Elizabet
      Robert DIXON/Elizabet    ┌─ Enter=See Full Record ─┐  ┌─ Esc=Cancel ─┐
      Robert DIXON/Elizabet

Copyright  1980, 1997 by Intellectual Reserve, Inc.  All Rights Reserved.
```

Warning

The IGI is an extremely valuable research tool, but remember that it is only an index. You should verify every entry by going to the original source to ensure accuracy.

Ancestral File

The Ancestral File contains lineage-linked information on more than twenty million people. With Ancestral File, you can print pedigree charts and family group sheets of families contained in the database. There are free published guides on the Ancestral File available online and in most Family History Centers. Two of these are *Contributing Information to Ancestral File* and *Correcting Information in Ancestral File*. The Ancestral File is available in the FamilySearch program at the Family History Center. You can also use it on the Internet at <http://www.familysearch.org>. There is no microfiche version of Ancestral File.

Research Tip

Search the Ancestral File for all of your family names. Each screen contains instructions. You may find complete family group records and pedigrees extending many generations. If someone has submitted information about your ancestors, it can save you years of work. However, the information you obtain will only be as good as the research of the person(s) who submitted it. There are still many errors in this database. If you find a name that interests you, you can find the name and address of the submitters. Contact each of them to find out what documentation they have and if they have found any new information about the family. You can also submit your own research to the database. Because the Ancestral File is used all over the world, it is a good way to let others know about your family.

Family History Library Catalog (FHLC)

Mastering the FHLC is your key to finding research materials available in the Family History Library. **The Family History Library Catalog is available in three formats.** The Web version is on the Internet at <http://www.familysearch.org/Search/searchcatalog.asp>. At the Family History Centers, the FHLC is available in

Sources

a computerized version (currently on compact disc) and on microfiche. At the time of this writing, a new computerized catalog was in the testing stages. This catalog may be in all Family History Centers by the time this book is published, so some of the search categories may be different from the ones you read here.

You can search the Catalog in several ways. The compact disc, microfiche, and Web versions of the catalog all have different search capabilities, so not all searches are available in each format. As of 1999 only the Surname and Locality (Place) searches are available in all three formats of the Family History Library Catalog.

- **Surname:** The Family History Library has a large number of books containing previous research. Search by your ancestor's surname to find histories and biographies of your family.

- **Locality:** Items are arranged by locality if the records are from a place or about a place. Search by the name of the place where your ancestor lived to find records pertaining to the locality. On the Web version of the FHLC, the Locality Search is called the "Place Search."

- **Subject:** Records are organized by broad topics such as religions, ethnic groups, occupations, types of records, etc. You will most often search by subject when you want to find general information about a topic.

- **Author/Title:** If you know the author or title of a book, this is the quickest way to see if the Family History Library has it. You will usually search by author or title when you want to see if the book you are seeking is available on microfilm or microfiche from the Family History Library.

- **Film/Fiche Number:** If you know the Family History Library's microfilm or microfiche number for the record you want, you can locate it quickly by searching by the number.

- **Call Number:** If you know the Family History Library call number for a book or periodical, you can search for the record using this number.

- **Computer Number:** Each record title in the FHLC has a computer number. Sometimes the computer number covers an entire collection of records (such as all films of the 1851 census of England and Wales). Other times it covers only one record. Searching by computer number is the fastest way to bring up a series of records. Computer numbers are used in all of the Family History Library's Research Outlines. They are not used in this book because at the time of this writing, computer numbers are not yet available in the Web version of the FHLC.

Two free four-page guides are available and extremely useful. These are *Family History Library Catalog (on compact disc)* and *Family History Library Catalog (on Microfiche)*. These are available online and are usually at Family History Centers.

Using the Family History Library Catalog

Let's start to search the FHLC. **First, use the Family History Library Catalog to look for published family histories or genealogies that have been done by someone else.** A distant relative may have already done much of the work for you. Then, look for local histories that may contain details about your ancestor or

Step By Step

his community. After looking through the many secondary and compiled sources, you are ready to look at original records on microfilm. The majority of the Family History Library's microfilm and microfiche materials are accessible to researchers at Family History Centers for a small fee.

Fiche/Film Number. Use the FHLC to search by fiche/film number for the following resources. These are the same references listed in the Libraries section of this chapter. If you are using the FHLC at a Family History Center, see if the FHC has each work. If not, you may wish to order missing ones so that they will be readily on hand any time you need to refer to them. Please note that one microfiche number may be assigned to a single fiche or to a set of fiche. Before ordering, see how many microfiche are covered by the fiche number you want.

> Marshall, *The Genealogist's Guide* (see page 36). FHL film 496451
> Whitmore, *A Genealogical Guide* (see page 36). FHL fiche 6054492
> Barrow, *The Genealogist's Guide* (see page 37). FHL fiche 6026284
> Lee, *Dictionary of National Biography* (see page 37). FHL fiche 6051262
> (a set of 278 fiche)

In addition to the ones above, you will want to consult the following biographical sources to see if your family is listed.

British Biographical Archive (New York: K.G. Saur, c1984). The first series is a collection of biographies that was originally contained in 324 different sources from all over England. It is easy to use. All biographies have been assembled into one alphabetical sequence, so just find the fiche number that contains your ancestor's surname. This series is available on a total of 1,160 fiche (FHL fiche numbers 6029709–732). There is also a recently released second series containing even more sources (FHL fiche numbers 6140789–814), so be sure to look at both sets.

British and Irish Biographies, 1840–1940 (Cambridge, England: Chadwick-Healey, 1984–). This is a large set of biographies on thousands of microfiche. These are biographies that were published between 1840 and 1940, so they are about people who lived earlier than that. There is an every-name index on fiche 6342001. The index alone is on 325 fiche!

Surname. Now search by surname to find books written about your family. Look for all of your ancestral surnames. As you read each entry, see if the family lived in the same area of England and during the same time period as your ancestors. You will see related surnames in the FHLC listing, but please note that the Family History Library Catalog gives only the primary surnames covered in the book.

Important

Locality or Place. This is the most important search feature of the Family History Library Catalog. To use the microfiche version of the FHLC, you must know how records are arranged. Locations are arranged from large to small. This means that records for the country are followed by records of each county, and then by the parishes and towns within them. All records pertaining to England are listed first. After the section for England, all counties are listed alphabetically. Records for the individual parishes and towns are at the end of each county's listings. To find records for the parish of Stamfordham in the county of Northumberland, look in the FHLC under England-Northumberland-Stamfordham.

Each locality's records are organized by subject. Subject headings used in the Family History Library Catalog are listed in the table below. It will be very helpful to be familiar with these headings. For example, you will notice that there is no heading called "Wills." If you want to find your ancestor's will, look under the category "Probate Records." There is also no heading called "Parish Registers." To see if the FHL has any parish registers for your ancestor's parish, look under the subject "Church Records." Parish registers for the parish of Stamfordham, Northumberland will be cataloged under England-Northumberland-Stamfordham-Church Records.

Start by looking for records in your ancestor's town or parish, then look for records of the county. Don't forget to search for records of England and also of Great Britain. For example, are there any published indexes to church records of the area? To find out, look under England-[County]-[Parish]-Church Records-Indexes. Then look for England-[County]-Church Records-Indexes. Then look under England-Church Records-Indexes.

Research Tip

Subject Headings Used in the Family History Library Catalog	
Almanacs	Manors
Archives and Libraries	Maps
Bibliography	Medical Records
Biography	Merchant Marine
Business and Commerce Records	Migration, Internal
Cemeteries	Military History
Census	Military Records
Chronology	Minorities
Church Directories	Names, Geographical
Church History	Names, Personal
Church Records	Naturalization and Citizenship
Civil Registration	Newspapers
Colonization	Nobility
Correctional Institutions	Obituaries
Court Records	Occupations
Description and Travel	Officials and Employees
Directories	Orphans and Orphanages
Dwellings	Pensions
Emigration and Immigration	Periodicals
Encyclopedias and Dictionaries	Politics and Government
Ethnology	Poorhouses, Poor Law, etc.
Folklore	Population
Gazetteers	Postal and Shipping Guides
Genealogy	Probate Records
Guardianship	Public Records
Handwriting	Religion and Religious Life
Heraldry	Schools
Historical Geography	Social Life and Customs
History	Societies
Inventories, Registers, Catalogues	Statistics
Jewish History	Taxation
Jewish Records	Town Records
Land and Property	Visitations, Heraldic
Language and Languages	Voting Registers
Law and Legislation	Yearbooks

Practice using the Locality Search feature of the Family History Library Catalog to find records for the places where your ancestors lived. Most Family History Center volunteers should be able to assist you.

Does the Library Have Materials That Are Not Listed in the Family History Library Catalog?

Yes. The library holds millions of books, periodicals, microfilms and microfiche covering a wide variety of subjects. The Family History Library Catalog tells you the names and volume numbers of these materials, but it does not give detail about what is in them. For example, the FHLC will list the name of a family history society's journal and give a brief description about it, but the FHLC will not tell you the names of the individual articles that have been published in the periodical. Therefore, many important materials lie buried in the Family History Library's collections.

To assist researchers with finding these resources, Frank Smith and a team of volunteers spent many years going through the books, periodicals, and microforms in the FHL's collections. **They produced an inventory called *Smith's Inventory of Genealogical Sources.*** It contains references to obscure genealogical information found in numerous printed sources in the Family History Library. The items are arranged by place, then by subject. The "General" listing is for subjects that do not apply to a particular place. Each subject listing is followed by a range-of-years listing so that you can find materials for the subject covering a

Printed Source

Smith's Inventory of Genealogical Sources: England	
v. 1, pt. 1. England general (subject)	v. 23, pt. 1. London (subject)
v. 1, pt. 2. England general (range of years)	v. 23, pt. 2. London (range of years)
v. 2. Bedford	v. 24. Monmouth
v. 3. Berkshire	v. 25. Norfolk
v. 4. Buckingham	v. 26. Northampton
v. 5. Cambridge	v. 27, pt. 1. Northumberland (subject)
v. 6. Cheshire	v. 27, pt. 2. Northumberland (range of years)
v. 7. Cornwall	
v. 8. Cumberland	v. 28. Nottingham
v. 9. Derby	v. 29. Oxford
v. 10. Devon	v. 30. Rutland
v. 11. Dorset	v. 31. Shropshire
v. 12. Durham	v. 32. Somerset
v. 13. Essex	v. 33. Stafford
v. 14. Gloucester	v. 34. Suffolk
v. 15. Hampshire	v. 35. Surrey
v. 16. Hereford	v. 36. Sussex
v. 17. Hertford	v. 37. Warwick
v. 18. Huntingdon	v. 38. Westmorland
v. 19, pt. 1. Kent (subject)	v. 39. Wiltshire
v. 19, pt. 2. Kent (range of years)	v. 40. Worcester
v. 20, pt. 1. Lancashire (subject)	v. 41, pt. 1. York (subject)
v. 20, pt. 2. Lancashire (range of years)	v. 41, pt. 2. York (range of years)
v. 21. Leicestershire	v. 41, pt. 3. York (other references by subject)
v. 22. Lincoln	

certain time period. The years from 1900 back to 1500 are divided into fifty-year periods. From 1500 to Saxon times (1066), they are divided into 100-year periods. You will, therefore, be able to search for detailed information such as a pedigree of a family living in Epsom, Surrey, or an article about Catholics in Northumberland from 1650 to 1700.

Smith's Inventory of Genealogical Sources: England is available in forty-one volumes on FHL microfiche 6110526. It is a set consisting of ninety-six fiche. The inventory is also available at the Family History Library in blue books in the British Reference Area. Volume numbers are given in the table on page 48. This source will save you many hours of research and will enable you to find materials that would be virtually impossible to locate otherwise.

SUMMARY

Step two of the research process is to use resources available in libraries in your area. Become familiar with the library and get to know the librarians. They will be able to help you further your research. You will then spend the majority of your research time using microfilms of original documents. Most of these are only held at the Family History Library, but they are accessible to you through your nearest Family History Center. Get to know how to use the International Genealogical Index, the Ancestral File, the Family History Library Catalog, and *Smith's Inventory of Genealogical Sources*. With these resources, you will be able to find countless references to your ancestors' lives in England.

WHERE DO I GO FROM HERE?

The examples in the rest of this book will give you good practice in reading and analyzing English documents. We will follow the paper trail left by the Telford and Dixon families through the generations. By reading each chapter, you will learn how to find the fascinating details of your own ancestors' lives.

If you are researching the time period between 1837 and the present, you will want to pay particular attention to the chapters on civil registration, census records, and probate records. See chapter six to get started.

If you are researching the period between 1538 and 1837, you will most often use records of the Church of England, including parish registers, bishop's transcripts, marriage licenses, and probate records. **Chapters ten and eleven will show you how to use them.**

For More Info

Remember, however, that there is no magic dividing line at 1837. Even if your ancestor left England long before that time, he usually left family and friends behind. You will want to learn to use the later records so you can find those people. You may even use these records to find cousins living in England today!

Bring this book with you to your nearest Family History Center, and let's find our English ancestors.

SIX

Civil Registration and Its Indexes

S ince 1 July 1837, births, marriages, and deaths in England and Wales have been recorded by governmental authorities. This system of re- cording is called "civil registration." More than 90 percent of all births have been registered, and the percentages are even higher for marriages and deaths. The system has grown increasingly more effective, and in the twentieth century very few events have gone unrecorded. Copies of all records are central- ized by the General Register Office (GRO) in London. The officer responsible for the records is the Registrar General. The birth, marriage, and death certifi- cates contain valuable family information that may not be available anywhere else. Best of all, they are indexed for the whole of England! This can help you locate an English ancestor when you don't know exactly where he lived. Civil registration records are an extraordinary resource for family historians.

WHY WERE THE RECORDS CREATED?

Notes

The British government since the mid-1600s has tried to implement a variety of systems to record births, marriages, and deaths. It was important to create documentation showing specific dates and relationships that would be legal in a court of law. Prior to the nineteenth century, the bulk of the population in England belonged to the Church of England, and its records were often used. With the George Rose Act of 1813, the local Church of England clergy was expected to record the births, marriages, and deaths of everyone in their commu- nity, but this was a problem in many parts of the country because of the growing number of dissenters. Clergymen were also reluctant to work as unpaid civil servants. To resolve these problems, the Births and Deaths Registration Act and the Marriage Act were both passed by Parliament in 1836 to create the civil registration system.

HOW WERE THE RECORDS CREATED?

To implement the civil registration system, England and Wales were originally divided into 27 regions. These regions were divided into 618 registration districts under the direction of Superintendent Registrars. By 1851 there were 623 registration districts. A registration district may contain several parishes. Conversely, a large city may have several registration districts. Each district was further divided into subdistricts, controlled by local registrars, with a total of 2,193 registrars in 1838.

Births and Deaths

From 1 July 1837, births and deaths were supposed to be reported to the local registrar by a relative or a friend or neighbor of the family. Births were often reported by the mother. Because she frequently waited until she had recovered from childbirth to report it, there is usually some delay between the time of birth and the time of registration. The family had up to six weeks to register the birth in person or in writing. From six weeks to six months, the person registering the birth had to appear personally before the registrar. From six months to one year, registration required personally appearing before the superintendent registrar, who took the information and signed the register. After one year, no birth could be registered without the written authority of the Registrar General. For these late registrations, proof of the event had to be provided by parties other than those involved, for example, the midwife, doctor, or siblings alive at the time and able to recall the event. Without this proof, a birth certificate could not be issued. It is therefore possible, although not common, for a birth to have been registered a whole year or more later than expected.

Deaths, however, were usually reported within two days and certified by a doctor within five days, or within fourteen days for unusual deaths requiring an inquest. Nobody could be buried without a registrar's certificate or a coroner's order, and if the undertaker performed a burial without one of these documents, he had to report the burial to the registrar within seven days. Therefore, very few deaths went unrecorded. If an inquest was held, the registration of the death would not occur until the inquest was complete.

Until 1874, the local registrar traveled around his district and requested the information regarding births and deaths. It was his responsibility to ensure that these events were recorded. Informants had to supply the details when asked. After 1874, someone present at the birth or death was required to go to the registrar to report the information and sign the register. Penalties for not reporting the events were introduced and were up to forty shillings per offense. If false statements were given and conviction occurred, the fine was not to exceed ten pounds or imprisonment without hard labor for a term not exceeding two years. Penal servitude for a term not exceeding seven years could also be given. These penalties did increase reporting.

The local registrar recorded the events and each quarter gave a copy to the Superintendent Registrar. Each quarter the Superintendent Registrar sent a copy of his records to the Registrar General at the General Register Office in London.

Marriages

Marriage records were compiled at the places where the marriages were performed. People could not be married anywhere they wanted; the marriage had to occur in an officially recognized place.

All ministers of the Church of England were authorized to perform marriage ceremonies. From 1837, it was the responsibility of the Church of England clergy to report marriages occurring in the Established Church. The churches kept two marriage registers. One was retained by the church and the other register, when filled, was forwarded to the Superintendent Registrar. It took several years in some places for a register to become filled, and in some rural areas the original 1837 register still has not been filled. However, each quarter an additional copy was made of all marriages and was forwarded to the Registrar General in London.

From 1837 to 1898, ministers from other religious denominations could perform marriages if the location was preregistered as a place for marriages and only if the local registrar was present. It was not the religious ceremony but the exchange of vows and the recording by the local register that made the marriage legal. After 1 January 1899, the presence of the local registrar was no longer necessary at a nonconformist marriage. However, a certificate or license was still required to be obtained in advance from the registrar, and the event had to occur in a preregistered location.

A couple could also be married by certificate or license obtained in the office of the superintendent registrar in the district in which they resided.

A certificate required seven days residency in the district. A license required fifteen days residency. If the man and woman resided in different districts, notice had to be given in both. Many Roman Catholics and other nonconformists obtained a certificate to avoid the publication of banns in the Church of England. All pending certificates were recorded in a "notice book," and the list was publicly available for anyone to read and have the opportunity to object to the wedding. A minimum notice of twenty-one days was required before the marriage could be held. After that time, the couple could marry within three months at the registrar's office or any registered marriage location. The Superintendent Registrar's license authorized an immediate marriage. It could be issued on the second day after the entry into the notice book, was valid for three months, and could be used in any preregistered marriage location, including the registrar's office, but not in any Church of England church or chapel. This was the first time since 1660 that a purely civil marriage ceremony was an option.

WHY SHOULD I ORDER A CIVIL REGISTRATION CERTIFICATE?

All of the certificates contain a lot of genealogically important information. Using these certificates you can find your ancestor's name, occupation, date and place of birth, parents' names including mother's maiden name, information about former marriages, spouse's name, date and place of marriage, date and place of death, cause of death, residences, and much more.

Important

For births and deaths, the date of registration determines when the event will appear in the index. Marriages were recorded at the time of the ceremony. So there is no distinction between the date of the event and the date of registration.

Ideally, you will obtain birth, marriage, and death certificates for all members of the family because together they will give you a more complete picture of your family. However, this can involve considerable expense, so try to get as many as you can reasonably afford. You may need certificates for events that occurred near census years to locate your family in the census. You may also need the birth certificate of the first child born in the family to help you locate the parents' marriage record.

To obtain the certificates, use the national indexes to births, marriages, and deaths.

BIRTH, MARRIAGE, AND DEATH INDEXES

Two different sets of indexes exist. Each Superintendent Registrar indexes the records for his district. A national index is created by the Registrar General. The national index is compiled at the end of every quarter from the birth, marriage, and death records from all of England and Wales. These are indexed by the date the certificate was recorded, not by the date the event occurred. The volume and page number reference in the national index refers only to the records at the General Register Office and is meaningless for the Superintendent Registrar's records. It is important to remember that this national index is the one readily available in North America.

Most of the indexes to the civil registration records are handwritten prior to 1866 and typeset starting in the March quarter of 1866. All indexes are available to the public. **You can search the national indexes at your nearest Family History Center.** They are recorded in two formats: microfiche indexes covering 1837 through 1983 and microfilm indexes covering 1837 through 1980.

Birth Indexes

Birth indexes provide surname, name or sex of child, Superintendent Registrar's district, and volume and page number. After September 1911, the mother's maiden name is included in the index. The given name (or forename) of the child is recorded as follows:

> 1 July 1837 to 31 December 1865: all forenames in full
>
> 1 January 1866 to 31 December 1866: first forename in full, initials of other forenames
>
> 1 January 1867 to 30 June 1910: first two forenames in full, initials of other forenames
>
> 1 July 1910 to 31 December 1965: first forename in full, initials of other forenames
>
> 1 January 1966 to date: first two forenames in full, initials of other forenames

Marriage Indexes

Marriage indexes provide surname, first name, Superintendent Registrar's district, and volume and page number. Brides and grooms are indexed separately. After March 1912, the surname of the spouse was included in the index. Again, the given names are not recorded the same in all time periods.

    1 July 1837 to 31 December 1865: all forenames in full

    1 January 1866 to 31 December 1866: first forename in full, initials of other forenames

    1 January 1867 to 30 June 1910: first two forenames in full, initials of other forenames

    1 July 1910 to date: first forename in full, initials of other forenames

Death Indexes

Death indexes provide surname, first name, Superintendent Registrar's district, and volume and page number. Starting in the March quarter of 1866, the age at death also appears. Names are recorded as follows:

    1 July 1837 to 31 December 1865: all forenames in full

    1 January 1866 to 31 December 1866: first forename in full, initials of other forenames

    1 January 1867 to 30 June 1910: first two forenames in full, initials of other forenames

    1 July 1910 to 31 March 1969: first forename in full, initials of other forenames

    1 April 1969 to date: first two forenames in full, initials of other forenames

WHAT DO I NEED TO KNOW BEFORE USING THE CIVIL REGISTRATION INDEXES?

Research Tip

The indexes are arranged in chronological order by quarter year. **So before using the civil registration indexes, you will need to know the name of your ancestor and the approximate date of the event (birth, marriage, or death).** As you have seen, the index for each record will give the name of the person, the Superintendent Registrar's district, and volume and page number. Please note that the place listed in the civil registration index is the name of the registration district, not the name of the parish.

If you are looking for a birth or death, a general search in the index may produce many people with the same name. Therefore, you must know an approximate location to narrow down your options. If you do not know the place where an event occurred, look for a marriage record first. A marriage search requires the names of both the bride and the groom, so a matching record will be easier to find.

HOW DO I FIND THE NAME OF THE REGISTRATION DISTRICT?

Internet Source

Before you go to the Family History Center to look at the civil registration index, you can use the Internet to find the name of the registration district. If you know the name of your ancestor's parish, look up the parish under "Index of Places in England and Wales" at <http://www.genuki.org.uk/big/eng/civreg /places/>. There is also an online list of registration district numbers at <http://

www.genuki.org.uk/big/eng/civreg/GROIndexes.html>. If all you know is the county where your ancestor was born and you want to know the names of the registration districts for that county, you can find them in "Registration Districts in England and Wales (1837-1930)" at <http://www.users.zetnet.co.uk/ blangston/genuki/reg>. Please remember that some registration districts cross county boundaries.

You can also find the name of the registration district in the Family History Center. Simply look up the name of the parish in *The Imperial Gazetteer of England and Wales* on fiche numbers 6020308–336. This gazetteer will tell you the name of the registration district. You can see nineteenth-century maps of the registration districts in *A Guide to the Arrangement of the Registration Districts Listed in the Indexes to the Civil Registration of England and Wales.* It is on fiche number 6020287.

Sources

HOW TO USE THE CIVIL REGISTRATION INDEXES AT A FAMILY HISTORY CENTER

There are three separate civil registration indexes: the birth index, the marriage index, and the death index. The names registered in each quarter are listed in strict alphabetical order by the way the name was spelled on the record.

As mentioned before, the indexes to civil registration are available on both microfiche and microfilm formats. The microfiche indexes are faster to use, but some of the indexes were poorly filmed, so you may need to double-check using the microfilm version. The microfiche indexes at the Family History Library cover 1837 through the end of 1983 on 21,537 fiche. The indexes are on the following microfiche numbers:

Birth Indexes 1837–1983	#6101914 to #6102499
Marriage Indexes 1837–1983	#6102500 to #6103085
Death Indexes 1837–1983	#6103086 to #6103671

Searching the Birth Indexes
As an example, let's search for the birth of Mary Telford who was born about 1841 in Westgate, Northumberland.

You probably do not have access to the Internet in the Family History Center, so we'll use *The Imperial Gazetteer of England and Wales* on fiche numbers 6020308 to 6020327 to find the name of the registration district for Westgate. Look at the example from *The Imperial Gazetteer* in Figure 6-1. You will notice that there are five places named Westgate. The first one is in Durham; the second one is in Kent. The third entry is for "Westgate, a hamlet in Belton parish, Lincoln." The fourth entry is for Westgate in the County of Northumberland. This is the place we want. The entry tells us that Westgate is in the Newcastle-upon-Tyne district. Notice that the entry for Westgate in Belton parish, Lincoln, does not give the district. If this was the place we wanted, we would need to look for the entry of Belton to find the name of the registration district.

Now that we have the registration district, we will look for Mary Telford,

Step By Step

WEST FIRLE, &c.   See FIRLE (WEST), &c.

WESTGATE, a chapelry in Stanhope parish, Durham; on the river Wear, 5¼ miles W of Stanhope r. station. It was constituted in 1867; and it has a post-office under Darlington. Pop., about 1,500. The living is a p. curacy in the diocese of Durham. Value, £250. Patron, the Bishop of D. There is a Primitive Methodist chapel.

WESTGATE, a hundred in St. Augustine lathe, Kent; containing 8 parishes and a part. Acres, 9,954. Pop. in 1851, 2,218. Houses, 467.

WESTGATE, a hamlet in Belton parish, Lincoln; 2 miles NNW of Epworth. Pop., 371.

WESTGATE, a township and a sub-district in New-castle-upon-Tyne district, Northumberland. The township lies on the river Tyne, within Newcastle borough; forms the NW suburb of N. town; is in N.-St. John parish; and comprises 210 acres of land and 19 of water. Pop. in 1851, 16,477; in 1861, 21,272. Houses, 2,786. The increase of pop. arose mainly from extension of the iron trade.—The sub-district includes two other townships of St. John and one of St. Andrew; and contains Newcastle workhouse. Acres, 2,778. Pop. in 1851, 21,388; in 1861, 37,477. Houses, 5,377.

WESTGATE, Canterbury. See HOLYCROSS-WEST-GATE.

WESTGATE-HILL, a hamlet in Tong chapelry, W. R. Yorkshire; 4¼ miles SW of Leeds.

WESTGATE-STREET, a village in the Isle of Thanet, Kent; 2 miles E of Margate. It has a coast-guard station.

WESTGATE-STREET, Surrey. See WESTCOTT.

WEST GILLING. See GILLING (EAST and WEST).

WEST-GREEN. a hamlet in the NE of Hants: 2

Figure 6-1
Example from *The Imperial Gazetteer of England and Wales*, showing multiple places called Westgate. The one we need is part of Newcastle-upon-Tyne.

born about 1841 in the district of Newcastle-upon-Tyne. The indexes are ar-ranged chronologically by quarter year. The quarters end in March, June, Sep-tember, and December. Since we don't know exactly when Mary Telford was born, we may have to search a few years before and after 1841. We'll start in the March quarter of 1841 and if we don't find the entry there, we will look in the June quarter, the September quarter, etc., until we find the correct birth. If we don't find her birth within about three to five years, we will begin again with the December quarter of 1840 and search backward. It is important that we record the date of each index as we search it to avoid missing a quarter and to avoid looking at an index more than once.

Sometimes infants were not named at the time of registration. If the child was not given a forename (first or given name) when the informant registered the birth, the entry will appear in the indexes at the end of the list for the parents' surname followed by "male" or "female." Since we are not certain that Mary was given a name at the time of registration, we will look for the name Mary and for "female."

If there are multiple entries for a particular surname with the same or consecutive page numbers, this may indicate twins. However, it is also possible that two different families with the same surname had children born about the same time.

In the December quarter of 1841, we find an entry that matches our criteria (see Figure 6-2). The entries are handwritten and sometimes difficult to read. The volume numbers can be especially difficult to read. You can see how it may be hard to distinguish an "X" from a "V" if the entries are faded or blurred. If they are, look at the table on page 58, "Codes for Areas and Volumes in the Civil Registration Indexes." The volume number for the county of Northumberland for this time period was XXV.

Look again at the example of the birth index in Figure 6-2. Mary Telford's name is about halfway down the page. It says that her birth was registered in the "Newcastle Tyne" district, volume XXV, page 377. Be sure to record the year and quarter of the index, the name as written, district, volume, and page. With this information, you can order her certificate. Instructions for ordering the certificate begin at page 65 in this chapter.

Searching the Marriage Indexes

You can find the names of the bride and groom and the approximate date and place of marriage before using the marriage indexes. **Use the information from a birth certificate to find the names of the parents, including the mother's maiden name.** Mary Telford's birth certificate (shown in the next chapter) tells

Research Tip

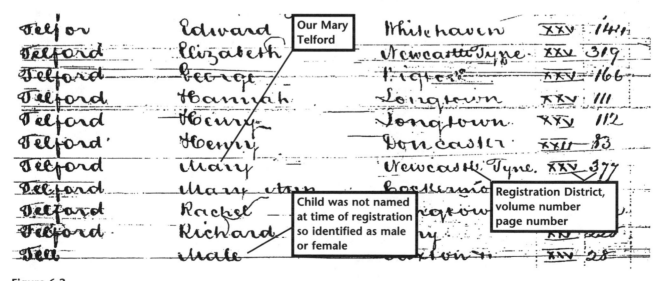

Figure 6-2
Telford birth entries from the Civil Registration Indexes for the quarter ending December 1841. This index covers births registered in October, November, and December 1841. Mary Telford was born in the Newcastle-upon-Tyne District, and her entry will be found on page 377 of volume XXV. Note that the index does not tell you her birth date, only the three-month time period in which her birth was registered.

Codes for Areas and Volumes in the Civil Registration Indexes

Roman Numerals (1837 to 1851)		Arabic Numerals and Letters (1852 to 1946)	
I-III	London & Middlesex	1a-1c	London & Middlesex
IV	London & Surrey	1d	London, Kent & Surrey
V	Kent	2a	Kent & Surrey
VI	Bedfordshire, Berkshire, Buckingham & Hertfordshire	2b	Hampshire & Sussex
		2c-2d	Berkshire & Hampshire
VII	Hampshire & Sussex	3a	Berkshire, Buckinghamshire, Hertfordshire, Middlesex & Oxfordshire
VIII	Dorset, Hampshire & Wiltshire		
IX	Cornwall & Devon	3b	Bedfordshire, Cambridgeshire, Huntingdonshire, Northampton & Suffolk
X	Devon & Somerset		
XI	Gloucester & Somerset		
XII	Essex & Suffolk	4a	Essex & Suffolk
XIII	Norfolk & Suffolk	4b	Norfolk
XIV	Cambridgeshire, Huntingdonshire & Lincolnshire	5a	Dorset & Wiltshire
		5b	Devonshire
		5c	Cornwall & Somerset
XV	Leicestershire, Northamptonshire, Nottinghamshire, & Rutland	6a	Gloucestershire, Herefordshire & Shropshire
XVI	Oxfordshire, Staffordshire Warwickshire & Berkshire	6b	Staffordshire, Warwickshire & Worcestershire
XVII	Staffordshire	6c	Warwickshire & Worcestershire
XVIII	Gloucestershire, Shropshire, Staffordshire, Warwickshire & Worcestershire	6d	Warwickshire
		7a	Leicestershire, Lincolnshire & Rutland
XIX	Cheshire, Derbyshire, Flintshire	7b	Derbyshire & Nottinghamshire
		8a	Cheshire
XX	Lancashire	8b-8e	Lancashire
XXI	Lancashire & Yorkshire	9a-9b	Yorkshire
XXII	Yorkshire	10a	Durham
XXIII	Yorkshire	10b	Cumberland, Northumberland & Westmorland
XXIV	Durham & Yorkshire		
XXV	Cumberland, Lancashire, Northumberland & Westmorland	11a	Glamorganshire, Monmouthshire & Pembroke
XXVI	Breconshire, Carmarthenshire, Glamorganshire, Herefordshire, Monmouthshire, Pembrokeshire, Radnorshire & Shropshire	11b	Anglesey, Breconshire Cardiganshire, Caernarvonshire, Carmarthenshire, Denbighshire, Flintshire, Merionethshire, Montgomeryshire & Radnorshire
XXVII	Anglesey, Caernarvonshire, Cardiganshire, Denbighshire, Flintshire, Merionethshire & Montgomeryshire		

us that her father's name was Walter Telford and her mother's maiden name was Mary Isabel Dixon. The birth certificate also gives us an address to use to locate the family in the census. Locating a census record before searching for the parents' marriage will often narrow down the time period to be searched. For example, the 1841 census record for Walter and Mary Telford (shown in chapter eight) indicates that Mary was not the first child. You should obtain the birth certificate for the first child to see if the parents were married at the time of the birth and also to see where they were living.

Searching the marriage indexes is more time-consuming than searching the birth indexes, because you must look for two names in each quarter. The good news is that this usually increases the likelihood that the entry you will find is the correct entry. There may be several Walter Telfords or several Mary Dixons, but there should be only one Walter Telford whose entry matches that of a Mary Dixon. Let's look for their marriage in the indexes.

The civil registration certificate of birth for the Telford's first child, Elizabeth, states that she was born in May 1840 and that her parents were married. They could have been recently married, so we will begin searching for the marriage in the June quarter of 1840 and work backward. **Always start by looking for the person with the less common name.** Since there are likely to be more Mary Dixons than Walter Telfords, we will look for his name first. If his name is not found in a quarter, we will not need to look for Mary Dixon in that quarter.

Tip

In the marriages registered in July, August, and September 1839 we find the name Walter Telford. See Figure 6-3. The entry reads

> Name: TELFORD, Walter
> Superintendent Registrar's District: Newcastle on Tyne
> Volume 25
> Page 263

It is easy to miss one of the parties if we forget that there are two columns

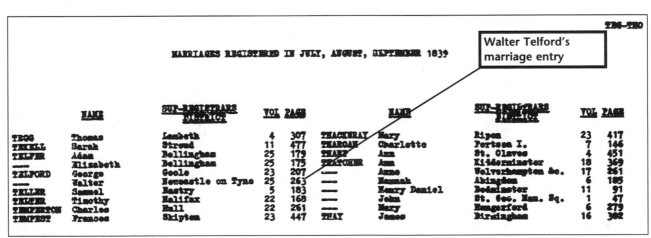

Figure 6-3
Walter Telford's marriage entry in the Civil Registration Index for September 1839. The index shows that he was married in the Newcastle-upon-Tyne District, and the certificate will be found in volume 25, page 263. Compare with entry for Mary Isabell Dixon in Figure 6-4. The entries for bride and groom must match.

```
                                    100.                                    DIP--XIB

              MARRIAGES REGISTERED IN JULY, AUGUST, SEPTEMBER, 1839

         NAME          SUB-REGISTRARS      VOL PAGE        NAME         SUB-REGISTRARS      VOL PAGE
                         DISTRICT                                          DISTRICT

DIPPLE     George      St. Geo. East        2   27    DIXON   Maria     Droitwich          18  269
DIPDALE    Edward      Stoke Damerel        9  484      ---   Martha    Hungerford          6  285
DIRKIN     Alexander   Wigton              25  141      ---   Mary      Leeds              23  284
DIRRICK    Edwin       Bristol             11  170      ---   Mary      Sculcoates         22  361
DISBURY    Eliza       St. Luke             2  520      ---   Mary      Tynemouth          25  358
DISBURY    Elizabeth   Faringdon                        ---   Mary      St. Martins         1  155
  ---      Marianne    Royston &c.                      ---   Mary      Durham             24   51
DISHER     Thomas      St. London                       ---   Mary Ann  Leeds              23  336
DISLEY     James       Manchester                       ---   Mary Ann  Sculcoates         22  391
DISLEY     Eleanor Christiana                            ---   Mary Ann  Newcastle on Tyne  25  259
                       Strand                            ---   Mary Ann  Faversham           5  238
  ---      Sarah       Exeter              10  123      ---   Mary Isabell Newcastle on Tyne 25 263
  ---      William     Market Bosworth     15  211    DIXON   Michael   Durham &c.         24   63
DISMON     George Robert St. Geo. East      2   45      ---   Moses     Nottingham         15  718
DISRAELI   Benjamin    St. Geo. Hanover Sq. 1   37      ---   Nancy     Keighley           23  226
DITCHAM    Eliza       Watford &c.         13  638      ---   Nancy     Clitheroe          21  199
```

> Mary Isabell Dixon's marriage entry

Figure 6-4
Mary Isabell Dixon's marriage entry in the Civil Registration Index for September 1839 shows she was married in the Newcastle-upon-Tyne District, and the certificate is found in volume 25, page 263. Compare with entry for Walter Telford in Figure 6-3. The entries have to match for you to have the correct marriage.

per page. The first column in Figure 6-3 ends with Thackuray, Hannah (not shown), and the next column continues with Thackuray, Mary. Be sure to look at both columns.

We will now look in the same quarter (September 1839) for the name Mary Dixon. You can see in our example (Figure 6-4) that there are five Marys, four Mary Anns, and one Mary Isabell. Mary Dixon is a common name! Even if we did not know that Mary's middle name was Isabell, we would still be able to easily identify the correct Mary Dixon by looking for the one who has the same registration district, volume number, and page number as Walter Telford. Please note that the volume and page number for the bride and groom must match exactly or you do not have the correct couple. The entry for Mary Isabell Dixon says

> Name: DIXON, Mary Isabell
> Superintendent Registrar's District: Newcastle on Tyne
> Volume 25
> Page 263

This is an exact match, so we'll order this certificate. Once you have found a precise match for the bride and groom, see page 66 in this chapter for how to order the certificate.

Step By Step

Searching the Death Indexes

The process for searching the death indexes is the same as searching for births. We will look for someone who died in the twentieth century to see how the format varies slightly from earlier indexes. We want to get the death certificate for the wife of Walter William Telford. Walter was the son of Walter Telford and Mary Isabel Dixon. His wife was Isabella.

See the illustration of the death index in Figure 6-5. Notice that the age at

315

DEATHS REGISTERED IN OCTOBER, NOVEMBER AND DECEMBER, 1937.   TEA-TEN

Name	Age	District	Vol	Page		Name	Age	District	Vol	Page
Teal, Ernest	28	Halifax	9 a	569		Teil, Mowbray J.	64	Exeter	5 b	114
— Sarah M.	54	Huddersfield	9 a	457		Telemaque, James H.	20	Romford	4 a	494
Teale, Frederick	72	Cheltenham	6 a	469		Telfer, Alice A.	71	Ulverston	8 e	972
— Mary E.	60			588		— Annie G.	57	Reading	2 c	412
— Richard	55			295		— Christina	58	Nthmbld.N.2nd.1C b		557
Teall, Ena G.W.	0			529		— John	49	Blackpool	8 s	712
Teanby, Jemima	79			287		Telfor, Janet	78	York	9 d	7
— William	70			589		Telford, Charles F.	0	Newcastle T. 10 b		60
Tear, Annie B.	39	Rugby	6 d	871		— Dora	41	Chester-le-S.10 a		510
Teare, Agnes	53	Liverpool N.	8 b	395		— George	25	Watford	3 a	1219
— Charles H.	57	Bournemouth	2 b	956		— Isabella	90	Newcastle T. 10 b		35
— Robert	67	Whitehaven	10 b	780		— Isabella	71	Barton	8 c	709
— Sarah J.	71	Liverpool N.	8 b	616		— Mary	65	Doncaster	9 c	838
Tearle, Sheila	0	Luton								
Tearrell, Alice A.	44	Rochford								
Teasdale, Eli	62	N.Bierley								
— Elizabeth	74	Gateshead								

Isabella Telford options

Ages at death were added to the index in 1866 but should only be used as an approximate guide, especially with the elderly. Accuracy there will depend upon the informant's knowledge.

Figure 6-5
Ninety-year-old Isabella Telford's death entry in the Civil Registration Index for the quarter ending December 1937. Her certificate will be found in Newcastle-upon-Tyne, volume 10b, page 35.

the time of death is given. Before 1866, no age is listed in the index. The age is often only an approximation, not your ancestor's exact age. We find two entries for "Telford, Isabella" in the quarter ending December 1937. The index tells us that one of them was ninety years old when she died and the other was seventy-one years old. The first one died in the district called "Newcastle T." This is the abbreviation for Newcastle-upon-Tyne. Because we have both an age and a district, this helps us to decide which certificate to order. We will order the one for the ninety-year-old Isabella Telford. You will see the death certificate in the next chapter.

If a particular surname has multiple entries with the same or consecutive page numbers, this may indicate deaths in the same family, e.g., mother and child dying in childbirth or siblings dying together. However, it is also possible that two different families with the same surname registered deaths close to another in time so that the entries appear on the same or consecutive pages.

WHY CAN'T I FIND MY ANCESTOR IN THE INDEX?

In most cases, if you follow the procedures outlined, you should have no trouble locating your ancestor. However, it is always *your* ancestor's name that somehow falls through the cracks. Let's look at the usual reasons for not finding our ancestors in the civil registration indexes and see what we can do.

Base Information Incorrect. This is probably the most common reason that you cannot find your ancestor. On what evidence are you basing your research? How reliable is that evidence? Just because something is in writing doesn't mean it's true! For example, often we are looking for a birth of a person based on his age in a census record or on a death certificate, both of which are unreliable. Information received from relatives is also often incorrect. Always reexamine the evidence that led you to believe that an event occurred in a particular time and place. Could an error have been made?

Technique

Spelling and Handwriting. The spelling of names is another common reason for not finding an entry in the indexes. There was no standardized spelling of names before the late nineteenth century. Names were spelled phonetically, so your ancestor may have spelled his name differently from the way you do. His name could also have been heard and recorded with a different spelling. Do not forget that many of our ancestors were illiterate. The person making the records wrote down what he thought he heard. We have seen forty or more spelling variations to some of our surnames. Be creative with spelling. If you want to find "creative" spelling variations, ask several children to spell the surname!

Another possibility is that the government indexer could have misread the registrar's handwriting and indexed the name under a different spelling. If the indexer misread the first letter of the surname, you could be in for a very long search. For example, the capital letters *S*, *L*, and *T* can look very similar and are commonly misread. In this case, you have to ask, Which letters of this name could be mistaken for other letters? Here's a suggestion for creative handwriting: give the surname to several doctors and see how they write it!

One last problem occurs on occasion: The name may have been left out of the index by mistake. In this case, write to the Superintendent Registrar and ask for a copy of the certificate.

Wrong Name. Your ancestor may not have been registered at birth under the name he later used. A child may not have been named at the time of registration and the parents did not return to the registrar upon making a decision. Instead of a given name, these children are listed as "male" or "female" and are found in the index after the children with forenames and that specific surname. A child could also be registered with two given names but was always known by the second one (middle name). A child might have been given one name at registration and a different one at baptism and the latter was used through life. This is rare, but it can occur. The person may also be listed under his or her nickname. You should always look for name variations. Your ancestor may have been listed in the birth record by one name and used a variation of the name for the rest of her life. **The best reference is *The Oxford Dictionary of English Christian Names*** (see page 68). This book gives variations and origins of names. It will help you find nicknames, former versions of the name that will appear in earlier records, and current variations. The book, though currently out of print, should be available by interlibrary loan. An inexpensive book that you should have on hand is *First Name Variants* (see page 68), which will give you name variations and nicknames.

In the marriage indexes, a woman who has been previously married will be listed under her former husband's surname, not her maiden name. The birth records of her children should indicate if there was a previous marriage. In the death index, she will usually be listed with the surname of her last husband. Make sure that you are not missing any marriages.

Wrong Place. Your ancestor may not have been born where he said he was born, and the marriage or death may not have occurred where you expect. Marriages usually occurred in the parish of the bride, so look for the marriage

Printed Source

there. After the marriage, the couple often went to live in the parish of the groom. A woman often went home to her mother to have the first baby. Births had to be registered in the district where the event occurred, so the birth registration of a first child will usually be in the district where his grandmother lived. A birth may also have occurred at a hospital in a different district, while the mother was away visiting relatives, or during travel. Your ancestor may not have died at home, but while working or traveling. Deaths most often occurred in the homes of relatives. Census records are a good resource for helping you find the various places where your ancestor lived.

The Event Wasn't Registered. In most cases, you can rule out this possibility if you are looking for a marriage or death record. Marriages were recorded by the clergy or registrar. Deaths were reported because a death certificate was necessary to obtain a burial permit. However, it is estimated that up to 15 percent of births before 1875 were not registered. Many parents did not know about the laws requiring registration or assumed that registration was not necessary because the child's baptism was recorded in a church register. They may even have intentionally not registered the birth. For example, parents who wanted to avoid child labor laws did not want the child's age recorded. The Birth and Death Act of 1874 required those present at a birth or death to report the event to the registrar. The Act introduced fines for not registering and penalties for late registration (i.e., later than forty-two days after the event). Therefore, after 1874, virtually all births, marriages, and deaths have been recorded.

If you cannot find a birth, search for a baptism. Baptisms were recorded in parish registers. See chapter ten for information on how to use these records.

Illegitimacy. You are almost guaranteed to find illegitimacy in your ancestry. Do not be dismayed about this; illegitimacy was common in England. If the person you are seeking was one of the oldest children in the family, consider this as a possibility. Illegitimate children will usually be recorded in the indexes with the mother's maiden surname. This may not be the surname that the person actually used. To find the mother's maiden name, obtain the birth certificate of one of the younger children. The mother's maiden name will be found on that certificate. Then search the civil registration index for the birth of the older child using the mother's maiden surname. Another problem associated with illegitimacy is that the child may have been born in a different parish than the later children in the family, so you may be searching in the wrong registration district.

Adoption. Prior to 1 January 1927 there was no such thing as legal adoption in England; the word was often used in cases of guardianship or foster-parenthood. After 1 January 1927 an adopted child will have two birth certificates. The first is a normal record of the original birth which has "adopted" written in the margin. The second gives his or her adoptive name, parents, and the court which granted the adoption order. There is a separate set of indexes connecting the two sets of birth records. Direct application needs to be made to the Registrar General, who will arrange a counseling session prior to the search for the original certificate.

Death Not Registered When It Occurred. The date of registration is important because this date, not the actual date of death, determines the entry of the

For More Info

death into the indexes. If you do not find the death registered in the quarter you are expecting, or even in the year, look further. The death registration may have been delayed because of an inquest, which may follow an accident, suspicious circumstances, suicide, or unexplained death. If a death has not been registered within a year of the date of death, then the death can only be registered with the authority of the Registrar General, and this will be noted in the column with the date of registration.

Event Not in England or Wales. Even though your ancestor lived in England, it is possible that his birth, marriage, or death did not occur there. Therefore, his name will not appear in the regular civil registration indexes. For marriages, the couple could have eloped and married in Scotland, Channel Islands, Isle of Man, or Ireland, where different rules apply. For deaths at sea near a coast, there is no rule governing whether the death should be registered by the local registrar or by the Registrar General of Shipping and Seamen. See the table below for suggestions of alternative indexes that may contain your ancestor's name.

Alternative Indexes

All of these indexes except numbers 5 and 23 are available on FHL microfiche numbers 6137109 to 6137491 and may be ordered through a local Family History Center.

1. Army chaplains' registers of births, marriages, and deaths from 1796 to 1880
2. Regimental registers of births in the United Kingdom (from 1761) and abroad (from 1790) up to 1924, plus indexed regimental registers of marriages
3. Army returns of births, marriages, and deaths abroad (1881–1955) and RAF returns from 1920
4. Consular records of births, marriages, and deaths 1849–1965
5. Adopted children's register (from 1927)
6. Marine registers of births (1837–1965) and deaths (1837–1950) on British merchant or naval ships
7. Deaths: Natal and South Africa Forces (Boer War), 1899 to 1902
8. First World War deaths (army) 1914–1921—officers
9. First World War deaths (army) 1914–1921—other ranks
10. First World War deaths (navy) 1914–1921—all ranks
11. Second World War deaths (RAF) 1939–1948—all ranks
12. Second World War deaths (army) 1939–1948—other ranks
13. Second World War deaths (army) 1939–1948—officers
14. Second World War deaths (navy) 1939–1948
15. Indian Services war deaths 1939–1948
16. U.K. High Commission records of birth, marriages, and deaths abroad, 1950–1965
17. Army, navy and RAF registers of births, deaths, and marriages (abroad), 1956–1965
18. Births and deaths in British civil aircraft from 1947–1965
19. Births, marriages, and deaths (military, civil and chaplains' registers) in the Ionian Isles (1818–64)
20. Births, marriages, and deaths in Protectorates of Africa and Asia, 1941–1965
21. Miscellaneous foreign registers of births, marriages, and deaths 1956–1965
22. Registers of births, marriages, and deaths abroad since 1966
23. Registers of stillbirths from 1 July 1927 (only available with consent of the Registrar General)

THE FAMILY RECORDS CENTRE

Location
1 Myddelton Street, London EC1R 1UW

Hours

Monday	9:00 A.M to 5:00 P.M.
Tuesday	10:00 A.M to 7:00 P.M.
Wednesday	9:00 A.M to 5:00 P.M.
Thursday	9:00 A.M to 7:00 P.M.
Friday	9:00 A.M to 5:00 P.M.
Saturday	9:30 A.M to 5:00 P.M.

Major holidays affecting these hours include: Christmas, New Year, Easter, May Day (first Monday in May) and Spring (usually last Monday in May). If you are planning to visit near these holidays, confirm hours in advance.

Contact information
Online at <http://www.pro.gov.uk/about/frc>
General enquiries at 0181 392 5300
Fax to 0181 392 5307

HOW DO I ORDER THE CERTIFICATE?

After you have tried the problem-solving techniques above, you should be able to locate your ancestor in the civil registration indexes. The records are all located at the General Register Office, which became part of the Office for National Statistics (ONS) in 1996. The Director of the ONS is also the Registrar General.

You can order the certificate by visiting the Family Records Centre in London, or you can order it by mail.

If you are planning a trip to England, you may want to go to the Family Records Centre for the experience. All of the birth, marriage, and death indexes are found there in large, heavy volumes. Once you have used them, you will see how much easier it is to use the microfilm and fiche indexes. The Family Records Centre also has census and other records.

You can find more about the Family Records Centre at its Web site <http://www.pro.gov.uk/about/frc>. You can also read about it in an inexpensive booklet by Audrey Collins called *Basic Facts About Using the Family Records Centre* (see page 68). This booklet describes the contents of the Family Records Centre and how to use it. It also includes a map and tells you the best public transportation routes. The address and hours of the Family Records Centre appear in the table above.

Most likely, you will be ordering by mail. If so, you are in luck! Mail order certificates are one of the few things in recent years where the prices have actually gone down! **You can download the form you need directly from the ONS Web site at <http://www.ons.gov.uk/ons_f.htm>.** You should also check

PURCHASE OF CIVIL REGISTRATION CERTIFICATES

In Person

Certificates can be purchased at the Family Records Centre in London for $6.50 each.

Postal Applications

You can download an application form in Word format from <http://www.ons.gov.uk/ons_usf.htm>.

Correspondence should be addressed to General Register Office, P.O. Box 2, Southport, Merseyside, PR8 2JD, United Kingdom.

Full certificate of birth, marriage, or death*	£11.00
Full certificate of birth, marriage, or death with ONS Index reference supplied	£8.00
Full certificate of adoption	£11.00

*Includes the cost of a three-year inclusive search, e.g., 1900–02.

Applications take six to eight weeks to process.

Priority Service

A priority service is available for the certificates to be mailed the next working day. The cost for a full certificate is £27.00, or £24.00 when the full ONS index reference information is supplied.

Priority service orders are accepted by
    Telephone: (+44) 151 471 4816
    Fax: (+44) 1704 550013
    E-mail: certificate.services@ons.gov.uk

Payment
Payment can be made using Visa, MasterCard, Switch, or Access cards. Credit cards are the cheapest and easiest way to make these purchases. Payment can also be made with an international money order or a check or draft payable to ONS and expressed in pounds sterling.

Warning

current prices there. Full details about ordering the certificate are included in the table above. **When you look at the Web site, you will see other choices not mentioned here, such as the option to order a short (abbreviated) certificate of birth. You do *not* want to order one of these.** Short birth certificates provide only the date and place of birth. They are of no genealogical use. They were introduced in 1947 to provide proof of age and to conceal details of illegitimacy. Order only the full certificate.

Since you have used the indexes, you should already have the ONS index information. The "ONS Index" is another name for the GRO Index that you have been using. Therefore, you will order the "full certificate of birth, marriage, or death with ONS Index reference supplied."

Please ensure that the information you put on the form matches what you have recorded from the index. The indexes are very specific. When you ask for Mary Telford's birth record with the reference such as December 1841 volume XXV page 377, the person receiving your application will first search for all films for the December 1841 quarter, then find volume XXV. He will

Portion of form, partially completed requesting a birth certificate for our Mary Telford. Notice that when you have done the indexing search yourself and have only one option you only include on the form the information from the index. If any other information is included and anything is incorrect the certificate will not be issued.

The other information lines are available if you have not done the index search, but have information about the individual and you are requesting that the ONS do a five-year search to find the certificate for you.

Similar forms are available for the marriage and death certificates.

Number of certificates required
___1___ Full Certificate   _____ Short Certificate

Please tick appropriate box
___X___ Birth Register   _____ Adoption Register

Particular of the person whose certificate is required. Remember, we need full details to ensure a positive search.

PLEASE COMPLETE IN BLOCK CAPTIALS

Surname at Birth ___TELFORD_____

Forenames__MARY_____

Date of birth_____

Place of birth_____

Father's surname_____

Father's forenames_____

Mother's maiden surname_____

Mother's forenames_____

	Reference information from GRO Index		
Qtr/Year	Vol. No	Page No.	District
DEC/1841	XXV	377	Newcastle Tyne

put this film in the machine and turn to page 377. This page will contain five birth entries (deaths also have five entries, while marriages contain two entries per page). If the information you supplied is correct, you will be sent a copy of the information photocopied onto a modern certificate. If any information is wrong (for example, the recorded name is Margaret), you will not receive the certificate.

Part of a sample form requesting the birth certificate for Mary Telford is illustrated above. The rest of the form requests information about you, such as name and address. Similar forms are available online for the marriage and death certificates.

Now, put your order in the mail! The civil registration certificates will provide valuable information that is often not obtainable anywhere else. When your first certificate arrives, it will be a big step in beginning to find your family history.

For More Info

AFTER I HAVE ORDERED THE CERTIFICATE, WHERE DO I GO?

Read chapter seven, Analyzing Civil Registration Certificates.

Sources

WHERE DO I FIND OUT MORE?

Bardsley, Alan. *First Name Variants*. 2nd edition. Birmingham, England: Federation of Family History Societies, 1996.

Collins, Audrey. *Basic Facts About Using the Family Records Centre*. Birmingham, England: Federation of Family History Societies, 1998.

Cox, Jane, and Stella Colwell. *Never Been Here Before? A Genealogists' Guide to the Family Records Centre*. Public Record Office Readers' Guide No. 17. Kew, Richmond, Surrey: PRO Publication, 1997.

Withycombe, E.G. *The Oxford Dictionary of English Christian Names*. New York: Oxford University Press, 1945.

SEVEN

Analyzing Civil Registration Certificates

T his chapter contains information about what should be on a birth, marriage, or death certificate. But, of course, we know that *your* certificate will be different. Together we will see that we never take anything at face value. Maybe your ancestor (or the person recording it) did not follow the rules. Maybe it's just the "law of genealogy" that dictates that critical information will be missing from your ancestor's documents. Therefore, we will try to outfox our ancestors who perhaps tried to make it challenging for us to find out the truth about them. We will look at each certificate separately and examine each item very carefully. We will learn to analyze each piece of information on the certificate and see what we can do when it does not match what we are expecting. We will see how we can use the information to lead us to other records. **Do not expect this chapter to be a light read; we have tried to find every reason for missing, unexpected, or inaccurate information.** You probably will not want to sit down and read this chapter for entertainment; just refer to it from time to time. It will help you to be skeptical with all documents you read.

Important

Compare the information on the certificate for your ancestor to the birth, marriage, and death certificates in this chapter. If you have found certificates among your family papers, they are likely to look like the illustrations here. If you obtain new certificates, they may look different. In 2000, the General Register Office is changing the appearance of the birth and death certificates but the content will be the same.

HOW TO READ AND ANALYZE ENGLISH BIRTH CERTIFICATES

The birth certificate contains a header and ten columns. Let's look at each part in detail.

Step By Step

Birth Certificate Heading

The heading on the certificate gives the name of the registration district and subdistrict in which the birth was registered. The county and the year in which the event was registered are also included.

In the birth certificate of Mary Telford (Figure 7-1), you can see that her birth was registered in 1841 in the subdistrict of Westgate, District of Newcastle-upon-Tyne in the County of Northumberland, Borough of Newcastle-upon-Tyne. This birth was recorded on page 353 of the GRO birth register.

Column 1: When and Where Born

First the GRO registration number. This is the entry number in the General Register Office birth register.

More importantly this column tells the date and place of your ancestor's birth, which may or may not match what you have from other sources. The information on the birth certificate is usually the most reliable. However, sometimes the informant lied about the date of birth so that it appeared to be within the six-week period of time allowed for penalty-free registration. If you have conflicting information from the family Bible or a baptismal entry, look at column eight to see if the registration date is approximately six weeks (forty-two days) from the recorded date of birth. The date of birth may also be incorrect because the informant did not remember the exact date or confused it with the birth date of another child in the family.

When a time of birth is recorded in this column the possibility of twins needs to be considered, so return to the index entries to see if there is another child with the same surname and the same or adjacent registration number.

Warning

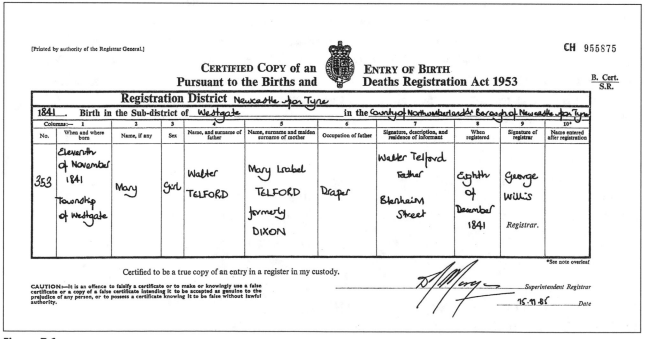

Figure 7-1

Birth Certificate for Mary, the daughter of Walter Telford and his wife Mary Isabel, formerly Dixon. Mary Telford was born 11 November 1841 in the district of Newcastle-upon-Tyne, Northumberland.

This column also contains the place of birth. In the early registrations this may only give the name of the town, for example "Township of Westgate." In urban areas, the addresses became more specific over time. In rural areas, only the name of the community is usually provided.

Notice the place of birth in column 1 and the address of the informant in column 7. The "Township of Westgate" is provided in column 1 of Mary Telford's birth record, but a more specific "Blenheim Street" is given for the address of her father, the informant. We will use the street address to find the family in the census.

From this certificate, we cannot determine if the child was born at home or somewhere else in the township. The mother may have left the community of residence to have her child. For example, a woman often went to her mother's home to have her first child. In this case, the address of the birth and the address of the informant (grandmother, who was present at the birth) may not match what you are expecting.

If the child is illegitimate and born in the workhouse, it is quite common for the master of the workhouse to be the informant. Therefore, the place of birth is the address of the workhouse and not the permanent address of the mother, who may live nearby or may come from several parishes away.

Column 2: Name, If Any

Column 2 is for recording the given name(s) of the child. This column may be blank if the informant did not name the child when registering the birth. Many children were registered with two forenames, but grew up using only the second one. The child's surname was not stated until 1968; prior to this the surname has to be assumed.

It is possible to change the name of a child given in column 2 by using column 10. Within the Church of England, baptismal names are regarded as more important than names given at civil registration. So names can be changed by baptism within one year of the date of registration. The actual recording of the name change can occur at any time afterward. When a name change occurs, the indexes should be updated to reflect the change.

Column 3: Sex

This will read "boy" or "girl" before 1969 and "male" or "female" after 1969. One would think that the sex of a child should be obvious, but unfortunately, it is not always that simple. Informants occasionally made mistakes and the recorder could have made an incorrect assumption based on the name of the child.

Column 4: Name and Surname of Father

This column tells you the name of the father, but it is also used to determine the surname of the child.

If the parents were married at the time of the birth, the full name of the father will be included in this column. If the couple was not married, column 4 will usually be blank. However, a clue to the father's identity may be found if a surname is added to the child's name in column 2, e.g., Mary Brown.

There were special rules regarding the registration of illegitimate children. From 1837 to 1875 the mother could name anyone as the father of her child. However, the father of an illegitimate child did not have to be mentioned. The Registration Act of 1875 stated that the father's name could only be included in this column if both the father and mother requested it and both signed the certificate as informants. Additional methods were introduced in 1953 so that an unmarried father could have his information included without being present to sign at registration.

If the mother became a widow before the birth of her baby, the father's name in column 4 will be followed by "(deceased)."

Column 5: Name, Surname, and Maiden Surname of Mother

The information in this column is very important because it tells you the name of the mother, her maiden name, and her name from any previous marriage.

Notes

There are several options here:

a. If the mother is not married, there will be a single surname, e.g., Jane Lord.

b. If the mother is married, there will be two surnames, e.g., Mary Isabel Telford formerly Dixon. Telford is the mother's married name and Dixon is her maiden name.

c. If the mother has been married more that once, all surnames may be shown, e.g., Mary Smith, late Brown, formerly White. (Mary's current married name is Smith, her former married surname was Brown, and her maiden name is White.)

d. If the mother is using a name that she is not legally entitled to use, it will be indicated by the use of "otherwise," e.g., Mary Black, otherwise Green, formerly White (Mary Black who also uses the surname Green, maiden name White.)

In 1969 the format of the registers changed so that it was not necessary for a woman with multiple marriages to have all her previous married names recorded on the child's birth certificate. For registration purposes, the maiden name actually means the surname the woman used at her first marriage.

Column 6: Occupation of Father (Rank or Profession)

"Rank or profession" tells you what the father did for a living. The occupation is very useful in helping you to distinguish him from other men with the same name. Generally the information given is for paid employment, but occasionally status will be indicated, such as "of independent means."

If there is no father in column 4, there will be no occupation. If a father's name is mentioned but a line is drawn through column 6, it can mean that the father had no occupation, or was unemployed at the time of registration, or the informant did not know what the father did.

If "(deceased)" appears in this column, it means that the father died before the baby was born.

Column 7: Signature, Description, and Residence of Informant

The name of the informant is important because this person is usually a relative of the child. It will also help you determine the reliability of the information on the certificate. **The people who can be informants include the following, in order of preference:**

a. Mother: She is the preferred informant. Information is expected to be accurate.

b. Father: If married to the mother, he is the second preferred choice.

c. A person present at the birth: This covers a long list of possibilities including midwife, grandmother, aunt, sister, or neighbor. The more remote the relationship, the more likely the information on the certificate is inaccurate.

d. The owner or occupier of the house or institution: This includes the master of the workhouse, matron of a hospital, or a relative or friend if the mother gave birth in that person's home.

e. The person in charge of the child (option added in 1875): This could include the father of an illegitimate child, the master of the workhouse if an unmarried mother died in childbirth, guardian of a foundling hospital, or any relative or neighbor who cared for the baby.

When the first six columns of information had been completed, the informant was supposed to verify the information and then sign in column 7. If the informant could not sign his name, he made an "X" or other mark, and the registrar completed it with "The mark of [the informant's name]." If this is found, it usually means that the informant could not read what was written and errors may exist. A signature does not guarantee that the informant could read, because many people learned to write their names but nothing else.

Column 7 also includes the address of the informant. This is valuable if it is the mother, father, or stated relative. If the mother or father was the informant, the address will usually be the home address of the child. If the mother had her baby away from home and a parent was not the informant, then this column may contain the address of another relative.

Column 8: When Registered

It is the date of registration, not the date of the event, by which the birth and death certificates are indexed. You will want to see how close the date of birth is to the date of registration. If it is close to the forty-two-day cutoff, be suspicious. Parents may have altered the birth date to avoid the fees for late registration. There were no checks on actual birth date until well into the twentieth century.

Column 9: Signature of Registrar

This column is only important if the registrar and the Superintendent Registrar have signed the certificate implying something is unusual, such as a late registration.

Column 10: Name Entered After Registration

This column is to allow a change of forename (given name), not surname, to be made to the certificate after registration. (See Column 2 description on page 71.)

Certificate Changes

If an error is found on a certificate (for example, the wrong date of birth), the certificate cannot be changed. Instead, after proof of the error, an annotation is made in the margin of the certificate and signed by the registrar and the superintendent.

Now That I Have Read the Birth Certificate, Where Do I Go From Here?

After you have recorded all of the information about the child's birth, the next step is usually to use the names of the father and mother to locate the parents' marriage record. Search the marriage indexes for the parents' names and order the marriage certificate. You will also use the place of birth or the address of the informant to find the family in the census returns. See chapter eight to find out more about the census.

Step By Step

HOW TO READ AND ANALYZE ENGLISH MARRIAGE CERTIFICATES

The marriage certificate has a header, eight columns, and a footer. We need to look at each item closely. We will look at the marriage certificate of Walter Telford and Mary Isabel Dixon in Figure 7-2.

Marriage Certificate Header

The heading on the certificate provides the name of the Registration District, which will match the entry found in the GRO Indexes. In our example, the Registration District is Newcastle-upon-Tyne.

Below the Registration District are two types of headings depending on whether the marriage occurred in the Church of England or at some other location, such as the Registrar's Office. You can see that the Telford-Dixon marriage occurred in the Church of England. The words *parish church* always indicate the Church of England.

Entry Number

The first unnumbered column on the certificate contains the entry number in the original marriage record book. It can range from one to five hundred and has nothing to do with the GRO reference number in their indexes.

Column 1: When Married

This is the date of the marriage that should be recorded on your pedigree chart and family group record. Since the marriage entry was recorded at the time it occurred, there is no separate registration date as there is for births and deaths.

Figure 7-2
Marriage Certificate for Walter Telford and Mary Isabel Dixon who were married 11 August 1839 at All Saints Church in Newcastle-upon-Tyne, Northumberland.

Column 2: Name and Surname

Column 2 contains the name and surname of the bride and groom at the date of the marriage. Their names at the time of the marriage may or may not be the names they were given at birth. In the past, the bride and groom were simply asked for their names and no documentary proof was needed. Occasionally, the bride or groom adopted a stepfather's surname. People might also use a mother's maiden name or a name chosen at random because they didn't like the one they were born with or wanted to hide their identity. Admittedly, the occurrence of name changes is small, but they do occur. Look at column 7, which contains the father's name. If his surname is different from that of his child, it may indicate a name change.

Recent certificates may give explanations of name changes, such as "Name changed by Deed Poll" or "formerly known as" or "otherwise."

Column 3: Age

This information is only as accurate as the bride or groom cared to make it. They were not asked for proof of age or identity unless they appeared to be under the age of consent. Legal consent was at age twenty-one. If the bride or groom was under twenty-one, the consent of the parent(s) or legal guardian(s) or the court was required. The parents of the minor child were notified separately that a notice to marry had been taken by their child. The parents were given time to object. If a parent stated an objection, the couple could not marry until reaching age twenty-one. This sometimes encouraged the bride or groom to say that they were older

Warning

than they were so that they could marry. The only exception to the consent rule was if a person had been married young with parental consent and had then become a widow(er) before reaching age twenty-one, he or she could then remarry without parental consent. Technically a marriage would not be legal if a couple needing parental consent married without it.

At the beginning of civil registration, fourteen-year-old males and twelve-year-old females could marry with parental consent. In the twentieth century, the legal marriage age was changed to sixteen with parental consent for both males and females. The age of consent was also dropped from twenty-one to eighteen.

Unfortunately, some marriage registers, including our illustration, simply state "of full age." Many registers will state both ages as "21" instead of using the words "of full age." If your certificate says "21" for the ages of the groom and bride, it means that they should be at least twenty-one. However, some people lied about their ages so that they didn't have to obtain parental consent. Therefore, the "of full age" or "21" in this column may be meaningless.

Column 4: Condition (Marital Status)
The marital status at the time of the marriage is often "bachelor" or "spinster" or "widow" or "widower."

\di'fin\ *vb*

Definitions

"Bachelor" usually means that the man had not been previously married. However, it is not uncommon for a widower to be listed as "bachelor." A widower is a man whose previous wife has died. Here "spinster" is not "old maid"; it means that the woman had never been married. A widow is a woman whose previous husband has died. Although widowers are often listed as bachelors, widows are never listed as spinsters. We can see in our illustration that Walter Telford has *probably* not been married before, and Mary Isabel Dixon has not been previously married.

Before August 1971, it was also possible for a previously married man or woman to appear again as "bachelor" or "spinster" if the prior marriage was void or annulled. An annulled marriage is considered to have never occurred.

Column 5: Rank or Profession (Occupation)
Column 5 provides the rank, profession, or occupation from paid employment. A woman may show no occupation even though many women had paying jobs. Our illustration indicates that Mary Dixon was employed as a dressmaker. If you find an occupation that you do not recognize, look for a description in *The Oxford English Dictionary* (2nd ed. Oxford: Oxford University Press, 1989).

Column 6: Residence at the Time of Marriage
The address at the time of marriage may be misleading. When a couple was getting married, one of them had to
   a. live in the parish for a Church of England wedding
   b. live in the district in which the nonconformist church was situated
   c. live in the district of the registrar's office

However, there are exceptions:

a. If a couple lived in one parish/district but regularly worshipped at a second church in a different parish or district, they could get married at the church providing the minister would verify that they worshipped there.

b. If a couple wanted to marry in a denomination for which there was no church or approved building in either of their districts, then the couple could choose the specific church of the correct denomination. This church might be many miles away.

If these exceptions did not apply and the couple wanted to get married outside of the district in which they resided, they obtained a marriage license. One of the partners established residency in the district seven days prior to applying for a marriage license at the registrar's office. The person did not need to stay at that address.

Therefore, remember that the address on the marriage certificate may not be the bride's or groom's usual place of residence.

Column 7: Father's Name and Surname

The man named in this column should be the natural father of the bride or groom. The only legal exception is for an adoptive father after 1926.

If either the bride or groom is illegitimate, this column might

a. be blank—because they do not know the father's name.

b. include the father's name, even though the person was not named on the birth certificate.

c. include a fictional name to avoid possible embarrassment from leaving a blank space.

If either father was dead at the time of the marriage, this column should, but does not always, state "deceased."

Column 8: Rank or Profession of Father

This column shows the father's occupation, although it may say "retired" in place of the specific occupation. With common surnames, occupations may be the only way to sort out which individual is your ancestor.

Marriage Certificate Footer

The footer can tell you a great deal about your family, so examine it carefully. There are six options with minor word changes:

a. For the Church of England or the Church in Wales: "Married in the ["parish church" or chapel name] according to the Rites and Ceremonies of the ["Established Church" or "Church of England" or "Church in Wales"]."

b. For all nonconformist churches or other religious groups (except Quakers or Jews): "Married in the [place] according to the rites and ceremonies of [religious group]." With this type of entry, examine the header and footer closely because the place and religious denomination do not have to match. For example, a person may be getting married according to the

Important

rites of the Congregational church, but the ceremony is taking place in a Presbyterian church because that is a registered facility for weddings, or because it's the only facility in the area big enough to hold the wedding party. The marriage entry will be recorded in the register of the denomination of the building, not the denomination of the church performing the ceremony. In the above example, the marriage will be recorded in the Presbyterian register.

c. "Married in the Register Office." In some areas and time periods, this can be a strong indicator of nonconformity, especially if one partner was Roman Catholic.

d. Jewish and Quaker marriages can be recognized by, "Married at [address] according to the usages of the ["Society of Friends" or "Jews"]," or "Married at [building name]," etc. These marriages may be in a registered building or at a private address.

e. A deathbed marriage can be recognized by, "Married at [private address or hospital] according to the rites and ceremonies of [religious group]" plus "conducted according to the Registrar General's licence."

f. A marriage in a prison or mental institution can be recognized by, "Married at [private address]" together with "according to the rites and ceremonies of [religious group]," but without mention of the Registrar General's license.

The end of the line under the main entry reads "by [process] after or by me [signature and title]."

There are seven options for process:

a. "By certificate" indicates an entry in a register office or nonconformist marriage register. It also indicates that the couple waited three weeks between giving notice and getting married.

b. "By licence" indicates an entry in a register office or nonconformist marriage register. It also indicates that the couple may have married with less than three weeks between giving the notice and getting married. The minimum was one clear working day. However, the license lasts three months, so the marriage wasn't necessarily done in a rush.

c. "After banns" can only be found in a Church of England marriage. It is equivalent to the certificate for the register office or nonconformist churches.

d. "By common licence" can only be found in a Church of England marriage. It allows for a marriage in a shorter space of time and has been issued by the bishop or his surrogate for the diocese of the church. It is equivalent to the license for the register office or nonconformist churches.

e. "By special licence" can only be found in a Church of England marriage. The license has been issued by the archbishop and allows the couple to marry in a church that is not the usual parish church of either party.

f. "By Registrar General's licence" on a marriage certificate usually signifies that one of the people getting married is dying. This license allows the marriage ceremony to take place at any location at any time of the day or night.

g. "By registrar's certificate" is very rare but does imply a Church of England ceremony. It can be issued, for example, when services in a church or chapel are so infrequent that the calling of banns and the marriage ceremony could not be completed within the required three-month time period.

So, what does Walter Telford and Mary Isabel Dixon's marriage certificate tell us? We know that they were married in the Church of England by license (spelled "licence" in England). Their certificate shows process option (b) above.

Signatures

The signatures at the bottom of the certificate should include those of the bride, groom, witnesses and officials. If your certificate came from the General Register Office, these signatures are *not* the original signatures. The original signatures are found in the marriage register at the place where the couple married and in the marriage register at the Superintendent Registrar's office. Many clergy required the couple to write their full names, and this may differ from their normal signatures.

The witnesses, two minimum, should be known to the bride and groom because they are performing a legal function and may need to be contacted later to verify the marriage. For many marriages, the witnesses are close relatives. We will want to find out if James Pearson and Nicholas Alderson are relatives of the bride and groom.

After the signatures of witnesses, the signature of the minister will appear. In Church of England marriages, the certificate will have one signature because the cleric conducts the ceremony and completes the registration. For a marriage in the Register Office or in a nonconformist chapel, there will be two signatures. One is for the person conducting the ceremony, and the other is the signature of the local registrar.

Because the Telford-Dixon marriage occurred in the Church of England, there is only one signature, that of Rob[er]t Green, Perp[etual] Curate.

To complete the certificate, a line should be drawn through the space at the end of the certificate outside the box containing all the details. This signifies that no corrections have been made to the original entry. Any corrections will be added to this space and the line omitted.

Now That I Have Read the Marriage Certificate, Where Do I Go From Here?

You may have an exact age of the bride and groom. **If the birth is after 1 July 1837 see the birth section in this chapter, if prior to this date, see chapter ten for information on finding church christening records.**

You should have an address to use to locate this couple in the census returns. The census will tell you a lot more about your family. For example, if the age

For More Info

For More Info

Step By Step

of the couple was listed as "21" or "of full age," the census may give you a more precise age. **See chapter eight to start using the census.**

HOW TO READ AND ANALYZE ENGLISH DEATH CERTIFICATES

Many genealogists ignore death certificates because they give less information than the certificates of birth and marriage. But death certificates are important for tracing medical histories and finding probate records, descendants, other relatives, and more. You will see now why you should get the death certificates of all members of your family. **We will examine the death certificate of Isabella Telford, who is a daughter-in-law of Walter and Mary Isabel Telford,** (see Figure 7-3).

Death Certificate Header

The death certificate header is identical to the birth certificate header.

Register Entry Number

The register number can range from one to five hundred, with five entries per page in the GRO registers. This means that five entries will have the same reference number. It is possible that two or more family members died at the same time and have the same reference number. Examples include a mother

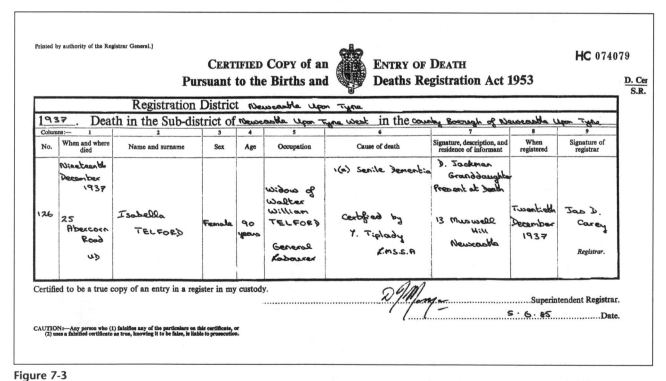

Figure 7-3
Death Certificate for ninety-year-old Isabella Telford who died on 19 December 1937 of senile dementia. She died at 25 Abercorn Road in Newcastle-upon-Tyne, Northumberland. Notice that the informant is a granddaughter, and the certificate provides her place of residence. This is a clue for further research.

and child dying in childbirth, two children dying of the same illness, or family members dying in an accident.

Column 1: When and Where Died

This is the date and place of death. It was recorded close to the time of the event, so record this information on your pedigree chart and family group record.

When a body is found and the precise date of death cannot be determined, the certificate may state "Dead body found on" or "On or about the fifth of February."

The place of death may not be the same as the place of residence of the deceased. Unless the informant is the spouse, you may not have an address for the usual place of residence. If the address given in this column is not recognized, find out what is at that address. It will be interesting to know whether it is the address of a relative, a place of employment, a hospital, or a prison.

Warning

Isabella Telford's certificate states that she died "Nineteenth December 1937" at "25 Abercorn Road UD." We can now look for a probate record; see chapter nine on how to do this.

The address also provides clues for further research. We will want to find out more about this address. Was this her home or was it the home of one of her sons or daughters? Is it an institutional address? If this was a family home, does the place still exist? Can we get a picture of where our ancestor lived? Who lives there now? We may want to see the home when we take our trip to England.

Column 2: Name and Surname

This is the name by which your ancestor was known at the time of death. It may or may not match the name given at birth. It is very common to have first names dropped or changed during life. Obviously, a married woman's surname at death will be different from the surname she was given at birth. For illegitimate children, their father's name may not be on the birth certificate, but they may nevertheless have used the surname of the father. After April 1969, a married woman's maiden name will be provided.

Isabella Telford is listed by her married name. We cannot tell by this certificate what her maiden name was.

Column 3: Sex

This should be obvious and is shown as "male" or "female," although recording mistakes are occasionally made.

Column 4: Age

The age at death on the certificate should always be viewed with suspicion. The deceased did not report her own age. It is known that ages got more exaggerated as the person got older. The informant, therefore, was only reporting what he or she believed about the age of the deceased. The most reliable ages are usually given by the parents or spouse of the deceased. Information reported by children or others is less reliable.

The age of Isabella Telford was reported as ninety years. This age is highly suspect because it is a round number and was reported by her granddaughter. But we now have an approximate date to begin searching for her birth record. Since she died in 1937, her birth should be sometime around 1847. This at least narrows down the range of years we will have to search. It is very unlikely that her age would be reported as ninety if she were only fifty-six!

Column 5: Occupation (Rank or Profession)

For a man of working age, his occupation should be shown. If the man was retired, the column may state his previous occupation as "retired underground miner," or it may just state that he was at that time "not in gainful employment" or "out of employment." The occupation given may not be consistent with other occupational evidence, especially if he was elderly, because it only indicates his occupation at the time of death.

For a wife or widow, there will usually be no reference to an occupation. The reference in this column will usually say "wife (or widow) of [husband's name, his occupation]." Only after 1969 are married women shown with an occupation of their own.

A single woman is more likely to have an occupation stated. The space could also be blank, or it might state "daughter of [father's name, his occupation]."

For a child, the column will state "Son/Daughter of [father's name, his occupation]," unless the child was illegitimate, in which case the mother's name would be substituted. Both parents' names will be given after 1969.

The rank or occupation of Isabella Telford is "Widow of Walter William Telford, General Labourer." This tells us that Walter Telford has already died and that we may start searching backward through the death indexes for his death. It also tells us his occupation. This is important because people changed occupations. We may have found him in an earlier record with a different occupation.

Column 6: Cause of Death

This information is very important for compiling the health history of your family. However, the cause of death on the certificate can be specific or vague depending upon the informant and the time period.

You can judge the accuracy of the information by seeing if the death is
a. uncertified
b. certified by a doctor
c. certified by a postmortem but without an inquest
d. certified following an inquest

During the early years of registration, all deaths were uncertified. The informant gave the cause of death as he saw it. The cause was simply given as pneumonia, measles, stroke, childbirth, etc. It is still possible to have an uncertified death recorded, but these are not common.

Idea Generator

By 1845, most causes of death were certified. When not certified, it means a doctor did not write a certificate of cause of death. In a poor family, the doctor was often not called for death because the family knew that nothing could be done and the doctor would have to be paid.

By 1875, the cause of death was described in clinical terms followed by "Certified by [name of doctor, doctor's qualifications]." This means that the doctor who signed the medical certificate was present during the last illness of the deceased and visited the deceased within the last fourteen days, or had seen the body after death. If no doctor met these criteria, the coroner had to be notified. The doctor or coroner determined the cause of death based on the medical knowledge of the time. You will usually need to look up old medical terms to find out their modern meanings.

We know from examining Isabella's death certificate that a doctor examined her and determined the cause of death.

Column 7: Signature, Description, and Residence of Informant

Column 7 gives the signature, description, and residence of the informant. This can be extremely valuable for researchers. The informant may have been a close relative of the deceased. The informant's information can help you determine the reliability of the information on the certificate.

In the early days of registration, the informant could be

a. someone present at the death

b. someone in attendance during the final illness

c. the occupier of the house

d. the master or keeper of an institution

Prior to 1875 relationships between the informant and the deceased are not usually stated. A name not recognized may be a married daughter, a granddaughter or grandson, a son-in-law, or any other relative likely to have a surname different from that of the deceased.

After 1875 the relationship of the informant to the deceased was given along with the notations "present at the death" or "in attendance." People who were not related but were present at the death still qualified, and the phrase "present at the death" will appear without any stated relationship.

A relative of the deceased is defined as anyone connected by blood or marriage. The term *relative* includes not only close relatives—such as brothers and sisters, daughters and sons, and grandchildren—but also the more distant in-laws, aunts and uncles, nieces and nephews, stepchildren and stepparents. A common-law spouse has no status in law for registration purposes and would be unable to register the death of a partner unless qualified under some other classification, such as being present at the death.

The more remote the relationship to the deceased, the less likely that the information given will be accurate.

The informant on Isabella Telford's death certificate is her granddaughter, D. Jackman, who lived at 13 Muswell Hill, Newcastle. We now will want to find out more about the granddaughter. Which of Isabella's children is the parent of D. Jackman? Why is she, rather than a child of Isabella, the informant? Is it because D. Jackman's mother or father is deceased, or is there another reason? Who else was living at 13 Muswell Hill? Is the granddaughter still living today? She may have some wonderful memories about our family. She or her children may have more information about the family and may even have family photos.

Column 8: When Registered
Registration is normally very close to death, possibly on the day of the death. Today only five days are allowed to register a death, fourteen days if a coroner's postmortem is required. Registration is usually quick because burials cannot take place without a death (or coroner's) certificate. However, there is no time limit with a coroner's inquest, and thus registration may occur months after the actual death.

In our illustration, the death was registered on the day after the death occurred.

Column 9: Signature of Registrar
Column 9 contains the signature of the registrar. If a death was registered a year or more after it occurred, this column will also contain the signature of the Superintendent Registrar.

For More Info

Now That I Have Read the Death Certificate, Where Do I Go From Here?
The search for the probate record comes next. See chapter nine if the death occurred in 1858 or after. See chapter eleven if the death occurred before 1858.

If you have a home address of the deceased or another relative, use this address to locate the family in the census returns. See chapter eight.

You have an approximate age to locate a birth certificate, as described earlier in this chapter, or a christening record (see chapter ten).

If you have the name of a surviving spouse or an indication that the spouse had died, use this information to find more about the spouse.

In general, after examining the civil registration certificates, see the census if you are looking for people alive before 1891 (soon to be 1901).

Sources

Where Do I Go for More Information?
Herber, Mark D. *Ancestral Trails: The Complete Guide to British Genealogy and Family History*. Baltimore, Md.: Genealogical Publishing Company, 1998.

EIGHT

Census

CENSUS BACKGROUND

The first national census was taken in England in 1801 to determine the size of the population, especially the number of available men for the Napoleonic Wars. A census has been taken every ten years since then, except for 1941 because of World War II. The 1801 to 1831 censuses were head counts of the population and did not record information about individuals. However, some enumerators did record names in order to count the numbers of the males and females that were to be tabulated.

Genealogically significant national census returns began in England in 1841. The 1841 and subsequent censuses theoretically contain the names of everyone in the country.

How Was the Census Taken, and Why Is It Important?

As we have seen, the administration of civil registration made it possible to collect information about everyone in England. The Registrar General was at the head of the system. He had a staff who maintained a central register of all births, marriages, and deaths. The country was divided into registration districts, each headed by a Superintendent Registrar. The registration districts were divided into subdistricts with a local registrar whose responsibility was to collect data on all births, marriages, and deaths in his subdistrict and to forward them to the superintendent registrar. Therefore, the local registrars were already prepared to collect personal data. Only one additional step was needed to take the census: Before each census was taken, the local registrars divided their subdistricts into enumeration districts and appointed temporary enumerators. Each census required a separate act of parliament until the Census Act of 1920 made provision for all future censuses.

The census was taken on a specific night, so it is a snapshot of society on

Notes

Census Dates	
Year	Census Date
1901	1 April
1891	6 April
1881	4 April
1871	3 April
1861	8 April
1851	31 March
1841	7 June

\di'fin\ *vb*

Definitions

Important

that particular date. **The sidebar shows the census date for each census from 1841 to 1901.**

To record the census, each enumerator was given a set of household schedules, an enumerator's book, and an instruction and memorandum book. The enumerator used the memorandum book to keep track of the schedules distributed and collected from each household. The enumerator left a household schedule with each householder. The schedule included instructions on how to complete it. The householders were instructed to list only those people who were actually present in the house on the census night.

On the morning after the census night, the enumerator collected the schedules. He was supposed to verify that they had been properly completed, and if not, he was supposed to ask for the missing details. If a schedule had not been done at all, the enumerator filled in the schedule for that house. After collecting and completing all of the household schedules, the enumerator copied them into his enumerator book. When he copied the information, the enumerator made a mark (/) at the end of each family in a dwelling. Multiple-family dwellings were common; two slashes (//) were used at the end of these. The enumerators used common abbreviations when referring to occupations. Some of the most frequently used abbreviations are listed in the sidebar below.

COMMON OCCUPATIONAL ABBREVIATIONS

Ind.	Person of independent means
F.S.	Female servant
M.S.	Male servant
Ag. Lab.	Agricultural laborer
J.	Journeyman
Ap.	Apprentice
F.W.K.	Frame work knitter
N.K.	Not known

After copying the schedules, the enumerator counted the houses and people, and filled in tables with this information. He then turned in the schedules and books to the registrar, who checked them and sent them to the Census Office in London.

At the census office, the clerks reviewed the enumerators' books and tabulated various statistics. They often made marks on the page as they checked each item. You will see many such marks on the microfilmed copies. Sometimes the marks make it appear as if your ancestor had placed a mark in the "Whether Blind, Deaf, and Dumb" column. Other times these marks make it difficult to read people's ages. The enumerators' books are on microfilm. The original householders' schedules were destroyed. That's just our luck; we'd really like to see those!

Knowledge of the census procedure is crucial to interpreting the census returns. Because the schedule listed only those actually present on census night, it is common to find incomplete families on the census. When someone is not listed with the family, it is important to not jump to the conclusion that he or she was deceased. The missing family member may be enumerated elsewhere because he was living there, temporarily working there, or merely visiting. For example, in the 1881 census of Goudhurst, Kent, Walter and Mary Price appear to be missing one of their unmarried daughters. She was, however, enumerated in the census of Herne, Kent, because she was a servant in another family's household. In the 1861 census of Ashford, Kent, Harriett Allan's occupation was listed as "Engine Driver's wife." Her children and mother were also recorded, but her husband was not listed with the rest of the family because he was working away from home on the census night. In the 1881 census of Croyden, Surrey, Margaret Forward was listed as "Wife," but her husband was not enumerated with the family. He appeared in the household of Charles Scriven as a "visitor."

Different types of errors can occur depending on who reported the information and who completed the census schedule. Some people intentionally lied on the householder's schedule. A few even evaded the census taker. If your ancestor was illiterate, his schedule could have been filled in by a child in the house, by a neighbor, or by the enumerator. If the enumerator recorded the information, he wrote down what he thought he heard. If someone other than the enumerator completed the schedule, the enumerator interpreted that person's handwriting when he copied the household schedule into the enumerator's book. There is no way to know who actually wrote the original information. So when reading census records, you will need to consider both regional accents and handwriting variations. Furthermore, the census return you see is from the enumerator's book and not from the original household schedule. Whenever someone copies information from one record to another, transcription errors are bound to creep in.

What Will the Census Records Tell Me?

If you had ancestors born in England, Wales, or Scotland from about 1770 onward, you should search for them or their relatives in the census returns of 1841 and later. Although the civil registration of births started in 1837, the census will get you back even earlier. It will tell you the age and birthplace of everyone recorded and will also tell you the names of the parents of children living at home. British census records are genealogical gold mines!

Technique

The 1841 census lists each member of the household who was present on the census night, and it gives the exact age for children under age fifteen and approximate ages rounded down to the nearest five for all others. Accept the ages with caution. People often lied or were mistaken about their ages. Women especially tended to give incorrect ages. Women in their thirties and forties tended to state their ages as younger than the true age, but older women often said that they were even older than they actually were! The rounding of ages in the 1841 census can make this very problematic. If a forty-two-year old woman stated her age as thirty-nine (and who doesn't?), her age in the census will appear as thirty-five. The census also lists each person's sex and occupation. The final columns indicate whether the person was born in the county where enumerated ("Y" for yes, "N" for no) or in another country ("I" for Ireland, "S" for Scotland, "F" for foreign parts).

The 1851 and later censuses add the exact ages (as reported to the census taker) for each member of the household, the relationship to the head of the household, and marital status. The most exciting part is that the exact place of birth (parish or town and county) was often provided for those who were not foreign born. The exact place of birth should have been recorded by the census enumerator or householder, but this was not always done.

The census is one record that reconstructs and documents a family, not just individuals.

Reminder

What Census Records Are Available, and Where Are They Located?

In the United Kingdom, the information given on the census is confidential for one hundred years. The 1891 census is the most recent census available to the public. The 1901 census will be open for inspection in January 2002. The 1841 to 1881 census returns are on microfilm, 1891 is on microfiche, and all are available at the Family Records Centre, Myddelton Street, London. They are also available through the Family History Library. The Family History Library assigns its own film and fiche numbers to the records, so you locate the census reel using the FHL film number. Remember to use both the Public Record Office (PRO) reference and the FHL film number on your census citations. You can order the film you need at any Family History Center.

What Do I Need to Know Before Searching the Census?

You will need to know how the census is organized and what the census references mean. Records at the Public Record Office are arranged by the governmental body responsible for the record. The government office known as the Home Office was responsible for the 1841 and 1851 censuses as well as for many other kinds of records. All records transferred to the PRO from the Home Office are given the lettercode HO. The Registrar General has been responsible for subsequent censuses. These records are assigned the lettercode RG.

To make it easy to find an exact page among the millions of records at the PRO, the records of a governmental body are divided by record type into classes, and the classes are further subdivided into pieces. Each piece is a box or folder containing several books or papers. Every folio is individually numbered.

The 1841 census is class number 107 of the Home Office records. It has been assigned the code HO 107. The piece numbers run from 1 to 1465. They are cited as HO 107/1 to HO 107/1465. Each piece is a box containing enumerators' books. The folio numbers in each enumerator's book are stamped in the upper right-hand corner. The enumerator's books originally had their own page numbers, so both the folio number and the page number are cited. As we will see later in this chapter, Walter Telford's 1841 census record was found in piece 824 of the census, in book 14, folio 9, page 13. It is cited as HO 107/824/14, f 9, p 13. Anyone, no matter where he lives, can easily locate a census record using this reference. It will be recorded this way whether you are using the census at the PRO or on microfilm

Census Lettercodes and Class Numbers	
Year	Codes
1901	RG 13
1891	RG 12
1881	RG 11
1871	RG 10
1861	RG 9
1851	HO 107
1841	HO 107

in the United States. However, since you will most likely be reading the census on microfilm from the Family History Library, we will record the Family History Library film number first, then the PRO reference.

The 1851 census continued the piece numbering of the 1841 census. It begins with HO 107/1466. Each piece was given a continuous series of folio numbers rather than separately numbering the folios of each enumerator's book. Therefore, it is easier to find records in the 1851 census, and they are easier to cite. You will need only the class number (HO 107), the piece number, folio, and page number.

The 1861 and later censuses are assigned class numbers RG 9, RG 10, etc. They are arranged similarly to the 1851 census. Again, cite the class number, piece number, folio, and page.

SEARCHING THE CENSUS

Normally you will begin with the most recent census available and work backward. Each census gives you clues to help you find the family in a previous census, so you should start with the 1891 census (or the 1901 census when it becomes available in 2002). However, because the 1881 census is entirely indexed and covers the whole of England, this is usually a better starting point.

Technique

Unfortunately, British censuses are often more difficult to search than U.S. census records because many places in the British census are not indexed by surname. You will need to know the name of the parish where your ancestor was living, and in cities you will need to have a street address. You can find an address from several sources, including civil registration certificates of birth, marriage, and death; family letters; probate records; city directories; and others.

You can obtain a form to record British census information from the Family-Search Web site. It is available in the Family History Library's SourceGuide at <http://www.familysearch.org/sg/Fbritish.html>.

There are many ways to locate your family in the census. In this chapter we will use a different method to find each census record and illustrate the importance of searching all census years. The methods presented are often interchangeable between census years. The following list will help you find specific options.

> What if I don't know where my ancestor lived?
> > 1881 British Census and National Index (CD-ROM and microfiche)
> Using the Family History Library Catalog to find street indexes
> > 1891 census as example
> Using the *Register of Towns Indexed by Streets* to find street indexes
> > 1871 census as example
> Using surname indexes
> > 1851 census as example
> What do I do if there is no index?
> > 1841 census as example
> Search all census years
> > 1861 census as example

Sources

See Also

What If I Don't Know Where My Ancestor Lived?

Never fear! **There is an incredible tool to get you started. It's the 1881 census index.** If you don't know the exact place of residence of your ancestor, begin with the 1881 census, because it is the only census that is completely indexed by surname. Not only that, but the entire census has been transcribed so that you can find all of the significant details right from the index. It's the dream of a lifetime for the family historian! Remember, however, that as good as this index is, we must still remember to verify the information by using the census returns on microfilm. **Review our Henry Goddard and Karl Marx example in chapter two (Figures 2-1 and 2-2).**

The 1881 census index is available in two formats. The microfiche edition is available through your local Family History Center. You can also purchase your own 1881 census index on CD-ROM and use it at home.

1881 BRITISH CENSUS AND NATIONAL INDEX ON CD-ROM

We'll look at the CD-ROM version first. You can search one national index that includes the names of everyone in England, Scotland, Wales, Channel Islands, and Isle of Man. You can then see a complete transcript of the census returns. If you do not have your own copy of the CD-ROM, see if a nearby Family History Center has this resource. Let's go step-by-step to see what we can find.

Step By Step

The 1881 British Census and National Index comes with a disc called the Family History Resource File Viewer. This is the program that is used to view the census discs. You will load the Viewer onto your computer, then you will load the National Index to 1881 British Census: Disc 1 and the 1881 British Census: Disc 1.

To begin the program, open the Resource File Viewer. Highlight "1881 British Census—National Index" and click "OK." The program will begin, and a screen will pop up that says, "Type Search Information." Here you will enter your ancestor's first and last names. We will look for the family of Walter Telford. We will enter "Walter" in the field for "First Given Name" and "Telford" in the "Last Name" field. Click "OK."

You would expect a name like Walter Telford to be relatively uncommon. But the search shows us that there were forty-five Walter Telfords in the 1881 census! One great feature of the CD-ROM version is that it will automatically search for the most common spelling variations and also variants of given names. For example, William, Wm., and Bill are all variants of the same name and will be listed together. The three spelling variations shown for this particular surname are Telfer, Telfor, and Telford. The names are listed in order of year of birth. Because of multiple options we must know more about Walter Telford than his name! We should at least have an approximate date of birth. If we know Walter's county of birth, or the name of the county where he was living in 1881, that is even better. In fact, if we know one of these places, we narrow our choices right from this screen. If we believe that Walter was born in the County of Northumberland, we can choose a person who was born in

CD Source

1881 BRITISH CENSUS AND NATIONAL INDEX

England, Scotland, Wales, Channel Islands, Isle of Man, and Royal Navy
This set contains twenty-five Compact Discs:

Family History Resource File Viewer (one disc)

National Index to 1881 British Census (eight discs)

1881 British Census (sixteen discs) divided into the following regions:
- East Anglia
- Greater London
- Midlands
- North Central
- Northern Borders and Miscellany
- Southwestern
- Scotland
- Wales and Monmouth

The entire set of twenty-five CDs is $33 plus applicable sales tax. Order from the Salt Lake Distribution Center at (800) 537-5971.

---

that county, go to the "Birth" column and click on "Nthu" (the abbreviation for Northumberland). This will bring up a list of only the people of that surname who were born in that county. We can do the same with the "Census" column and further modify the list to contain only those with that surname who were born in Northumberland and who were living there at the time of the census. In our example, everyone who was born in Northumberland was also living there at the time of the 1881 census. In this case, clicking on the "Census" column will not narrow down the search; it will take us directly to the census.

You should now be able to narrow your selection to a few choices by looking at the "Relationship" column and the "Year" column. The relationship to the head of household is stated in the former. The "Year" column contains the person's approximate year of birth. Would Walter have been old enough to be a head of household? Was he still living with his parents, or was he living with someone else? We know that our Walter was probably born between 1840 and 1850, so in 1881 he would have been old enough to be the head of household. There are four Walter Telfords who were born in this time period—one each born about 1844, 1846, 1849, and 1850. We will click on each one and see what happens.

Technique

If we select the Walter Telford who was born about 1844, we see that "Nthu" is underlined and in color. This means that it is linked to further information. Double click on either column across from Walter's name. This brings up a screen that says "Insert 1881 British Census Northern Borders Region Disc 1 in the CD-ROM drive. Then click OK." We remove the National Index CD from the drive and replace it with the Northern Borders Region Disc 1. We then click "OK," and Walter's census record appears.

The screen is split into two sections. The top section repeats the information from the index, but adds more precise place names. Instead of a birthplace of "Nthu" we see that Walter was born in Newcastle O T. The census place was Westgate. If this looks like a good possibility for our ancestor, we view the screen below that contains extracts from the census. The full census reference is listed first. It tells us that Walter was living at 40 Buckingham St. in Westgate, Northumberland, England. The source is FHL film 1342217 and the PRO reference is RG 11 piece 5048, folio 51, page 23. Under the reference is Walter's information. The head of household is listed in bold. The head of household is Walter Telford, married, age 37, male, born in Newcastle OT, Northumberland. Living at the same address is Isabella Telford, married age 35; Walter W. Telford, age 13; Mary J. Telford, age 14; Dorothy J. Telford, age 10; Thomas Telford, age 9; Robert A. Telford, age 5; Edward Telford, age 4; and Margaret A. Telford, age 1. All of them were born in "Newcastle On Tyne."

You will notice that relationships and occupations are not listed. These details are very important. Press the F9 key or click on the "Show Details" icon on the toolbar to see each person's occupation and relationship to the head of the household. With this information you should be able to identify your family. We have the right family on the first try! (OK, we didn't pick a fair example. You know that you will not find *your* ancestor on the first try. It's the law of genealogy that *your* ancestor will be the last one!)

But this index has more. We can also see who were the Telfords' neighbors. Click on the word "Neighbors" at the top of the screen. We can now move household by household in the census by using the black arrows on the toolbar. We can also scroll up and down the list to see the many households that were listed before and after the Telfords on the census returns. Use the scroll bar to the right of the census information to do this. You will always want to look at neighbors because relatives and close friends often lived nearby.

This index is a fantastic tool, but remember that it is only a transcription of the census. You will want to see the census return on microfilm. You can order the film you want at your nearest Family History Center. You already know the correct film number from the census transcription.

Warning

1881 CENSUS INDEX ON MICROFICHE

You can use the 1881 census index on microfiche at any Family History Center. A national index is available, as well as an index for each county. There are four main sections to each county: the surname, birthplace, and census place indexes, and the census as enumerated. The "census as enumerated" is a transcript of the census. There are also microfiche for miscellaneous notes, a list of vessels and ships, and a list of institutions. A complete listing of microfilm numbers appears in the following table.

England 1881 Census Index Microfiche Numbers							
County	Surname Index	Birthplace Index	Census Place Index	Census as Enumerated (Transcript)	Misc. Notes	List of Vessels & Ships	List of Institutions
Bedford	6086201	6086202	6086203	6086204	6086205	6086206	6086207
Berkshire	6086208	6086209	6086210	6086211	6086212	6086213	6086214
Buckingham	6086215	6086216	6086217	6086218	6086219	6086220	6086221
Cambridge	6086222	6086223	6086224	6086225	6086226	6086227	6086228
Cheshire	6086229	6086230	6086231	6086232	6086233	6086234	6086235
Cornwall	6086236	6086237	6086238	6086239	6086240	6086241	6086242
Cumberland	6086243	6086244	6086245	6086246	6086247	6086248	6086249
Derby	6086250	6086251	6086252	6086253	6086254	6086255	6086256
Devon	6086257	6086258	6086259	6086260	6086261	6086262	6086263
Dorset	6086264	6086265	6086266	6086267	6086268	6086269	6086270
Durham	6086271	6086272	6086273	6086274	6086275	6086276	6086277
Essex	6086278	6086279	6086280	6086281	6086282	6086283	6086284
Gloucester	6086285	6086286	6086287	6086288	6086289	6086290	6086291
Hampshire	6086292	6086293	6086294	6086295	6086296	6086297	6086298
Hereford	6086299	6086300	6086301	6086302	6086303	6086304	6086305
Hertford	6086306	6086307	6086308	6086309	6086310	6086311	6086312
Huntingdon	6086313	6086314	6086315	6086316	6086317	6086318	6086319
Kent	6086320	6086321	6086322	6086323	6086324	6086325	6086326
Lancashire	6086327	6086328	6086329	6086330	6086331	6086332	6086333
Leicester	6086334	6086335	6086336	6086337	6086338	6086339	6086340
Lincoln	6086341	6086342	6086343	6086344	6086345	6086346	6086347
Middlesex	6086348	6086349	6086350	6086351	6086352	6086353	6086354
Monmouth	6086355	6086356	6086357	6086358	6086359	6086360	6086361
Navy, Royal	6086362	6086363	6086364	6086365	6086366	6086367	6086368
Norfolk	6086369	6086370	6086371	6086372	6086373	6086374	6086375
Northampton	6086376	6086377	6086378	6086379	6086380	6086381	6086382
Northumberland	6086383	6086384	6086385	6086386	6086387	6086388	6086389
Nottingham	6086390	6086391	6086392	6086393	6086394	6086395	6086396
Oxford	6086397	6086398	6086399	6086400	6086401	6086402	6086403
Rutland	6086404	6086405	6086406	6086407	6086408	6086409	6086410
Shropshire	6086411	6086412	6086413	6086414	6086415	6086416	6086417
Somerset	6086418	6086419	6086420	6086421	6086422	6086423	6086424
Stafford	6086425	6086426	6086427	6086428	6086429	6086430	6086431
Suffolk	6086432	6086433	6086434	6086435	6086436	6086437	6086438

| **England 1881 Census Index Microfiche Numbers—*continued*** | | | | | | | |
County	Surname Index	Birthplace Index	Census Place Index	Census as Enumerated (Transcript)	Misc. Notes	List of Vessels & Ships	List of Institutions
Surrey	6086439	6086440	6086441	6086442	6086443	6086444	6086445
Sussex	6086446	6086447	6086448	6086449	6086450	6086451	6086452
Warwick	6086453	6086454	6086455	6086456	6086457	6086458	6086459
Westmorland	6086460	6086461	6086462	6086463	6086464	6086465	6086466
Wiltshire	6086467	6086468	6086469	6086470	6086471	6086472	6086473
Worcester	6086474	6086475	6086476	6086477	6086478	6086479	6086480
York	6086481	6086482	6086483	6086484	6086485	6086486	6086487
Isle of Man	6086495	6086496	6086497	6086498	6086499	6086500	6086501
Guernsey	6103711	6103712	6103713	6103714	6103715	6103716	6103717
Jersey	6103718	6103719	6103720	6103721	6103722	6103723	6103724
Instructions	6086835	——	——	——	——	——	——

Step By Step

Let's find Walter Telford in the microfiche index and see how the fiche compares to the CD-ROM version of the 1881 census. We know that Walter Telford was living in Northumberland, so we will start with the surname index for that county. You can see in the table above that the surname index for Northumberland is on FHL microfiche 6086383.

The surnames on the fiche are in strict alphabetical order, so you will need to consider spelling and name variations when searching for your ancestor. The header on each page tells us the first name appearing on the page. We go through the fiche until we get to the surname Telford, then to the page that has Walter's name. He appears on page 07439 (see Figure 8-1). The index itself gives us significant information. The headings are surname, forename, age, sex, relationship to head [of household], marital condition, census place, occupation, name of head [of household], county and parish where born, note, and the PRO reference and GSU [FHL] film number. Walter is the fourth entry from the bottom of the page. It says that Walter Telford is 37, male, the head of the household, married, living in Westgate, occupation cellerman, born in parish/town of Newcastle OT, county of Northumberland, and that his census return can be found in RG 11/5048, folio 51, page 23. You will use this reference to find the family in the "Census as Enumerated" section. The FHL film number is 1342217. This is great information, so why would we need more than one index?

Suppose that we want to find all of the people with the surname of Telford who were born in Newcastle-upon-Tyne and who were living anywhere in Northumberland in 1881. The 1881 census index table tells us that the birthplace index is on FHL microfiche 6086384. Now look at Figure 8-2. Here we find the Telfords who were born in the parish of Newcastle, Newcastle OT, or Newcastle-upon-Tyne. We use this index to find where families have moved

1881 CENSUS-SURNAME INDEX, COUNTY: NORTHUMBERLAND

TELFORD , Robert PAGE: 07439

CENSUS DATA © BRITISH CROWN COPYRIGHT 1987
MICROFICHE EDITION OF THE INDEXES © COPYRIGHT 1990, BY CORPORATION OF THE PRESIDENT OF THE CHURCH OF JESUS CHRIST OF LATTER-DAY SAINTS.

Annotations: "Title of particular census index and location" — "Source numbers so you can find original census entries" — "Walter Telford's entry"

SURNAME	FORENAME	AGE	REL./COND.	PLACE	OCCUPATION	NAME OF HEAD	CO	PARISH	PIECE/ROLLS	FOLIO NO	PAGE NO	FILM NUMBER
TELFORD	Robert	6			Scholar	TELFORD, John	NTM	Ulgham	5119	105	16	1342236
TELFORD	Robert	5			---	TELFORD, Esther	NTH	Rothbury	5137	62	2	1342240
TELFORD	Robert	1			---	TELFORD, Geor			5117	12	18	1342236
TELFORD	Robert	8x			---	TELFORD, Pete			5077	59	46	1342226
TELFORD	Robert A.	5			Scholar	TELFORD, Walt			5048	51	23	1342217
TELFORD	Robert B.	4	M Son	- Jesmond	---	TELFORD, Robe			5070	80	8	1342224
TELFORD	Robert J.	5	M Son	- Newcastle On T+	Scholar	TELFORD, Robe			5057	11	13	1342220
TELFORD	Robert L.	8	M GSon	- Cowpen	Scholar	LEE, Joseph			5093	35	37	1342230
TELFORD	Robert Phillips	1	M Son	- Wingates	---	TELFORD, John			5138	81	3	1342240
TELFORD	Robert S.	13	M Son	U Corsenside	Scholar	TELFORD, Eliz	NTM	Newcastle	5112	24	9	1342234
TELFORD	Ruth	18	F Daur	- Haydon	Scholar	TELFORD, Jame			5106	69	8	1342233
TELFORD	Sarah	26	F Serv	U Whitley	Gen Serv (Dom)	DENISON, Joseph			5083	54	38	1342228
TELFORD	Sarah B.	1	F GDau	- Seghill	---	CARR, Thomas	NTM	Seghill	5090	117	32	1342229
TELFORD	Sarah E.	4	F Daur	- Prudhoe	---	TELFORD, Robert	NTM	Ovingham	5101	48	51	1342232
TELFORD	Sarah Isabel	10	F Daur	- Prudhoe	Scholar	TELFORD, John	NTM	Mickley	5101	63	8	1342232
TELFORD	Sarah J.	10	F Vist	- Berwick Hill	---	HALL, William	NTM	Prudhoe	5097	82	5	1342232
TELFORD	Septimus	54	M Serv	U Featherstone	Farm Serv (Do+	HUTCHINSON, Matthew	NTM	Melkridge & Haltwhis+	5109	92	3	1342234
TELFORD	Stanley Living+	6	M Son	- Throckley	Scholar	TELFORD, Thos.	NTM	Haydon Bridge	5098	134	49	1342231
TELFORD	Susan	20	F Serv	U Newcastle On T+	Domestic Serv	KENDRICK, Joseph	NTM	Allentown	5059	48	29	1342220
TELFORD	Thomas	65	M Head	M Shilbottle	Carter	Self	NTM	Rothbury	5120	47	13	1342257
TELFORD	Thomas	62	M Head	M Elswick	Brush Manufac+	Self	---	Newcastle	5052	49	14	1342218
TELFORD	Thomas	56	M Head	M Prudhoe	Coal Miner	Self	CUL	Barcastle	5101	31	17	1342232
TELFORD	Thomas	43	M Head	M Hexham	Lead Miner	Self	NTM	Acomb	5104	9	9	1342233
TELFORD	Thomas	42	M Head	M Corbridge	Dom Coachman	Self	NTM	Bellingham	5102	27	11	1342232
TELFORD	Thomas	33	M Head	M Prudhoe	Coal-Miner	Self	NTM	Bellingham	5101	46	48	1342232
TELFORD	Thomas	29	M Head	M Newcastle On T+	Cabinet Maker	Self	KEN	Dover	5057	17	26	1342220
TELFORD	Thomas	27	M Head	M Hurton	Roadman (Lab)	Self	NTM	Chirton	5077	106	16	1342226
TELFORD	Thomas	27	M Head	M Wallsend	Blacksmith	Self	NTM	Corbridge	5072	39	28	1342225
TELFORD	Thomas	26	M Son	U Alnwick	Agricultural +	TELFORD, Henry	NTM	Rock	5123	15	5	1342232
TELFORD	Thomas	24	M Head	M Prudhoe	Coal Miner	Self	NTM	Rothbury	5101	70	21	1342232
TELFORD	Thomas	19	M Son	- Corbridge	Pipe Maker	TELFORD, Robert	NTM	Corbridge	5102	54	13	1342232
TELFORD	Thomas	15	M Son	U Shilbottle	Carter	TELFORD, Thomas	NTM	Shilbottle	5120	47	13	1342257
TELFORD	Thomas	12	M Son	- Throckley	Scholar	TELFORD, Thos.	NTM	Haydon Bridge	5098	134	49	1342231
TELFORD	Thomas	11	M Son	- Corbridge	Scholar	TELFORD, Thomas	NTM	Kirkwhelpington	5102	27	11	1342232
TELFORD	Thomas	9	M Son	- Westgate	Scholar	TELFORD, Walter	NTM	Newcastle O T	5048	51	23	1342217
TELFORD	Thomas	6	M Son	- Wallsend	Scholar	TELFORD, George	NTM	Willington	5072	15	29	1342225
TELFORD	Thomas	5	M Son	- Ulgham	Scholar	TELFORD, John	NTM	Ulgham	5119	105	16	1342236
TELFORD	Thomas	4	M GSon	- Lesbury	---	YOUNG, Alexandr.	NTM	Bilton	5121	54	6	1342237
TELFORD	Thomas	1m	M Son	- Coanwood	---	TELFORD, William	NTM	Haltwhistle	5109	86	5	1342234
TELFORD	Thomas	9m	M Son	- Prudhoe	---	TELFORD, Robert	NTM	Ovingham	5101	48	51	1342232
TELFORD	Thomas Hy.	29	M Head	M Morpeth	Hay Merchant	Self	NTM	Alnwick	5114	74	28	1342235
TELFORD	Thomas Hy.	1	M Son	- Morpeth	---	TELFORD, Thomas Hy.	NTM	Morpeth	5114	74	28	1342235
TELFORD	Thomas J.	5	M Son	- Corsenside	Scholar	TELFORD, Elizabeth	NTM	Corsenside	5112	24	9	1342234
TELFORD	Thomas W.	13	M Son	- Newcastle On T+	Scholar	TELFORD, Peter	CUL	---	5059	123	9	1342220
TELFORD	Thos.	44	M Head	M Throckley	Joiner	Self	NTM	Allendale	5098	134	49	1342231
TELFORD	Thos. Robert	8	M Son	- Prudhoe	Scholar	TELFORD, Wm.	DUR	Willington	5101	77	36	1342232
TELFORD	Walter	71	M FatL	W Tynemouth	Labourer	TELFORD, Ann	NTM	No Shields	5082	23	40	1342227
TELFORD	Walter	37	M Head	M Westgate	Cellerman	Self	NTM	Newcastle O T	5048	51	23	1342217
TELFORD	Walter	35	M Head	M Tynemouth	Mariner	Self	NTM	North Shields	5080	103	19	1342227
TELFORD	Walter	32	M Head	M Prudhoe	Deputy Oven H+	Self	NTM	Corseside	5101	36	27	1342232
TELFORD	Walter	21	M Son	U Stannington	Agricultural +	TELFORD, Elizabeth+	NTM	Ponteland	5095	72	7	1342231

+ = SEE ORIGINAL CENSUS FOR FULL DATA   m = MONTHS   w = WEEKS   d = DAYS   > = GREATER THAN   < = LESS THAN
M = MARRIED   U = UNMARRIED   W = WIDOW(ER)   D = DIVORCED   O = OTHER
N = SEE MISCELLANEOUS NOTES

Figure 8-1
The microfiche version of 1881 Census—Surname Index gathers in one listing all the people with the same surname within the county. It then arranges the entries by forename and then age. Copyright © 1999 by Intellectual Reserve, Inc. Census data © British Crown copyright 1999. All rights reserved.

within the county. For example, Walter Telford, his wife, and children are listed with birthplaces of "Newcastle OT." The census place was Westgate, indicating that they were found in Westgate at the time of the 1881 census. The families of James Telford and of William Telford also contain people who were born in Newcastle-upon-Tyne (this time the name of the parish is spelled out). William Telford and his sister Ann were in Newcastle on Tyne All Saints, truncated as "Newcastle On Tyne A+." The "+" at the end of the entry means that the place name was too long to fit in the field. The James Telford family was in Elswick at the time of the census. Your ancestors may have moved within a city, a county, or across the country. This index can help you find them. You can see that this is a phenomenal tool for locating migrating ancestors!

Now let's look at the census place index. The Northumberland census place index is on FHL microfiche 6086385. We use this index to see all of the Telfords who were living in Westgate in 1881 and to find where they were born. Examine Figure 8-3. There were twenty-four people in Westgate with the surname of

SURNAME	WHERE BORN		[Title of particular census index and location]	AGE	S E X	RELATION- SHIP TO HEAD	MARITAL CONDITION	CENSUS PLACE	N O T E	REFERENCES			
	CO	PARISH					NAME OF HEAD			PIECE RG11/	FOLIO NO	PAGE NO	O.S.U. FILM NUMBER
TELFORD	NTM	Newcastle		34	F	Serv	M CURRY, Joseph			5059	85	4	1342220
TELFORD	NTM	Newcastle		4	F	Daur	- TELFORD, John			5048	84	13	1342217
TELFORD	NTM	Newcastle		1	F	Daur	- TELFORD, John			5050	28	12	1342218
TELFORD	NTM	Newcastle		45	F	Wife	M TELFORD, John			5101	63	8	1342232
TELFORD	NTM	Newcastle		40	M	Head	M Self			5111	11	15	1342234
TELFORD	NTM	Newcastle	John Wm.	12	M	SerC	- CURRY, Joseph			5059	85	4	1342220
TELFORD	NTM	Newcastle	Margaret	7	F	Daur	- TELFORD, John			5048	84	13	1342217
TELFORD	NTM	Newcastle	Margaret	2	F	Daur	U TELFORD, Robert			5463	125	16	1342222
TELFORD	NTM	Newcastle	Robert	26	M	Son	U TELFORD, William			5047	152	31	1342217
TELFORD	NTM	Newcastle	Sarah	26	F	Serv	U DENISON, Joseph	Whitley		5083	54	38	1342228
TELFORD	NTM	Newcastle O T	Dorothy J.	10	F	Daur	- TELFORD, Walter	Westgate		5048	51	23	1342217
TELFORD	NTM	Newcastle O T	Edward	4	M	Son	- TELFORD, Walter	Westgate		5048	51	23	1342217
TELFORD	NTM	Newcastle O T	Isabella	35	F	Wife	M TELFORD, Walter	Westgate		5048	51	23	1342217
TELFORD	NTM	Newcastle O T	Margaret A.	1	F	Daur	- TELFORD, Walter	Westgate		5048	51	23	1342217
TELFORD	NTM	Newcastle O T	Mary J.	14	F	Daur	- TELFORD, Walter	Westgate		5048	51	23	1342217
TELFORD	NTM	Newcastle O T	Robert A.	5	M	Son	- TELFORD, Walter	Westgate		5048	51	23	1342217
TELFORD	NTM	Newcastle O T	Thomas	9	M	Son	- TELFORD, Walter	Westgate		5048	51	23	1342217
TELFORD	NTM	Newcastle O T	Walter	37	M	Head	M Self	Westgate		5048	51	23	1342217
TELFORD	NTM	Newcastle O T	Walter W.	13	M	Son	- TELFORD, Walter	Westgate		5048	51	23	1342217
TELFORD	NTM	Newcastle On Tyne	Agnes H.	5	F	Daur	- TELFORD, James	Elswick		5051	25	50	1342218
TELFORD	NTM	Newcastle On Tyne	Ann	53	F	Sis	U TELFORD, William	Newcastle On Tyne A+		5062	8	10	1342221
TELFORD	NTM	Newcastle On Tyne	James	2	M	Son	- TELFORD, James	Elswick		5051	25	50	1342218
TELFORD	NTM	Newcastle On Tyne	Marion B.	7	F	Daur	- TELFORD, James	Elswick		5051	25	50	1342218
TELFORD	NTM	Newcastle On Tyne	Mary S.	33	F	Wife	M TELFORD, James	Elswick		5051	25	50	1342218
TELFORD	NTM	Newcastle On Tyne	William	49	M	Self	U Self	Newcastle On Tyne A+		5062	8	10	1342221
TELFORD	NTM	Newton	John	48	M	Head	M Self	East Matfen		5098	34	5	1342231
TELFORD	NTM	No Shields	Ann	70	F	Wife	M TELFORD, Joseph	North Shields		5074	25	41	1342225
TELFORD	NTM	No Shields	Ann	27	F	Wife(Head)	M Self	Tynemouth		5082	23	40	1342227
TELFORD	NTM	No Shields	Isabella	11	F	Daur	- TELFORD, Peter	Chirton		5077	59	46	1342226
TELFORD	NTM	No Shields	James	52	M	Bord	M FLETT, Robert	Chirton		5075	60	28	1342225
TELFORD	NTM	No Shields	James	8	M	Son	- TELFORD, Peter	Chirton		5077	59	46	1342226
TELFORD	NTM	No Shields	Peter	3	M	Son	- TELFORD, Peter	Chirton		5077	59	46	1342226
TELFORD	NTM	No Shields	Robert	8m	M	Son	- TELFORD, Peter	Chirton		5077	59	46	1342226
TELFORD	NTM	No Shields	Walter	71	M	Fatl	W TELFORD, Ann	Tynemouth		5082	23	40	1342227
TELFORD	NTM	No Shields	Walter	5	M	Son	- TELFORD, Peter	Chirton		5077	59	46	1342226
TELFORD	NTM	North Shields	Annie	10	F	Daur	- TELFORD, Wm.	Prudhoe		5101	77	36	1342232
TELFORD	NTM	North Shields	Walter	35	M	Head	M Self	Tynemouth		5080	103	19	1342227
TELFORD	NTM	Ovingham	Ann	9m	F	Daur	- TELFORD, Joseph	Prudhoe		5101	42	40	1342232
TELFORD	NTM	Ovingham	Elizabeth	11m	F	(Daur)	- TELFORD, John	Prudhoe		5101	50	56	1342232
TELFORD	NTM	Ovingham	Henry	18	M	Son	U TELFORD, James	Prudhoe		5101	54	64	1342232
TELFORD	NTM	Ovingham	Henry	7	M	Son	- TELFORD, Thomas	Prudhoe		5101	31	17	1342232
TELFORD	NTM	Ovingham	Nichols Jane	2	F	Daur	- TELFORD, Joseph	Prudhoe		5101	42	40	1342232
TELFORD	NTM	Ovingham	Jane	6	F	Daur	- TELFORD, John	Prudhoe		5101	50	56	1342232
TELFORD	NTM	Ovingham	Jane	2	F	Daur	- TELFORD, Thomas	Prudhoe		5101	46	48	1342232
TELFORD	NTM	Ovingham	Jane Ann	7	F	Daur	- TELFORD, Robert	Prudhoe		5101	48	51	1342232
TELFORD	NTM	Ovingham	Jasper C.	1	M	Son	- TELFORD, Walter	Prudhoe		5101	36	27	1342232
TELFORD	NTM	Ovingham	Margaret A.	5	F	Daur	- TELFORD, Thomas	Corbridge		5102	27	11	1342232
TELFORD	NTM	Ovingham	Mary	16	F	Daur	U TELFORD, Thomas	Prudhoe		5101	31	17	1342232
TELFORD	NTM	Ovingham	Mary H.	3	F	Daur	- TELFORD, John	Prudhoe		5101	50	56	1342232
TELFORD	NTM	Ovingham	Nicholas H.	1	F	Daur	- TELFORD, Robert	Prudhoe		5101	48	51	1342232
TELFORD	NTM	Ovingham	Peter	4m	M	Son	- TELFORD, Thomas	Prudhoe		5101	46	48	1342232

+ = SEE ORIGINAL CENSUS FOR FULL DATA   M = MONTHS   W = WEEKS   D = DAYS   > = GREATER THAN   < = LESS THAN   M = MARRIED   U = UNMARRIED   W = WIDOW(ER)   N = SEE MISCELLANEOUS NOTES
D = DIVORCED   O = OTHER

Figure 8-2
The microfiche version of 1881 Census—Birthplace Index gathers all the people of a particular surname and arranges them first by county of birth, then parish of birth, then forename and age. This pulls all the Telfords born in Newcastle together, but notice the place variations creating three separate listings: Newcastle, Newcastle O T, Newcastle On Tyne. Copyright © 1999 by Intellectual Reserve, Inc. Census data © British Crown copyright 1999. All rights reserved.

Telford. Look at the "Where Born" column. Most of these Telfords were born in Newcastle, but some were born in Bellingham, Hexham, Ingoe, and even Scotland. You will use this section to find the birthplaces of missing family members. You may find children missing from your family group records. It will also give you additional places to search for records of your family.

The fourth major section is the census as enumerated. This is a transcript of the census. You will find the census transcript by referring to the Public Record Office reference on the index pages. Whether you used the surname index, the birthplace index, or the census place index, you will find the same references. Walter Telford is listed in all three indexes with the PRO reference RG 11, piece 5048, folio 51, page 23. The entire 1881 census is RG 11, so all we need to locate the family are the piece, folio, and page numbers. The Northumberland Census-As-Enumerated is on FHL microfiche 6086386. The piece numbers are

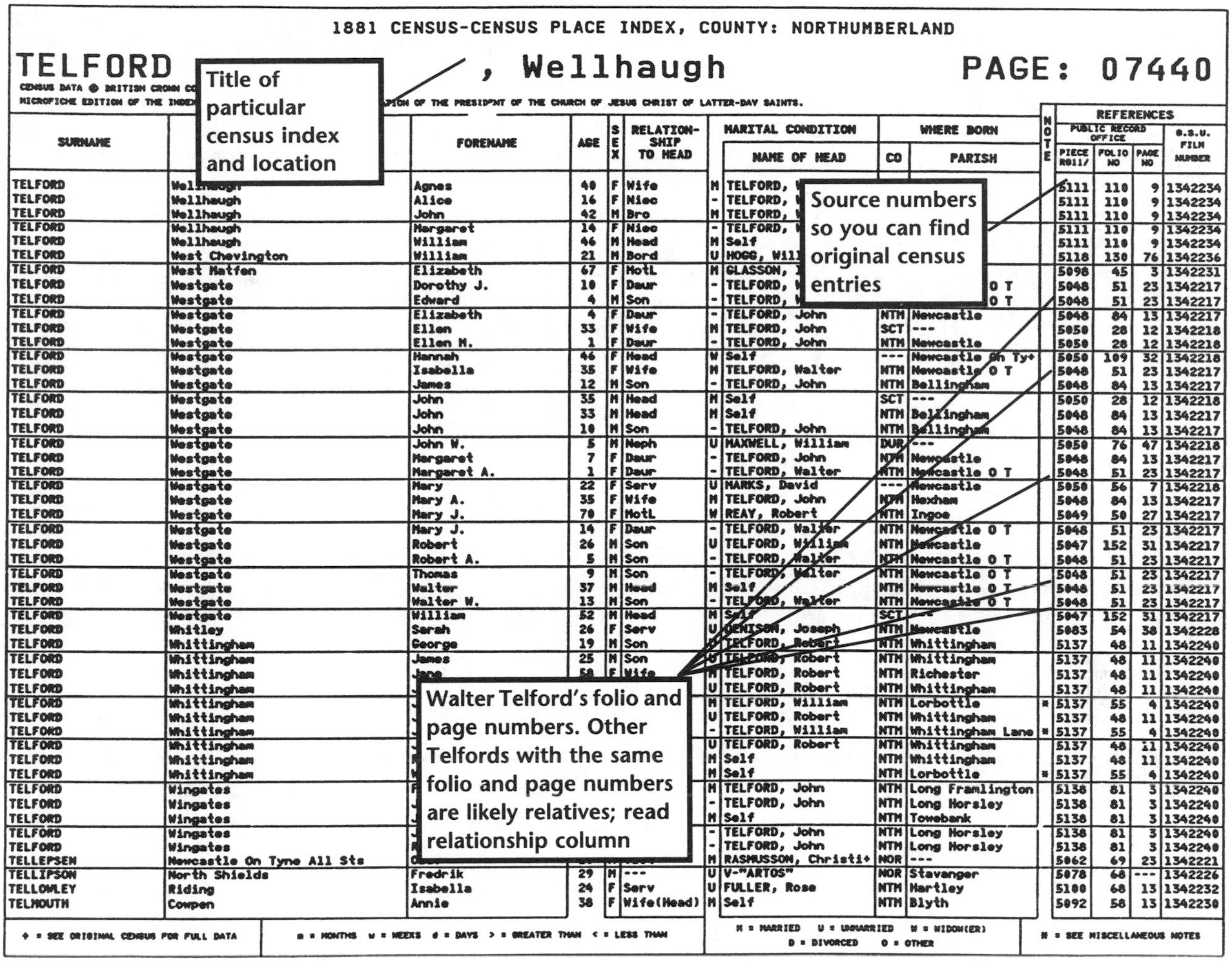

Figure 8-3
The microfiche version of the 1881 Census—Census Place Index gathers all the people of a specific surname together who are residing at the time of the census in a specific community. Within the community they are then listed by forename and age. Copyright © 1999 by Intellectual Reserve, Inc. Census data © British Crown copyright 1999. All rights reserved.

at the top of each fiche. We scan the tops of the pages until we come to 5048, 51, 23 (see Figure 8-4). Here all the census information is neatly typed. There is no handwriting to worry about! On the microfiche, each column of the census is transcribed in the order that it appeared on the census return. You can easily scan the adjacent households and see them all at once. This is an advantage over the CD-ROM version. Here you see that the Telford family is split between two pages of the census transcription. Walter Telford is found at the third entry from the bottom on the first page. He was found at "40 Buckingham +" If there is not enough room in any field, the information is truncated; this is the major drawback to the microfiche version. We need to look at the full entry on microfilm to see the complete address. Because the 1881 British census CD-ROM does not truncate fields, we have seen from the CD that the full address is 40 Buckingham St. But here is everything we need: the name of Walter Telford, his sex, age, marital status, occupation, and birthplace. The names, relationships, marital status, ages, sex, and occupations of other members of

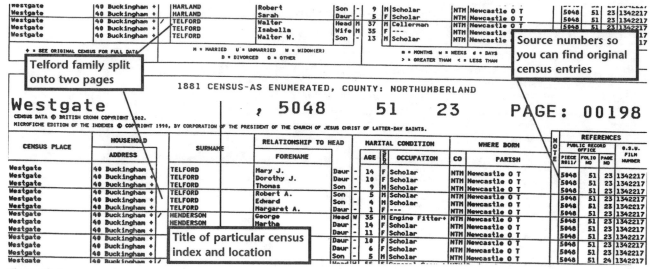

Figure 8-4

The microfiche version of the 1881 Census—As Enumerated is a transcription of the census. The order of the names is arranged as if you were walking the streets with the census taker, so you get to see who your ancestor's neighbors were and what they did for a living. Copyright © 1999 by Intellectual Reserve, Inc. Census data © British Crown copyright 1999. All rights reserved.

For More Info

Reminder

Sources

the household are all listed in full. In the British census, we should find the exact parish of birth! This is great stuff! It is far better than the information on the U.S. census, where we will find only the state of birth. We expect to find the exact place of birth, and when we do, **we can go to the records of that parish to trace the family further. See chapter ten for details.**

If you look at the copy of the census schedule on microfilm, you will see very little difference between it and the transcript. The census page on microfilm contains the full citation information, but it is not all in one place. The PRO class and piece number—"RG 11/5048"—are found in the box below the census page. The folio number is stamped in the upper right corner of the census, and the page number is typed in the upper right corner. The full citation is FHL film 1342217, PRO reference RG 11/5048, f 51, p 23.

Because this index is so complete, many people will be tempted to go no

MICROFICHE INDEXES TO THE 1881 BRITISH CENSUS

Surname index: Use this index to find all people with a particular surname in the 1881 census. Search by surname.

Birthplace index: Use this index to find all of the people with identical surnames who were born in a particular parish. Search by surname, then by parish of birth.

Census place index: Use this index to find all people with the same surname who were found in matching census locations. Search by surname, then by census place.

further. You, however, know that even the best indexes and transcripts are no match for the source. **You will *always* go back to the original source, if possible.**

HOW DO I FIND MY ANCESTOR IN THE OTHER CENSUS YEARS?

We have spent a lot of time looking at the 1881 census because the various indexes are some of the most powerful tools currently available in the field of family history. By starting with the 1881 census indexes, we can more easily find our ancestors in the 1891 and 1871 censuses and then go from there to other records.

The majority of the British census is not indexed, and there is no nationwide index other than the one to the 1881 census. However, many private individuals and family history societies in England have produced some census indexes for their areas.

You can find out what census indexes exist for your ancestor's place by using *Marriage and Census Indexes for Family Historians* (see page 117). This booklet is arranged by county and lists all known census indexes. It tells the type of index (surname or street index), where it is located, the time period covered, and cost. This information can save you considerable research time. The book is periodically updated, so be sure that you have the latest edition.

Many of the family history societies have Web sites on the Internet. A Web site may have a list of the census indexes and how to order them. Because the societies are members of the Federation of Family History Societies, you can obtain a listing of societies for each county at <http://www.ffhs.org.uk/memb ers/England.htm>. Each society name is linked to its Web site, so you can go immediately to the site to see what's available.

When no indexes are available, you will need to search page by page through the entire district. Although this may seem tedious, you will do your most effective research when searching every page because you will notice other people with the same surname. You will also notice relatives with different surnames, such as married daughters, whom you would never have found if you had gone directly to your ancestor's entry. In many parishes, it can take less than one hour to go through the entire census page by page. The results will pay off handsomely!

Technique

FINDING THE CORRECT MICROFILM NUMBER FOR ENGLISH CENSUSES

Even if you cannot find a census index that contains your ancestor's name, you can still locate him on the census. First, you need to know the name of the parish where your ancestor resided. You can obtain the name of the parish (and sometimes an exact address) from civil registration certificates of birth,

Sources

Timesaver

marriage, and death. **Once you know the name of the parish, go to the Family History Center and use the** *Index of Place Names Showing the Library Microform Numbers for the 1841–1891 Census Records of England, Wales, Channel Islands and the Isle of Man: Arranged by Names of Places and Showing the Parish in Which Situated.* You can see why this is called the "Census Register." It can be found on microfiche number 6024509. All Family History Centers have this set of microfiche. The register lists all places in England and will tell you the microfilm or fiche numbers for each census year.

Using the Family History Library Catalog to Find Street Indexes

For large cities, it is impractical to search page by page, so you will need a street address. We have an address from the 1881 census, and we can sometimes use this address to find our ancestors in 1891. Let's see what happens with Walter Telford. He was living in Westgate, Newcastle-upon-Tyne in 1881. His address was 40 Buckingham Street.

We turn to the Census Register on fiche 6024509 and look for Westgate. The places are listed alphabetically. Westgate appears on page 1151 of the register (see Figure 8-5). Because there are often several places in England with the same name, you will want to check the parish and county columns to make sure you have located the correct place. In our example, Westgate is in the parish of Newcastle-upon-Tyne—St. John, located in the county of "NHUMB," which we know is Northumberland. You will see columns for each census year with the film or fiche numbers for that census listed underneath. If there is an asterisk (*) next to the census microfilm number, there is a surname index available for that place. A plus sign (+) next to the film number means that there is a street index available. An equal sign (=) means that both surname and street indexes are available. Many of the surname indexes are not available

*** K 06 ***   *** K 06 ***

ALPHABETICAL INDEX TO 1841-1891 CENSUS OF ENGLAND, WALES, ISLE OF MAN, AND CHANNEL ISLANDS						JAN 1993	PAGE 1,151		
PLACE	PARISH		1841	1851		1861	1871	1881	1891
	TOWNSHIP	COUNTY	FILM	FILM	PAGE NO.	FILM	FILM	FILM	FICHE #
WESTGATE	NEWCASTLE UPON TYNE-ST JOHN	NHUMB	438887	087082+		543190+	848423+	1342219+	6099307+ 4
			438887	087082+		543190+	848421+	1342218+	6099302+ 3
			438887	087082+		543191+	848422+	1342219+	6099303+ 4
			438887	087082+		543191+	848420+	1342217+	6099301+ 3
			438887	087082+		543190+	848423+	1342219+	6099311+ 3
			438887	087082+		543190+	848423+	1342219+	6099313+ 3
			438887	087082+		543190+	848423+	1342219+	6099307+ 4
			438887	087082+		543190+	848423+	1342219+	6099310+ 4
WESTHALL	WESTHALL	SUFF	474635	207454	709-726	542769	830794	1341457	6096595 3
WESTHAM	WESTHAM	SUSS	464163	193540	15-43	542662	827479	1341246	6095880+ 2
WESTHAMPNETT	WESTHAMPNETT	SUSS	474674	193557	388-411	542672	827516	1341275	6095954 3
WESTHIDE	STOKE EDITH	HEREFS	288818	087378	332-340	542873	835342	1341624	6097169+ 4
WESTHOPE	DIDDLEBURY	SHROPS	474585	087383		542876	835391	1341630	6097194 2
WESTHORPE	WESTHORPE	SUFF	474638	207444	210-220	542763	830771	1341448	6096568 5
WESTHOUGHTON	DEANE	LANCS	306925	087217	1-154	543032+	842054+	1341913+	6098217+ 3
			306925	087217	1-154	543032+	842054+	1341913+	6098216+ 3

Figure 8-5
The Census Register, found on fiche 6024509, lists all places alphabetically. For each census year, the film numbers for that location are given. Some locations, like Westgate, are on more than one film number.

```
                    Family History Library Catalog 21 Sep 1999        Page 1
                                   **Full Display**

        CALL NUMBER
        BRITISH
        REF Q AREA
        942
        X22s
        1891

        AUTHOR
        Great Britain.  Census Office.

        TITLE
        Street index, 1891 census, England and Wales.

        FORMAT
        24 v.

        NOTES
        Typescript (photocopy).
        Arranged numerically by district number.

        CONTENTS
        v. 1. Paddington, Kensington, Fulham, Chelsea, St. George Hanover
           Square, Westminster, Marylebone, Hampstead, Pancras, Islington,
           Hackney, St. Giles, Strand, Holborn, London City -- v. 2. Shoreditch,
           Bethnal Green, Whitechapel, St. George in the East, Stepney, Mile
           End Old Town, Poplar, St. Savior Southwark, St. Olave Southwark,
           Lambeth, Wandsworth, Camberwell, Greenwich -- v. 3. Lewisham,
           Woolwich, Epsom, Guildford, Farnham, Croydon, Kingston, Richmond,
           Bromley, Dartford, Medway -- v. 4. Tunbridge, Maidstone, Thanet,
           Dover, Elham, Hastings, Eastbourne, Brighton, Steyning, Portsea
           Island, Isle of Wight -- v. 5. Christchurch, Southampton, South
           Stoneham, Reading, Brentford, Hendon, Barnet, Edmonton -- v. 6.
           Wycombe, Northampton, Wellingborough, Peterborough, Bedford, Luton,
           West Ham, Romford, Ipswich, Yarmouth, Norwich -- v. 7. Highworth,
           St. Thomas, Newton Abbot, Totnes, Plymouth, Stoke Damerel,
           Barnstaple, Redruth, Penzance, Axbridge, Bath, Bedminster -- v. 8.
           Bristol, Barton Regis, Gloucester, Stroud, Cheltenham, Hereford,
           Atcham, Wolstanton, Stoke upon Trent, Burton upon Trent -- v. 9.
           Lichfield, Cannock, Wolverhampton, Walsall, West Bromwich, Dudley,
           Stourbridge, Kidderminster, Worcester, Kings Norton, Birmingham --
           v. 10. Aston, Coventry, Warwick, Leicester, Lincoln, Caistor,
           Glanford, Mansfield, Basford -- v. 11. Nottingham, Shardlow, Derby,
           Belper, Chesterfield, Stockport, Macclesfield, Altrincham -- v. 12.
           Runcorn, Northwich, Nantwich, Chester, Birkenhead, Liverpool, Toxteth
           Park, West Derby, Prescot -- v. 13. Ormskirk, Wigham, Warrington,
           Leigh, Bolton, Bury, Barton upon Irwell -- v. 14. Chorlton, Salford,
           Manchester, Prestwich, Ashton under Lyne -- v. 15. Oldham, Rochdale,
           Haslingden, Burnley, Blackburn -- v. 16. Chorley, Preston, Fylde,
           Lancaster, Ulverston, Barrow-in-Furness, Wharfedale, Keighley --
           v. 17. Huddersfield, Halifax, Bradford -- v. 18. Hunslet, Bramley,
           Leeds, Dewsbury, Wakefield, Pontefract -- v. 19. Barnsley, Wortley,
           Ecclesall Bierlow, Sheffield, Rotherham, Doncaster, York, Sculcoates,
           Hull -- v. 20. Scarborough, Middlesbrough, Darlington, Stockton,
           Hartlepool, Auckland, Lanchester, Durham, Easington, Chester-Le-
           Street -- v. 21. Sunderland, South Shields, Gateshead, Newcastle,
```

> **Newcastle Street Index in Volume 21**

Figure 8-6A
Family History Library Catalog entry for communities that have street indexes for the 1891 census. Continued on page 102.

on microform, but the street indexes are available on microfiche.

To find a street index for the 1891 census, look in the Family History Library Catalog for England-Census-1891-Indexes. You will find the listing of microfiche numbers for the 1891 census street indexes. You can see this in Figure 8-6B. The catalog descriptions tell the areas covered by each street index volume. Newcastle is in volume 21, which is on FHL microfiche 6036601. We will examine how to use a street index in the next section, so let's go directly to the 1891 census page.

As you can see on the census page in Figure 8-7 Walter Telford didn't move! This census is cited as FHL fiche 6099301, PRO reference RG 12/4191, f 75, p 30. Compare this census to the one we found in 1881, Figure 8-4. Because these censuses were taken at the same time of year, we would hope to find everyone's

Sources

```
              Family History Library Catalog 21 Sep 1999        Page 2
                            **Full Display**

        Tynemouth, Morpeth, Carlisle -- v. 22. Cockermouth, Whitehaven,
        Kendal, Bedwelty, Newport, Cardiff -- v. 23. Pontypridd, Merthyr
        Tydfil, Bridgend, Neath, Swansea -- v. 24. Llanelly, Holywell,
        Wrexham, Carnarvon.
     Also on microfiche.   Salt Lake City : Filmed by the Genealogical
        Society of Utah, 1993.   131 microfiches ; 11 x 15 cm.

                                                             BRITISH
     ADDITIONAL FORMATS                                      FICHE AREA
     Vol. 1.  (6 fiche) ------------------------------------------ 6036581
     Vol. 2.  (5 fiche) ------------------------------------------ 6036582
     Vol. 3.  (6 fiche) ------------------------------------------ 6036583
     Vol. 4.  (5 fiche) ------------------------------------------ 6036584
     Vol. 5.  (4 fiche) ------------------------------------------ 6036585
     Vol. 6.  (6 fiche) ------------------------------------------ 6036586
     Vol. 7.  (6 fiche) ------------------------------------------ 6036587
     Vol. 8.  (6 fiche) ------------------------------------------ 6036588
     Vol. 9.  (6 fiche) ------------------------------------------ 6036589
     Vol. 10. (5 fiche) ------------------------------------------ 6036590
     Vol. 11. (5 fiche) ------------------------------------------ 6036591
     Vol. 12. (6 fiche) ------------------------------------------ 6036592
     Vol. 13. (5 fiche) ------------------------------------------ 6036593
     Vol. 14. (5 fiche) ------------------------------------------ 6036594
     Vol. 15. (6 fiche) ------------------------------------------ 6036595
     Vol. 16. (6 fiche) ------------------------------------------ 6036596
     Vol. 17. (6 fiche) ------------------------------------------ 6036597
     Vol. 18. (5 fiche) ------------------------------------------ 6036598
     Vol. 19. (6 fiche) ------------------------------------------ 6036599
     Vol. 20. (5 fiche) ------------------------------------------ 6036600
     Vol. 21. (5 fiche) ------------------------------------------ 6036601
     Vol. 22. (5 fiche) ------------------------------------------ 6036602
     Vol. 23. (5 fiche) ------------------------------------------ 6036603
     Vol. 24. (5 fiche) ------------------------------------------ 6036604

     THIS RECORD FOUND UNDER
         1. England - Census - 1891 - Indexes
         2. Wales - Census - 1891 - Indexes


     Family History Library Catalog Copyright © 1987, Mar 1997 by
     The Church of Jesus Christ of Latter-day Saints.  All Rights Reserved.
```

Newcastle Street index in volume 21

Figure 8-6B
Continued from page 101.

age to be exactly ten years more than it was at the time of the previous census. But, of course, we don't find anything of the sort. Walter was 37, he is now 48; Isabella was 35, now 44; Robert was 5, now 16; and Margaret was one year old, now 10. These ages, however, are close. You will often notice considerable differences in ages from one census to the next. The family has changed in other ways. Walter and his sons all have different occupations from the previous census. Furthermore, Walter W., Mary J., and Dorothy J. are not with their parents, so we need to look elsewhere in the census to find them.

Tracing all family members from census to census will show you a lot about their changing lifestyles.

Using the *Register of Towns Indexed by Streets* to Find Street Indexes

We saw how to find a street index for the 1891 census by using the Family History Library Catalog. **For other years, you can also use the *Register of Towns Indexed by Streets* to locate street indexes.** It covers the years 1841–1881, but it does not contain the names of all towns that have street indexes. The register is arranged by census year and is available on FHL microfiche 6026692. Follow these steps:

1. Find the desired census year, listed chronologically.
2. Find the name of your ancestor's town, listed alphabetically. If there is

Sources

Step By Step

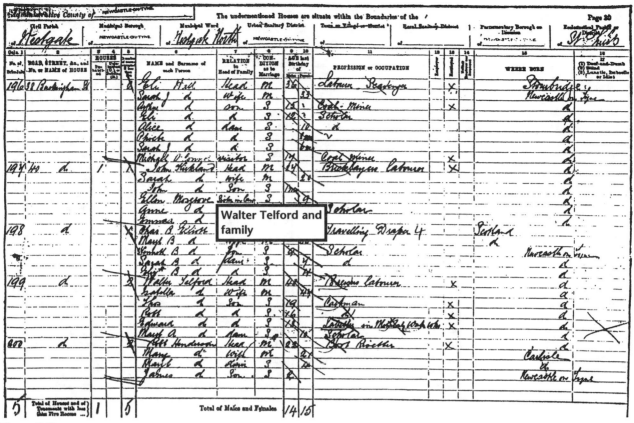

Figure 8-7
1891 Census page for 40 Buckingham Street, Westgate, Newcastle-upon-Tyne. Observe that Walter Telford's family is one of four families living at this address.

more than one town with the same name, be sure that you are looking at the one in the correct parish and county.

3. Across from the name of the town is a column labeled "Indexed Under." This contains the district under which your town is indexed. Write down the district, volume number, microfiche number, and part number of the street index. Order the microfiche number that you recorded. Keep the entire reference; you will use it when the microfiche arrives.

4. When the microfiche of the street index arrives at the Family History Center, locate the correct volume and part number in the set. The volume and part numbers are noted at the top of each fiche.

5. When you find your ancestor's street in the index, record the reference number(s) for that street. Return to the first page of the district. This page will list the reference numbers along with the appropriate microfilm number of the census. Order the census microfilm from the Family History Library.

We will show how to find Walter Telford in the 1871 census using this process. It is somewhat cumbersome, but worth the effort.

Searching for Buckingham Street in Westgate, Newcastle-upon-Tyne, Northumberland, in 1871, we use the *Register of Towns Indexed by Streets* on FHL

Case Study

```
                                                          -25-

                                                            Ref Q 942 X2s  1871
TOWN                     |PARISH                    |COUNTY  |INDEXED UNDER |VOLUME |MICROFICHE |PARTS
                         |                          |        |              |       |           |
Weetslade or Weetslet    |Longbenton                |Nhumb   |Tynemouth     |  14   | 6054455   | 1-2
Wellow                   |Wellow                    |Som     |Bath          |   1   | 6054442   | 2-3
Welsh St. Donats         |Welsh St. Donats          |Glams   |Cardiff       |   3   | 6054444   | 2
Welsh Whittle            |Standish                  |Lancs   |Chorley       |   4   | 6054445   | 1
Welton                   |Welton                    |Yorks   |Scuicoates    |  13   | 6054454   | 2-3
Wenvoe                   |Wenvoe                    |Glams   |Cardiff       |   3   | 6054444   | 2
Werneth                  |Stockport                 |Ches    |Stockport     |  14   | 6054455   | 2
Wervin                   |Chester-St. Oswald        |Ches    |Chester       |   3   | 6054444   | 3
West Acklam              |West Acklam               |Yorks   |Stockton      |  14   | 6054455   | 2
West Bretton             |Silkstone                 |Yorks   |Wortley       |   5   | 6054446   | 1
West Bromwich            |West Bromwich             |Staffs  |West Bromwich |  15   | 6054456   | 1
West Clayton             |High Hoyland              |Yorks   |Wortley       |   5   | 6054446   | 1
West Derby               |West Derby                |Lancs   |West Derby    |  15   | 6054456   | 1-2
West Ella                |Kirk Ella                 |Yorks   |Sculcoates    |  13   | 6054454   | 2-3
West Ham                 |West Ham                  |Essex   |West Ham      |  16   | 6054457   | 3
West Hartford            |Horton                    |Nhumb   |Tynemouth     |  14   | 6054455   | 1-2
West Newbiggin           |Bishopton                 |Durham  |Stockton      |  14   | 6054455   | 2
West Town                |Backwell                  |Som     |Bedminster    |   1   | 6054442   | 2
Westbury-Upon-Trym       |Westbury-Upon-Trym        |Gloucs  |Clifton       |   4   | 6054445   | 2
Westerfield              |Westerfield               |Suff    |Ipswich       |   6   | 6054447   | 1-2
Westgate                 |Newcastle Upon Tyne-St. John |Nhumb |Nwcstle U Tyne| 11   | 6054452   | 3-4
Westhoughton             |Deane                     |Lancs   |Bolton        |   2   | 6054443   | 1-2
Westminster              |Westminster               |London  |Westminster   |   7   | 6054448   | 2-3
Westoe                   |Jarrow                    |Durham  |South Shields |  14   | 6054455   | 1-2
Weston                   |Weston                    |Som     |Bath          |   1   | 6054442   | 2-3
Weston Favell            |Weston Favell             |Nhant   |Northhampton  |  12   | 6054453   | 1
Weston In Gordano        |Weston In Gordano         |Som     |Bedminster    |   1   | 6054442   | 2
Weston Peverell          |Plymouth-St. Andrew       |Devon   |Plymouth      |  12   | 6054453   | 3
```

Figure 8-8

The 1871 *Register of Towns Indexed by Streets,* on fiche 6026692, lists the towns that have been indexes, the parish in which they are located, and where to find the index. It shows that Westgate is in the parish of Newcastle-upon-Tyne, St. John, and that the index will be found in volume 11, fiche number 6054452, parts 3 and 4.

fiche 6026692. We first look for the census year 1871, then for the town of Westgate; see Figure 8-8. The *Register* indicates that the street index for Westgate will be found in

Nwcstle U Tyne, Vol. 11, Fiche 6054452, Parts 3–4.

We record and retain the index information, and then order fiche 6054452 which is a multifiche set. "Parts 3–4" means that the street will be found on the third and fourth fiche of the set. When fiche 6054452 arrives, we search for Buckingham Street in volume 11, fiche 3 and 4 of the Newcastle-upon-Tyne district. The page that contains Buckingham Street is shown in Figure 8-9. We find

Supt. Registrar's District 553; Subdistrict 1B; Enumeration District 4; Subdistrict 1D; Enumeration District 7.

On the same microfiche, we return to the first page of the Newcastle-upon-Tyne district (Figure 8-10) and find that Subdistrict 1B, Enumeration District

STREETS INDEX TO 1871 CENSUS

GATESHEAD & NEWCASTLE UPON TYNE

STREET	SUPT. REGISTRAR'S DISTRICT	SUB-DISTRICT	ENUMERATION DISTRICT
Browns Place	552	1C	10
Bruces Yard	552	2F	19
Brunel Street	553	1m	28
Brunel Terrace	553	1L	26
Brunell Street, Back	553	1J	21
Brunswick Place	553	2F	22
Brunswick H	552	2K	35
		2L	36
Brunswick Ter	552	2E	16
Bryson Street	553	5A	4
Buck Bank	552	3B	7
Buckingham Street	553	1B	4
		1D	7
Buckingham Street, Upper	553	1D	7
Buckinook	552	4D	12
Bulmer Street	553	2C	10
Burdon Lane	553	5D	14
Burdon Place	553	5D	14

[Buckingham Street is in two different subdistricts]

Figure 8-9
The street index for the 1871 census lists alphabetically all streets in a locality. It gives the number of the registrar's district, the subdistrict, and the enumerator's district. Turn to the key shown in Figure 8-10 to locate the actual film needed. Note that Buckingham Street is found in two different subdistricts.

4 is on FHL film number 848421. Subdistrict 1D, Enumeration District 7 is on FHL film 848422. This method gives us the enumeration district instead of the folio number, so we will first search for Enumeration District 4 on film 848421.

Using this information, we can find the Telfords on the film. They were recorded on folio 81 of the census. Even though we found the entry in Enumeration District 4, we do not cite this; we cite the census the usual way. It is cited as FHL film 848421; RG 10/5070, f 81, p 27. Look at the Telfords in this census, Figure 8-11. Walter Telford, occupation cartman, is 27 years old. He is listed with his wife Isabella, daughter Mary Isabell age 4, son Walter William age 3, daughter Dorothy age 2, and son Thomas. Their surnames are not "do"; **that is an abbreviation for** *ditto*.

You will notice that the age of Thomas is "6 mo." Because he was six months

Important

STREETS INDEX TO 1871 CENSUS

NEWCASTLE-UPON-TYNE

Registrar's District	Sub-District	Enumeration District	Microfilm Number
553	1 a	1 - 2	848,420
553	1 b	3 - 4	848,421
553	1 c	5 - 6	848,421
553	1 d	7 - 9	848,422
553	1 e	10 - 11	848,422
553	1 f	12 - 13	848,423
553	1 g	14 - 16	848,423
553	1 h	17 - 19	848,423
553	1 j	20 - 22	848,424
553	1 k	23 - 24	848,424
553	1 l	25 - 26	848,424
553	1 m	27 - 29	848,425
553	1 n	30 - 31	847,385
553	1 o	32 - 33	847,385
553	1 p	34 - 36	847,385
553	2 a	2 - 4	847,386
553	2 b	5 - 8	847,386
553	2 c	9 - 11	847,386

Buckingham Street in subdistricts 1b and 1d on two films

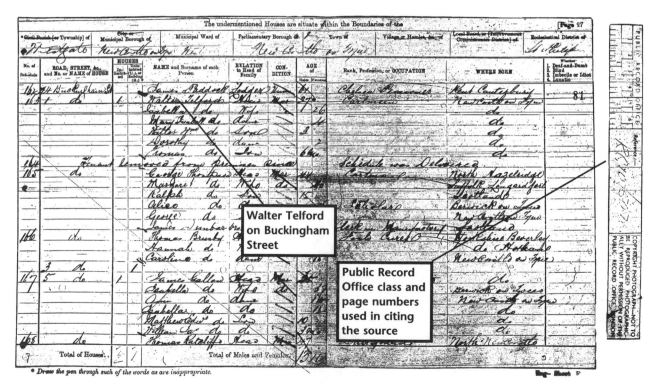

Figure 8-10
Information from the 1871 street index, shown in Figure 8-9, is used to identify a specific film on which your ancestor's street appears.

Figure 8-11
Page from the 1871 census showing Walter Telford and family living on Buckingham Street.

old on 3 April 1871 (the date the census was taken), his birth should have been recorded in the December quarter 1870. We should be able to easily find his name in the civil registration birth indexes. We can also estimate the marriage date of the parents at about 1865–1866, about one year before the birth of the oldest child. However, we are not certain that Mary Isabella was the first child. There could have been other children born previously who were not listed with the parents on the census return. Also, as we know, parents were not always married one year before the first child. But 1865–1866 is a good estimate with the facts we now have. We do not expect to find Walter and his wife together in the 1861 census, because we suspect that they were not married at the time. Our next step is to go back to civil registration to get more information about the family.

Using Surname Indexes

Surname indexes are available for many locations in the 1851 census. There are two places to search to see if there is one for your locality. Visit the Web pages of the member societies of the Federation of Family History Societies at <http://www.ffhs.org.uk/members/England.htm>. From the GENUKI Web site, you can visit the Web page for the appropriate county family history society. You can also look up the appropriate county in *Marriage and Census Indexes for Family Historians* (see page 117).

Sources

Check the Internet to see if there is a surname index from the Northumberland and Durham Family History Society to find the Telfords in 1851. You can find an index for Newcastle-upon-Tyne, Westgate Ward (HO 107/2404, Folios 1–630), Registration District 552/1. This book is listed as number N10 on the Northumberland and Durham Family History Society Web page at <http://www.geocities.com/Athens/6549/Books.html>.

In this case we will be looking for Walter Telford as a child with his parents, Walter Telford and Mary *Isabella* Dixon. Another Walter and another Isabella! It can get confusing! The surname index is shown in Figure 8-12.

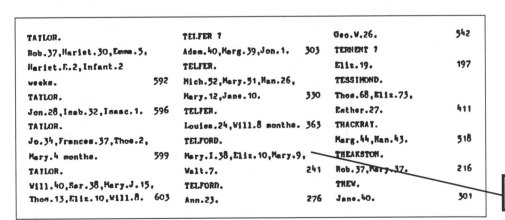

Figure 8-12
Look for surname indexes produced by local family history societies in England. The indexes often cover a relatively small area. Our Mary I. Telford example is from the 1851 census index for Newcastle-upon-Tyne—Westgate Ward, produced by the Northumberland and Durham Family History Society.

The surname index says
TELFORD
Mary.I. 38, Eliz. 10, Mary. 9, Walt. 7.   241

This looks like the correct family, but the father, Walter, is missing from the index. So we will look on microfilm for Mary Isabella Telford and family in Newcastle-upon-Tyne, Westgate Ward, Registration District 552/1 at HO 107/2404, folio 241. A search in the Family History Library Catalog under England Census 1851 produces a list of film numbers organized by district. The films begin with number 0087787. We are told from the surname index what the Registration District number is—552. So we will order the film that contains district 552.

The 1851 census is the only one in the Family History Library Catalog that is not listed by piece number. Now let's assume that your surname index gave you a citation with the class, piece and folio number, e.g. HO 107/2404, folio 241, but did not give the location or the district number. This situation is a distinct possibility, so let's examine how to convert this into a film number. **You can check the online catalog of the Public Record Office at <http://www.pro .gov.uk/finding/catalogue/> or order the 1851 Census Class List on fiche 6036975–81 at a Family History Center. Both lists are organized by class and piece number in numerical order. For each piece number, it provides the registration district, the registration subdistrict, the parish and the hamlets included in this census piece. After identifying the name of the parish, return to the Family History Library Catalog and search for the parish. Under the topic "Census," it will list for the 1851 census the appropriate film number for that parish. One registration district may cover one to four films.**

In our example we find that piece number 2404 is the first part of registration district 552 on FHL film 87082. All we have to do is go to folio 241 on film 87082 and look for the Telfords. But we don't find them there! If this happens, always look at the previous folio. The Telfords are actually located on the second page of folio 240.

Look at the example of the 1851 census at Figure 8-13. This census shows again why you will want to check all census records. In this record, we find other relatives that we had not previously seen. The head of the household is Edward Chatto. Although the census surname index listed Mary I. Telford, a more complete name is found in the census: Mary Isabella Telford is listed as sister-in-law of Edward Chatto. If she is Edward's sister-in-law, it could mean that she is the sister to Edward's wife, Dorothy Jane. You will notice that Dorothy Jane Chatto and Mary Isabella Telford were both born in Northd. Stamfordham. Mary Telford's marital status is married (not widowed), but where is her husband Walter? Her occupation appears to be "Drepmaker," but the word is actually *Dressmaker*. (Double s was formerly written with a long s followed by a short s and is often misread as the letter *p*.) Mary's age is 38 years, which means that she was born about 1813—before civil registration records started. We will want to search for her baptismal record in the church records of the parish of Stamfordham (see chapter ten). Elizabeth Telford, age

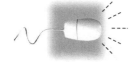

Internet Source

CD Source

1851 CENSUS INDEX ON CD-ROM

If your ancestor lived in Devon, Norfolk, or Warwick, then you are lucky. For these three counties only, there is a complete 1851 census index with the same format as the 1881 census index. You can purchase this single CD for $5 plus applicable sales tax. Order from the Salt Lake Distribution Center at (800) 537-5971.

37

No. of House...	Name of Street, Place, or Road, and Name or No. of House	Name and Surname of each Person who abode in the house, on the Night of the 30th March, 1851	Relation to Head of Family	Condition	Age of Males Females	Rank, Profession, or Occupation	Where Born	Whether Blind, or Deaf-and-Dumb
140	38 Villa Place	Margaret Turton	Head	U	28	Dress Maker	London	
141	39 Villa Place	Edward Chatto	Head	Mar	50	Tailor	North Allenton	
		Dorothy Jane do	Wife	Mar	41		North Stanfordham	
		Mary do	Daur	U	2		Durham Shotley Bridge	
		Mary Isabella Telford	Sister-in-law	Mar	38	Dress Maker	North Stanfordham	
		Elizabeth Telford	Niece	U	10	Scholar	North Newcastle	
		Mary do	Niece	U	9	do	do do	
		Walter do	Nephew	U	7	do	do do	
		John Tempsdley	Lodger	U	19	Ironmonger	North ...	
		Michael Patterson	do	U		Millwright	Durham Shotley ...	
142	30 Villa Place	Francis Bones	Head	Mar	57	Agent Sheriffs Officer	North Newsham	
		Elizabeth do	Wife	Mar	57		North Tobridge	
		John do	Son	U	26	Painter (House)	North Newburn	
		Rachel do	Daur	U	22	Dress Maker	do do	
		Mary do	Daur	U		... Maker	do do	
		Elizabeth do	Daur	U		Bonnet Trimmer	do do	
		Sarah do	Daur	U		...	do do	
		Hannah do	Daur	U		do do	North Newcastle	
		Francis do	Son	Mar		Weaver	do do	

(The annotation box at left reads: **Mary Isabella Telford and her children**)

Figure 8-13

This page from the 1851 census for Westgate, in Newcastle-upon-Tyne, provides a good example of why you should locate all census records for your family. Here we see Mary Isabella Telford living with her married sister and brother-in-law.

10, is listed as "Niece." Because her relationship applies to the head of the household, it means that she is Edward Chatto's niece—and probably Mary Telford's daughter. There are three children listed with Mary: Elizabeth, Mary, and Walter. Walter is seven years old. This matches the information we know about the Telford family. But we do not know why the husband Walter is not listed with his family. Is he alive? Does he have an occupation that requires travel? Is he listed elsewhere in the census? Is Mary Isabella merely visiting her sister? Why doesn't Mary have any children younger than age seven? Is she really a widow and listed incorrectly as married? We need to find this family in the 1861 census to see if Walter and Mary are listed together in that census. We will want to find them in the 1841 census to see Walter's occupation at that time. We will want to look at civil registration indexes. Do we find a death entry for Walter Telford? We should look at the civil registration certificates of his children's marriages, because Walter's occupation will be recorded on his child's marriage certificate. The certificate may also indicate "deceased." We can answer a lot of questions when we use census and civil registration records together.

It is much easier to find a family in the census when we have a surname index. You should try to obtain one if possible. **If no surname index is available, use the street indexes. These indexes will make your research a lot faster.**

Timesaver

What Do I Do If There Is No Index?

If neither surname index nor street index is available, you will have to search the old-fashioned way: page by page. But believe it or not, when there is no index you will do better research. It will take you longer to find your ancestor, but you will find out much more about your family. **When searching each page you'll find all kinds of clues that you would never have found if you looked only at your ancestor's entry.** So as you search the census, be sure to extract the entries for everyone of your surname.

For large cities, however, it is impractical to search every page. We'll show you how to find someone in a city. **Let's find the 1841 census record for Walter and Mary Telford.** We know from the civil registration certificates that they were probably living on Blenheim Street, Westgate, in 1841. The 1841 census is quite different from the later ones, so this example will show how the 1841 census differs and also how to find someone in a city when there is no index.

We turn to the Census Register on fiche 6024509 and look for Westgate. See Figure 8-5 and look at the column "1841 Film" for Westgate. The film number 438887 is given. In the column for the 1851 census, the film number 087082 has a + after the number. Therefore, the Family History Library has a street index for that census. We know that there is also a surname index for that census year because we used one in the previous example. But the Family History Library does not have a surname or street index for 1841. This does not mean that an index doesn't exist; it means only that the FHL does not have one. If there are no indexes, we will have to roll through film number 438887 looking for Westgate and then for Blenheim Street. Unfortunately, this is not an easy process. It can be especially difficult in the 1841 census because the 1841 census was recorded in pencil and many of the pages are barely readable.

There are several Enumeration Books on the film, each with its own title page. We will want to look at each title page because the title pages contain the name and description of the area being enumerated. It is important to pay attention to the Enumeration Book number and not to the enumeration district number. The book numbers are consecutive on the film, and each may contain several districts. For example, on this film Enumeration Book 4 contains parts of enumeration districts 5, 17, 12, and 14. You can see how difficult it might be locate a census record if you extract the enumeration district number instead of the book number.

We are looking for the township of Westgate, so we will skip the Enumeration Books for any other township. When we get to a book for Westgate township, we will usually want to roll page by page. However, we can often narrow down the most likely books by reading the descriptions on the title pages.

The Telfords were found in Westgate Enumeration Book 14, which contains enumeration district 11. The description of the district mentions Blenheim Street (see Figure 8-14). But so did enumeration districts 9 and 10. When you see a street mentioned, it may not be the only book that contains that street.

Before we do anything else, we will want to record where we found the census return. Always do this *first*, because once you start reading the census record, you may get so excited that you will forget to record where you found

Tip

Case Study

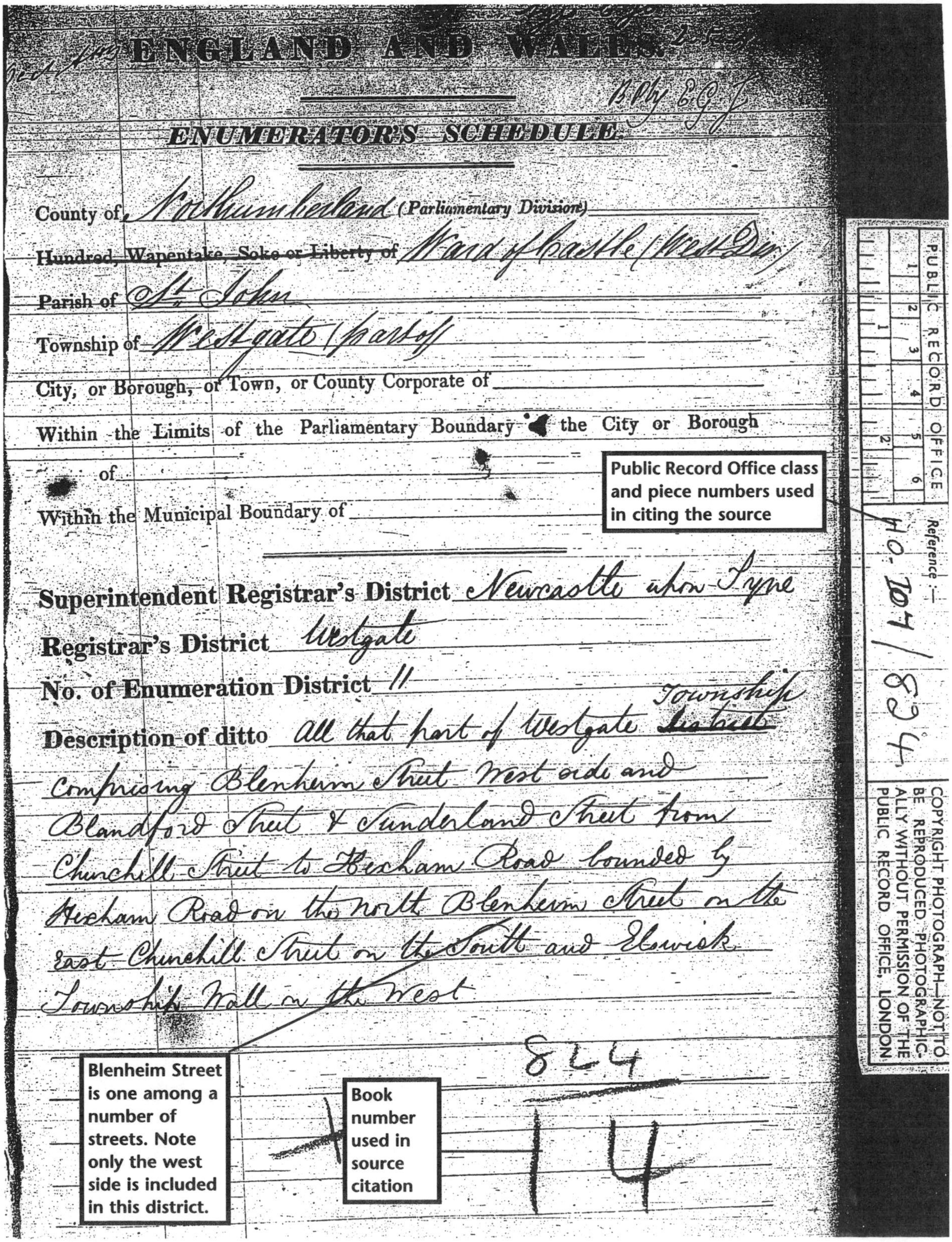
ENGLAND AND WALES.

ENUMERATOR'S SCHEDULE.

County of Northumberland (Parliamentary Division)

~~Hundred, Wapentake, Soke or Liberty of~~ Ward of Castle (West Div)

Parish of St. John

Township of Westgate (part of)

City, or Borough, or Town, or County Corporate of

Within the Limits of the Parliamentary Boundary of the City or Borough of

Within the Municipal Boundary of

Superintendent Registrar's District Newcastle upon Tyne

Registrar's District Westgate

No. of Enumeration District 11

Description of ditto All that part of Westgate ~~District~~ Township comprising Blenheim Street West side and Blandford Street & Sunderland Street from Churchill Street to Hexham Road bounded by Hexham Road on the north Blenheim Street on the east Churchill Street on the South and Elswick Township Wall on the West

824

14

PUBLIC RECORD OFFICE 1 2 3 4 5 6

Reference:— H.O. 107/824

COPYRIGHT PHOTOGRAPH—NOT TO BE REPRODUCED PHOTOGRAPHICALLY WITHOUT PERMISSION OF THE PUBLIC RECORD OFFICE, LONDON
Public Record Office class and piece numbers used in citing the source
Blenheim Street is one among a number of streets. Note only the west side is included in this district.
Book number used in source citation

Figure 8-14
Details from the first page of each census Enumerator's Book in 1841. Note the description showing the order in which the census enumerator walked the streets.

it. Remember that the 1841 census is not cited the same as other censuses. To record the 1841 census, you will need five pieces of information: the class code, piece number, enumeration book number, folio, and page number. Do not record the enumeration district number. The class code for the entire 1841 census is HO 107. The piece number in which this record was found is 824. The Enumeration Book number appears as part of a fraction on the title page. In this case, the title page has the fraction 824/14, so the book number is 14. The folio number is stamped in the upper right corner of the folios. A page without a folio number is the reverse side of the previous folio. The Telfords were found on page 13, which was the reverse side of page 12, folio 9. The full reference is HO 107/824/14, f 9, p 13 (Class code HO 107, piece 824, book 14, folio 9, page 13). We will record it like this:

FHL film 438887, PRO reference HO 107/824/14 f 9, p 13.

Now that we have properly cited the census, we can get to the fun part and examine the census itself. You can see in Figure 8-15 that the 1841 census doesn't give the same detail as the later censuses. In the first column, the place is recorded as Blenheim Street. There are no uninhabited houses recorded on this page. The column for names has a very specific title: Names of each Person who abode therein the preceding Night. In this column we find Walter Talford, Mary Do, and Elizabeth Do. The surname is not spelled the way we expect it, but we know that spelling variations are normal. Again, *Do* means "ditto." The column for ages states that Walter is 20 and that Mary is 25. Because the ages in the 1841 census are rounded down to the nearest five, it means that Walter is between the ages of 20 and 24, and Mary is between the ages of 25 and 30. The ages for children under fifteen are not rounded, so Elizabeth's age should be correct. The "Profession, Trade, Employment, or of Independent Means" column indicates that Walter's occupation is "Draper."

The last section, "Where Born," is the most disappointing part of the 1841 census. The record indicates only whether or not each person was born in the county where the census was taken. If "y" is recorded, then you have at least narrowed down the county of birth. If "n" is recorded in this column, it means that the birth occurred in another county of England or Wales (but you don't know which one). If the person was born outside of England and Wales, the birthplace is recorded in the next column as "S" for Scotland, "I" for Ireland, and "F" for foreign parts (which means anywhere else in the world). The first man on this page was born in foreign parts. That isn't too useful, except you now know he was probably not born in England, Ireland, Scotland, or Wales. We always hope that all of our ancestors in the 1841 census lived long enough to be recorded in the 1851 census so that we can find more precise places of birth!

After you have read the 1841 census, reexamine your family records to make sure that you have all census records for your family and that you have obtained the necessary civil registration certificates. If you have these, you should have a basic outline of your family in the nineteenth century, and you're ready to move on to probate records to fill in some details.

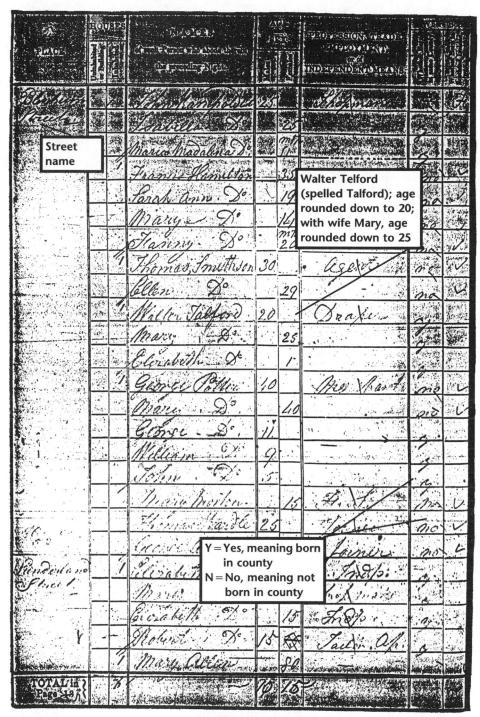

Figure 8-15
1841 census entry for Walter Talford (Telford), wife Mary, and daughter Elizabeth living on Blenheim Street in Newcastle-upon-Tyne. Note that the ages of the adults are rounded down to the nearest five years. The only indication of place of birth is whether it was within or outside of the county.

SEARCH ALL CENSUS YEARS

Census records containing names are available for 1841, 1851, 1861, 1871, 1881 and 1891, with 1901 to be released in January 2002. **You need to search for the family in all years. This process gives you details of family movement plus clues to birth, marriage and death dates.**

Important

In the above examples, the 1861 census is not shown because the information it contains is the same as the 1851, 1871, and 1881 censuses. For 1861, name indexes are rare, but check with the county Family History Society to see if one is available for your area. If your ancestor is in an urban area, you should follow the procedural steps listed above at "Using the *Register of Towns Indexed by Streets* to Find Street Indexes."

When we follow those steps, we find in 1861 that Mary Isabella Telford and her seventeen-year-old unmarried son Walter are living with Edward and Dorothy Jane Chatto, just as they were in the 1851 census.

However, there are differences. In 1851 the family was at 39 Villa Place, but in 1861 they are at 27 Villa Place. Did the family move, or were the houses renumbered (which was common in the 1850s)? Mary Isabella Telford is now listed as a widow, thus suggesting a ten-year window in which her husband Walter died. Mary Isabella's daughters Elizabeth and Mary are not in the house, suggesting they may have left to get married or to work. For Edward and Dorothy Chatto, this census confirms the eleven-year difference in their ages and shows that they have another daughter, Elizabeth, now nine years old, in the household.

The 1861 citation for Mary Isabella Telford is FHL Film 0548191, RG 9/3812, folio 7, page 12.

Each census will help you discover more about your family, so it is important to find your ancestors in all census years.

SUMMARY

We have located Walter Telford in the 1891, 1881, and 1871 censuses as an adult. We also found him as a child living with his mother in the 1851 and 1861 censuses. He was not born at the time of the 1841 census, so we located his parents and sister. We used a different method to locate each census record.

Normally you start with the most recent census and work backward in time. However, if you don't know where your ancestors lived, begin with the 1881 census indexes. They will make your research so much simpler. **You can find census records using the following methods:**

Step By Step

1. Using the 1881 British Census and National Index on compact disc. It is available for purchase from the Salt Lake Distribution Center and may also be available at a Family History Center.
2. Using the 1881 census index on microfiche available at a Family History Center. Microfiche numbers are provided in the table on pages 94–95.
3. Using the Family History Library Catalog and a street index.
4. Using the *Register of Towns Indexed by Streets* (FHL fiche 6026692) and a street index.

5. Using a surname index. To see what indexes are available, consult *Marriage and Census Indexes for Family Historians*. You should also consult the Web site of the family history society that covers the area where your ancestor lived.

6. Searching without an index. Use the Census Register on FHL fiche 6024509 to find the appropriate film number.

Technique

WHY CAN'T I FIND MY ANCESTOR IN THE CENSUS?

You can't find the address. For a rural area this is not a problem; you just search line by line through the district. However, in an urban area this could involve a major search. If the street was a short one, or in a bad neighborhood, the census taker may have skipped it. The street may also have changed its name from one census to the next or from the time of a certificate to the time of the census. The street may not have existed at the time of the census or was under construction. In addition, the houses may have been renumbered; this was especially common in the 1850s. In some urban areas there may be two streets with the same name and numbers indexed together. If you have found a family at one address, you may not know that there is another street with the same name.

To solve these problems, you will need local maps, preferably contemporary, to see what is near the address you are trying to locate. **The Godfrey maps and Ordnance Survey maps mentioned in chapter three, *Uniqueness of English Research*, may provide a good starting point.**

See Also

Your ancestors may have moved. There was a great deal of mobility as a result of the Industrial Revolution. Movement is also likely around certain stages of life: marriage, childbearing, widowhood, and divorce. You can get a more accurate address by obtaining a civil registration certificate for an event that occurred close to a census year. Also look at a city or trade directory that was published one or two years after the census date. Directories took a year or longer to publish, so the addresses they contain are not current.

Your ancestor may not have been present in the household on the census night. The census shows the people who were present in the house on the census night, not necessarily the ones who normally lived there. Certain occupations, such as railroad workers, sailors, and soldiers, required working away from home. Fishermen may have been at sea on the census night and were enumerated in the first port where they arrived after the census day. Builders and laborers may have been working in another town. Wealthy people may have been traveling and took their servants with them. Your ancestor may be absent for a reason that has nothing to do with his occupation. The 1861 census was taken on Easter Sunday, so the family may have been gathered somewhere to celebrate. Your ancestor could have been visiting family or friends or assisting someone who was sick. People in institutions (hospitals, jails, workhouses) were enumerated in the schedule of the institution. If children are missing from the family, it could indicate death, marriage, or apprenticeship. Children may also have been in boarding school or working as servants in another household. In fact, if your ancestor was away from home for any reason, he should be enumerated elsewhere unless he was avoiding the enumerator.

Your ancestor may be present in the household but not listed. Popular belief in some parts of the country, especially with the early census, was that unbaptized children should not be listed, so many young children are omitted. Young children may also have been omitted to avoid charges of overcrowding.

Your ancestor is not indexed the way you expect. If you are using a surname index, there could be several reasons that you do not find your ancestor. The name could be spelled differently on the census return and, therefore, in the index. This is especially common with names that begin with vowels or the letter *H*. Be creative when thinking of ways the surname could have been spelled.

The indexer may have misinterpreted the handwriting on the census. If the first letter of the name was misread, it can be very difficult to locate your ancestor in the index. Write out the name and think about what other capital letters look similar.

Your ancestor could be listed in the index and on the census film under a different name. For example, when a widowed mother has remarried, her children may be listed under the surname of the stepfather.

The indexer may have missed the entry altogether. If you are relatively certain that your ancestor should appear in a place, proceed as if there were no index: Search every page!

A few of the census returns have been lost or destroyed. This is not common, but there are a few places where the census has not survived. There will be gaps in the class list, and other census returns will be needed to locate the family.

Base information is incorrect. You may be relying on incorrect information. For example, you may be trying to locate a census record of a child using the place of birth given in a later census. The birthplace given may be incorrect, because many people did not know where they were actually born and gave the place where they remember growing up. Some people gave the place of baptism instead of the place of birth. Some stated their birthplace as their current location, when they were actually born somewhere else, out of fear of being removed from their new home under the Poor Laws. Always reexamine your evidence and ask yourself, How reliable is it?

CAUTIONS FOR USING AND INTERPRETING CENSUS INFORMATION

Warning

It is important to locate families in all census years. The information in the census can be unreliable, but conflicting information will often come to light when you examine different years. Always question the reliability of the data. Remember:

- Any given piece of information may be incorrect.
- Be suspicious of reported ages.
- Names used by an individual may not be the same as those found in civil registration or church records.

- Names of places and people may be misspelled or spelled as they sound.
- Individuals missing from a household should be listed elsewhere in the census.

WHERE TO FIND OUT MORE ABOUT THIS TOPIC

Family History Library, *Resource Guide: 1881 British Census Indexes.* Guide number 34933000.

Gibson, Jeremy, and Elizabeth Hampson. *Marriage and Census Indexes for Family Historians.* 7th ed. Baltimore, Md.: Genealogical Pub. Co.,1998.

Higgs, Edward. *A Clearer Sense of the Census.* Public Record Office Handbook No. 28. London: HMSO, 1996.

Lumas, Susan. *The Census Returns of England and Wales.* An Introduction to Series. Federation of Family History Societies, 1992.

Lumas, Susan. *Making Use of the Census.* 3rd ed. Public Record Office Readers' Guide No. 1. London: PRO Publications, 1997.

Sources

AFTER SEARCHING THE CENSUS, WHAT SHOULD I DO NEXT?

Return to civil registration indexes to obtain the necessary certificates for family members that you have found on the census. Civil registration certificates help you find more census records; census records help you find more civil registration certificates. Used together, civil registration certificates and census records will give you more complete family information. Both will indicate addresses, occupational changes, and other important details. **See chapter six on civil registration indexes.**

Look at probate records. When someone disappears from the census, you can sometimes find the date and place of death, her heirs, and more by searching the national probate indexes. **See chapter nine on post-1857 probate records.**

Begin searching parish registers. The censuses of 1851 and onward give your ancestor's parish of birth. You can search parish registers to obtain earlier records of your family. **See chapter ten to find out how to use parish registers.**

For More Info

NINE

Post-1857 Probate Records

\di'fin\ *vb*

Definitions

an you imagine how great it would be if you could locate the will of anyone in the United States by checking a nationwide index? Well in England, you can! From 1858, all probate records in England and Wales have been processed in one central court system. There is a nationwide descriptive probate calendar (like an index, described later) that gives the name of the deceased, the date of death, the court where the probate was granted, the names of the executors, and more! It's another dream come true for genealogists.

WHAT IS PROBATE?

Probate is the process by which a court proves the validity of a will and gives the executor the authority to carry out the terms of the document. The authority to carry out the intentions of a will is called the Probate Act.

If the deceased did not leave a will, then the court appoints an administrator. The estate is then distributed to those who are legally entitled to inherit.

See the box on page 119 for definitions of terms you may encounter during your search of probate records.

Who Could Make a Will?

From 1837, males and females had to be over twenty-one to make a will.

A married woman, before the Married Woman's Property Act of 1882, could not make a will without her husband's consent unless her marriage settlement allowed her to do so. Prior to 1882, the courts assumed that all she owned belonged to her husband. This does not mean that you shouldn't look for wills of women. Wills could be made by widows or spinsters, and both groups frequently named large numbers of legatees.

\di'fin *vb*

Definitions

PROBATE TERMS

Codicil: A signed and witnessed amendment to an existing will.

Executor/Executrix: Man/woman appointed by the testator to execute the provisions of the will.

Holograph Will: A will written in the testator's own handwriting.

Intestate: A person who dies without a will or for whom a valid will has not been found.

Last Will and Testament: A written statement, usually signed and witnessed, of a person's wishes regarding the disposal of his property after death. The last will and testament is commonly called a will.

Legatee: A beneficiary; a person who is given something in a will.

Letter of Administration: A grant to administer the estate of a person who died without a will.

Letter of Administration With Will Annexed: A grant to administer the estate of the deceased when the executor of a will cannot or refuses to act or if the will does not name an executor.

Nuncupative Will: An oral will before three credible witnesses expressing the dying person's wishes. After 1838, these were only valid for soldiers on active military service and seamen at sea.

Testator: The person writing the last will and testament.

Who Kept the Records?

Prior to 1858, probate was the responsibility of the Church of England. The Probate Act of 1857 took the probate process away from the church courts and established a governmental system for registering all wills and administrations in England and Wales. A Principal Probate Registry was established in London along with forty-one district courts. Copies of all wills and administrations from the district courts were forwarded to the Principal Probate Registry.

Notes

How Were the Records Created?

When a person died, the executor would take the will, or a request for a letter of administration if the deceased died without a will, to the principal registry in London or to one of the district courts situated in the major cities and towns around England and Wales. Since 1926, there have been no jurisdictional boundaries to the district registries, which has made it much easier for executors who reside in another part of the country to probate a will.

At the court, the executor took an oath stating that he was the executor named in the will of the deceased, and then gave details on when the person died. Most estates were probated within three years. If the time lapse between death and request for probate was greater than three years, the executor would need to give an explanation for the delay.

The executors of an estate had to be over the age of twenty-one. If a will named a minor as an executor and the executor had not turned twenty-one at the time of the deceased's death, an administrator would be appointed. If a will named an executor and that executor was already dead, was incapable, or chose not to probate the will, then another person would be appointed to administer the estate. In this case, a letter of administration with will annexed was granted. The person seeking to obtain the probate act had to post a bond, with two sureties, for an amount equal to double the value of the assets in the estate.

If a person died intestate (without a will), a letter of administration would be granted to the next of kin. The next of kin does not include the surviving spouse, but is usually a child or sibling. The courts preferred to grant a letter of administration to one individual. However up to three administrators could be appointed providing they had equal claims on the estate. Once the administrator was appointed, the estate would then be distributed according to law. The Probate Act of 1857 standardized estate distribution rules throughout England. Prior to this, distribution was often by local custom.

The original will was deposited in the registry. A copy of the will was given to the executor to carry out the terms of the will. When the executor completed the probate process, a second copy of the will was sent to the Principal Probate Registry in London. These copies were used to make the index for all of England and Wales.

What Will Probate Records Tell Me?

These are very important documents providing evidence of links to previous generations. Wills usually name the widow, children, sons-in-law, and often other relatives, friends, and employees. They provide information that usually allows you to differentiate people of the same name from one another. They will tell you about your ancestors, their station in society, and their life.

Important

Most of your ancestors probably did not have a will, so don't be discouraged if you don't find one. Women who had wills were usually widows or spinsters and may have had little property to leave, but they often named lots of family members. However, do not assume that your ancestors were not wealthy enough to leave a will. There are wills for a wide range of people, from the landed gentry to farm laborers, doctors, soldiers, sailors, tradesmen, and maiden aunts. In other words, anyone could have left a will. Furthermore, even if your ancestor did not make a will, he may have been named in the will of another person. These documents are so valuable in establishing relationships and in describing your ancestor's life that you must look for them.

What Probate Records Are Available, and Where Are They Located?

Many older reference books refer to post-1857 probate records as the Somerset House wills because the indexes and the records were housed there from 1858 to 1998. The indexes are now at First Avenue House, 42–48 High Holborn, London

WC1V 6HA, and can be searched on-site. All indexes and probate records are accessible to the public with no relationship to the decedent required.

At your nearest Family History Center, you have access to the following records:

Probate Calendar (1858–1957) Search by film/fiche number. First film number is 0215221.

Principal Registry (1858–1925) Search by film/fiche number. First film number is 1836412.

Wills

Administrations with will annexed

District Courts (1858–1899 and 1900–1925 First film number 1239289 for the earlier period and 1566070 for the later period.)

Wills

Administrations with will annexed

Most administrations are not available on microfilm.

Sources

What Do I Need to Know Before Searching Post–1857 Probate Records?

You first need to know the difference between the nationwide probate calendar and a probate index. People who died from 1858 onward anywhere in England or Wales are included in the probate calendar. **The full name of the calendar is "Calendar of the grants of probate and letters of administration made in the Principal Registry: and in the several district registries of Her Majesty's Court of Probate."** It's another long title; we will simply call it the probate calendar. The probate calendar is not the same as an index. It will not give you the volume and page number of your ancestor's will. Instead, it will tell you which court handled the probate. In addition, it will give you details that may or may not be found in the will. You will want to make a copy of the calendar, and then you will want to get a copy of the will or administration. The will tells you the details about your ancestor's property and the beneficiaries.

Sources

In order to use the probate calendar, you will need to know your ancestor's name and enough information about him to distinguish him from other people with the same name. An approximate date of death will be helpful, but if you don't have any idea when your ancestor died, you can search the calendar year by year. It's a great tool.

Even if you believe that your ancestor probably did not leave a will, you should always check. It is equally important to look for wills of brothers and sisters of your ancestors, especially those who never married or who died childless. To show you how important these can be, we will examine not a will of one of the Telford/Dixon ancestors but the will of an unmarried cousin. His name is Dixon Dixon, and he died in 1859. The first question you might ask is, What kind of parent would name his child Dixon Dixon? Actually, the man's name was originally Dixon Brown, but he changed his surname in order to inherit property. He had no children of his own.

Research Tip

Technique

How Do I Find the Film I Need?

You can locate the probate calendar in the Family History Library Catalog using either of the following methods:

1. Search under England—Probate Records—Indexes.
2. Search by film number. Use film 0215221 at a Family History Center to obtain the full list of film numbers. This search is more difficult if you are using the Internet version of the FHLC, because you cannot currently scroll through the list of film numbers. Microfilm numbers for the records are as follows:

1858–1864 Film numbers 0215221 to 0215266
1864–1901 Film numbers 0251172 to 0251383
1901–1957 Film numbers 0251384 to 0251667

The film listing can be hard to interpret unless you know that the probate calendar is arranged by calendar year, then in alphabetical order by the surname of the deceased.

Search the catalog in the following order:

1. Year
2. First letter(s) of the surname of your ancestor

An estate is recorded in the year in which probate is registered. This may or may not be the same as the year in which death occurs. However, most estates are registered within a few months of the death.

On the films for 1858 through 1870 the wills and administrations are separated, so you will need to look at two sections of a microfilm or two different films. From 1871, the wills and administrations are combined into one alphabetical sequence.

We want to see if there is a will or administration for Dixon Dixon who died in 1859. We will look for the film for 1859 that contains the surnames beginning with the letter *D*. Look at the catalog entry in Figure 9-1. You can see that we will order film 215228, "Vol. 7–9 D–F Wills and Admins. 1859."

Step By Step

READING THE CALENDAR

The difficult part is finding the correct film. Once the film arrives, the process is easy. The calendar is arranged in strict alphabetical order by surname, then by given names(s). Just roll through the film to the name you want. Remember that before 1870, you will have to check two sections—the will section and the administration section.

An entry for Dixon Dixon appears in 1859. The example on page 124 is an annotated extraction of the calendar.

The probate calendar provides you with enough details to clearly identify your ancestor, even if he had a common surname. Details often in the calendar but not in the will include the following: decedent's occupation, place of last residence, date and place of death (this is never included in a will); value of the estate; name of the court in which the estate was probated; and name, place of

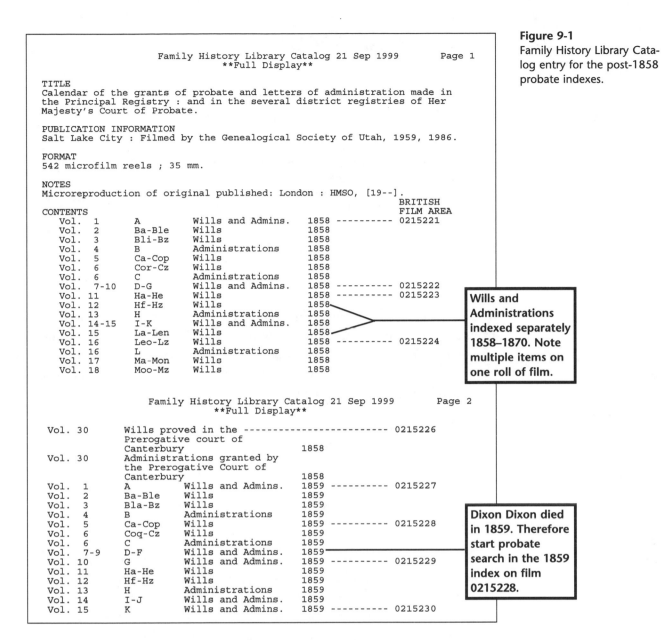

```
              Family History Library Catalog 21 Sep 1999      Page 1
                             **Full Display**

    TITLE
    Calendar of the grants of probate and letters of administration made in
    the Principal Registry : and in the several district registries of Her
    Majesty's Court of Probate.

    PUBLICATION INFORMATION
    Salt Lake City : Filmed by the Genealogical Society of Utah, 1959, 1986.

    FORMAT
    542 microfilm reels ; 35 mm.

    NOTES
    Microreproduction of original published: London : HMSO, [19--].
                                                              BRITISH
    CONTENTS                                                  FILM AREA
        Vol.  1      A          Wills and Admins.  1858 ---------- 0215221
        Vol.  2      Ba-Ble     Wills              1858
        Vol.  3      Bli-Bz     Wills              1858
        Vol.  4      B          Administrations    1858
        Vol.  5      Ca-Cop     Wills              1858
        Vol.  6      Cor-Cz     Wills              1858
        Vol.  6      C          Administrations    1858
        Vol.  7-10   D-G        Wills and Admins.  1858 ---------- 0215222
        Vol. 11      Ha-He      Wills              1858 ---------- 0215223
        Vol. 12      Hf-Hz      Wills              1858
        Vol. 13      H          Administrations    1858
        Vol. 14-15   I-K        Wills and Admins.  1858
        Vol. 15      La-Len     Wills              1858
        Vol. 16      Leo-Lz     Wills              1858 ---------- 0215224
        Vol. 16      L          Administrations    1858
        Vol. 17      Ma-Mon     Wills              1858
        Vol. 18      Moo-Mz     Wills              1858



              Family History Library Catalog 21 Sep 1999      Page 2
                             **Full Display**

    Vol. 30          Wills proved in the ------------------------ 0215226
                     Prerogative court of
                     Canterbury               1858
    Vol. 30          Administrations granted by
                     the Prerogative Court of
                     Canterbury               1858
    Vol.  1      A          Wills and Admins.  1859 ---------- 0215227
    Vol.  2      Ba-Ble     Wills              1859
    Vol.  3      Bla-Bz     Wills              1859
    Vol.  4      B          Administrations    1859
    Vol.  5      Ca-Cop     Wills              1859 ---------- 0215228
    Vol.  6      Coq-Cz     Wills              1859
    Vol.  6      C          Administrations    1859
    Vol.  7-9    D-F        Wills and Admins.  1859
    Vol. 10      G          Wills and Admins.  1859 ---------- 0215229
    Vol. 11      Ha-He      Wills              1859
    Vol. 12      Hf-Hz      Wills              1859
    Vol. 13      H          Administrations    1859
    Vol. 14      I-J        Wills and Admins.  1859
    Vol. 15      K          Wills and Admins.  1859 ---------- 0215230
```

Wills and Administrations indexed separately 1858–1870. Note multiple items on one roll of film.

Dixon Dixon died in 1859. Therefore start probate search in the 1859 index on film 0215228.

Figure 9-1
Family History Library Catalog entry for the post-1858 probate indexes.

residence, and usually occupation of the executors or executrix. The executors are often related, although the relationship may not always be stated. In the Dixon Dixon example, Thomas George Smith is his brother-in-law.

The calendar after 1966 does not name the executors. During World War II the Principal Probate Registry was evacuated to Llandudno, so many ancestors have their estates probated in Wales.

OBTAINING A COPY OF THE WILL

The probate calendar gives the date of probate and the name of the court. The format for the court is "proved (or granted) at the Principal Registry," "proved in London," "proved at [district court name]," or "[district court name]."

The arrangement of the will differs depending upon whether it is registered

1859 Probate Calendar Entry for Dixon Dixon	
DIXON DIXON Esq.	Name of decedent
Effects under £40,000	Value of estate
6 May 1859	Date of Probate
The Will of Dixon Dixon late of Unthank in the Country of **Northumberland** Esquire deceased who died on or about 9 March 1859 at Newcastle-upon-Tyne in the said County was proved at **Newcastle-upon-Tyne** by the oaths of the Reverend John Dixon Clark of Belford Hall in the said County Clerk the Nephew and Thomas George Smith of Togston in the same County Esquire the Executors.	Last place of residence Rank or profession Date and place of death Name of probate court Name, profession, place of residence and possibly relationship to deceased of executor or executrix

in the principal probate registry in London or in one of the district courts. The Family History Library has only microfilmed the wills and the administrations with will annexed. The administrations themselves have not been microfilmed. You will need to write to England to obtain copies of the administrations, and this is explained later in the chapter.

Principal Registry

Technique

Search for the will by these items in the following order:
1. Year of probate
2. Month of probate
3. First letter of surname (Women are listed after all of the men.)
4. Date of the month of probate

For each month, all estates are in alphabetical order by the first letter of the surname, then arranged by date for the month. All of the men are listed first, then the women. The organization of wills is repeated the next month. Therefore, wills registered in January are organized men with surnames beginning A through Z then women with surnames beginning A through Z. This set will be followed by wills for February arranged in a similar manner.

District Court

Technique

Search for the will by these items in the following order:
1. Year of probate
2. Month of probate
3. First letter of surname
4. Court

Therefore, to find Dixon Dixon's will in the district court of Newcastle-upon-Tyne, we will search for 1859, then for the month of May (the month when the estate was probated), then for the letter *D*, then for the court Newcastle-upon-Tyne.

For the district courts, the estates are arranged alphabetically by surname, then by courts in alphabetical order. In the year 1859, month of May, all the surnames beginning with D for the court of Bangor will be followed by the surnames beginning with D in Bedford, and so on. Once we get to D and Newcastle-upon-Tyne, we will look for our ancestor's name. The probates within that court may not be in strict alphabetical order, but this does not matter because generally there are not many records to search for in any given court. Once we have seen all surnames beginning with D for all courts for the month of May, we will begin the surnames beginning with D for the month of June.

In searching the films, make sure you are in the correct year, correct month, and the first letter of your ancestor's surname. Then search for the name of the court, and finally find the surname of interest. The names of the forty district courts are listed alphabetically in the table to guide you.

Research Tip

Locations of District Probate Registries in Alphabetical Order As Found on Probate Films			
Bangor	Chichester	Lichfield	Peterborough
Birmingham	Derby	Lincoln	St. Asaph
Blandford	Durham	Liverpool	Salisbury
Bodmin	Exeter	Llandaff	Shrewsbury
Bristol	Gloucester	Manchester	Taunton
Bury St. Edmunds	Hereford	Newcastle-on-Tyne	Wakefield
Canterbury	Ipswich	Northampton	Wells
Carlisle	Lancaster	Norwich	Winchester
Carmarthen	Leicester	Nottingham	Worcester
Chester	Lewes	Oxford	York

EXAMPLE

The index tells the court in which the estate was processed. In our example, Dixon Dixon's will was registered in May 1859 in Newcastle-upon-Tyne.

Search the Family History Library Catalog by film/fiche number using film number 1239289 to get a complete listing of films covering the years 1858 through 1899. For surnames beginning with D in May 1859 for Newcastle-upon-Tyne, we need film 1278834.

As you read through the abstract of the will, you will notice that Dixon Dixon is a single unmarried male of some standing in the community, leaving bequests to nieces and nephews, brother-in-law, servants and charitable organizations. From this one document, you not only learn about his lifestyle and what was important to him, but you are also able to construct a large family tree. Each individual mentioned can now be located in other documents, such as the census and civil registration.

You should obtain copies of all wills and letters of administration for your ancestors as well as for other family members. Combine the copy of the will with the information from the probate calendar for a more complete picture of the time and place of death, plus information on the executors. Together they will help you fill in lots of details about the lives of your ancestors.

Technique

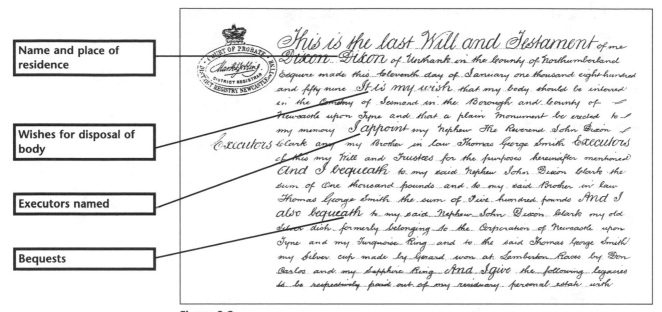

Name and place of residence

Wishes for disposal of body

Executors named

Bequests

Figure 9-2
This is the first page of Dixon Dixon's three-page will written in 1859 and proven the same year in the Principal Probate Registry.

Abstract of Will

DIXON DIXON

Will written 11 January 1859
District—Newcastle on Tyne

Residence   —of Unthank in the county of Northumberland
Rank or profession   —Esquire
Burial Wish   —interment in the Cemetery of Jesmond in the Borough and
                              County of Newcastle upon Tyne
                             —with plain monument
Executors   —my **nephew The Reverend John Dixon Clark**
                             —my **brother-in-law Thomas George Smith**

Bequests
— to my said **nephew John Dixon Clark**
  - one thousand pounds
  - my old silver dish formerly belonging to the Corporation of Newcastle
    upon Tyne
  - my turquoise ring

— to my said **brother-in-law Thomas George Smith**
  - five hundred pounds
  - my silver cup made by Gerard won at Lamberton Races by Don Carlos
  - my sapphire ring

Figure 9-3 (continued on page 127)
Notice the wealth of information given in this abstract of all details from the will of Dixon Dixon.

— to my **niece Jane Margaret Atkinson, wife of The Reverend William Atkinson**
  - interest and annual proceeds from two thousand pounds at four pounds per centum per annum
  - upon her death to my godson George Dixon Atkinson, son of the said William Atkinson.

— to my **niece Julia Kite, wife of The Reverend Frederick Robert Kite**
  - interest and annual proceeds from two thousand pounds at four pounds per centum per annum
  - upon her death to her child or children who attain the age of twenty-one in such shares and proportions as determined by Julia's will or by default in equal proportions.

— to my **niece Jane Davies, wife of The Reverend Charles Davies**
  - interest and annual proceeds from two thousand pounds at four pounds per centum per annum
  - upon her death to her child or children who attain the age of twenty-one in such shares and proportions as determined by Jane's will or by default in equal proportions.

Power is given to the trustees to invest the above three legacies in Parliamentary stocks or funds of Great Britain or upon securities in corporation or chartered company and to move the funds as appropriate.

— to my **sister-in-law Isabella Smith**
  - five hundred pounds

— to my servants living with me at the time of death
  - one years wages in addition to what may be due to them

— One hundred pounds to the General Infirmary at or near Forth Banks, Newcastle upon Tyne
— One hundred pounds to the Eye Infirmary in Newcastle upon Tyne
— to **Susan Lowrie of Benton**, in the county of Northumberland, my former housekeeper
  - annuity of twenty pounds during her life, paid quarterly

— to **Richard Morrison**, now living with me
  - annuity of twenty pounds during his life, paid quarterly

Above two annuities to be charged against my estate and other herditaments situate in the parish of Long Benton, county of Northumberland, to be paid from the annual rents and profits.
— to my **nephew Robert Brown, son of my late brother Robert Brown**
  - ten thousand pounds
— to my **nephew Ralph Brown, son of my late brother Robert Brown**
  - ten thousand pounds minus any indebtedness to me
— to my **nephew Dixon Brown, son of my late brother Robert Brown**
  - ten thousand pounds

Clauses for appointment of contingent trustees

Witnesses:
John Leadbitter
Peter Milligan, his Clerk

Figure 9-3 continued from page 126

WHAT WILL BE REVEALED IN LETTERS OF ADMINISTRATION

Letters of Administration in England are usually not as good as wills, but they contain valuable information. The letter of administration will state the name of the deceased, usual place of residence, and the date and place of death. For the administrators, you will find the name, address, occupation and any relationship to the deceased. The administrator does not have to be related but could be a major creditor. The administration will not name the beneficiaries, but you can obtain this information from Death Duty Registers. See chapter eleven on pre-1858 probate records for more information about these records.

You may be tempted to ignore probate documents other than wills, but you should always locate letters of administration because they do confirm the date and place of death and can provide information on potential relatives. For example, we have a letter of administration of a woman who lived on the southeast coast of England. The family story was that her husband had abandoned his aging wife. The letter of administration for her estate gave the husband's address in Wales. If this woman had left a will, her husband probably would not have been mentioned. The letter of administration provided the only clue to his whereabouts. Records like these provide fascinating leads to further research. Did he have a mistress? Did he have another family in Wales?

ADDITIONAL STRATEGIES

The FHL does not have the following records on microfilm: calendars after 1957, administrations at the principal registry since 1858, wills and administrations in principal registry and district courts since 1925.

What are the options if a search is needed for one of these?

In June 1998 the Probate Department of The Principal Registry of the Family Division was relocated to

> First Avenue House
> 42–49 High Holborn
> London WC1V 6NP
> Telephone: 0171 9367000

One option is to hire a London researcher to examine the indexes on your behalf and obtain copies of relevant documents. The search process in the printed volumes is quick, and copies are inexpensive when obtained on-site.

To obtain by mail copies of the registered will or letter of administration contact

> Probate Registry
> Duncombe Place
> York YO1 2EA
> Telephone: 01904 624210

WHY CAN'T I FIND MY ANCESTOR IN THE CALENDAR?

Not everyone left a will or a letter of administration. That does not mean you should not look; you should. These are easy records to check, and the indexes are all printed. The percentage of people being recorded increases over time, especially as the quantity and value of disposable property increases. The chances that your ancestor left an estate will increase the higher he was in the social strata and the greater the value of his possessions or land. However, don't forget that even the common laborer and soldier had estates to leave. **Not even all the wealthy left wills.** Usually the affluent did leave wills. However, sometimes your ancestors had nothing to dispose of because they had already distributed their property before death. Records of the younger generation may mention the origin of these items as they were passed to future generations. Your ancestor may also have had nothing to dispose of because he, or especially she, was living from life interests or annuities. In this situation look for the wills of the older generation.

If you are checking before 1871, the wills and administrations are listed separately. Be sure you have looked through both sections.

You didn't look late enough. Yes, most estates go through probate in the first three years, but some don't. Continue checking through the indexes. The estate may not have been probated until after the death of the spouse. If a widow was left with young children, there may have been no need to go through probate until the children were adults. So keep looking.

WHERE TO FIND MORE ABOUT THIS TOPIC

Cox, Jane. *Affection Defying the Power of Death: Wills, Probate & Death Duty Records.* An Introduction to Series. Federation of Family History Societies, 1993.

McLaughlin, Eve. *Somerset House Wills From 1858.* 5th ed. McLaughlin Guides, 1994. Although the location of the records has changed, this book will tell you how to use the wills. The records have moved from Somerset House to First Avenue House.

AFTER SEARCHING THE PROBATE RECORDS, WHAT SHOULD I DO NEXT?

If you find mention of other family members who were born, married, or died after 1837, return to civil registration. Obtain the necessary certificates for additional family members that you have found. Use any addresses given in the probate and civil registration records to locate the families in the census records. Notice that this search process is becoming circular. Probate records will often lead you to identifying a more complete family and finding more distant relatives. They may give you the names of married children. From this information you return to civil registration and census returns.

Examine the probate records carefully. Are there children you expected to find that are not included in the probate records? This could be an indication that you should search for a death in the civil registration indexes.

The information contained on a letter of administration is limited. However, for cases over seventy-five years old, the distribution of an estate can be followed through the Death Duty Registers. Unfortunately, the post-1857 registers have not been microfilmed. You can see them at the Public Record Office in Kew, Surrey, England.

The nonfamily bequests in the probate are important; they may indicate a lot about what was important to your ancestor. For example, if your ancestor left property to a person to whom he was not related, it may tell you how he felt about his servants, work associates, or other important people. Sometimes illegitimate children are mentioned without stating the relationship. Gifts to an institution may tell you about your ancestor's religious beliefs, charities he supported, his health, his occupation, or other information about his way of life. For example, Dixon Dixon gave a bequest to the General Infirmary and the Eye Infirmary (see Figure 9-3). Might he have had eye problems? The location of the charity may indicate the place of origin of your ancestor. Follow up on these clues.

For More Info

If the people mentioned in the will were born, married, or died before the beginning of civil registration (1837), the next step is to use church records to look for them. **Parish registers of the Church of England contain records of baptisms, marriages, and burials for your earlier ancestors. We will find out how to use these records in the next chapter.**

TEN

Parish Registers

P arishes are the fundamental unit of the Church of England. In 1538, Thomas Cromwell, Vicar-General of Henry VIII, ordered all parishes to keep records of all baptisms, marriages, and burials in their area. These parish registers are some of the most exciting records in all of genealogy.

WHAT ARE THE PARISH REGISTERS, AND WHY ARE THEY SO IMPORTANT?

The parish registers of England are theoretically records of the membership of the Church, but because the Church of England was the official church, it had responsibility for the record keeping and social welfare of everyone residing within its boundaries.

It was in everyone's best interest that these records were properly kept. This included the country, the Church, and your ancestors. One reason the country wanted the registers kept was to help determine the size of the population for fiscal and military purposes. The Church and your ancestors saw these records as the only way to prove the validity of a marriage, prove the right to inheritance, and to be assured of poor relief. Therefore, the parish registers contain entries for many of your ancestors who did not consider themselves to be members of the Established Church. If your ancestor was Catholic, for example, he often would have a child baptized in the Catholic church and then have the ceremony repeated in the Church of England.

Early Origins of Parish Records

The earliest records were written on loose sheets of paper. Around the end of Queen Elizabeth I's reign, many of these records were deteriorating. Therefore, a new law went into effect in 1597 requiring that parish records be maintained in parchment books. Parchment is made from sheepskin and lasts much longer than paper. The clergy were given the option to record all entries from the beginning of the parish registers (1538) or from the beginning of Queen Elizabeth I's reign (1558). Therefore, you will find that entries before 1597 were recorded in the same handwriting because they were copied from the original records. You will also find many parish registers dating from 1558. Another important act that year required parishes to forward an annual copy of the parish registers to the bishop of the diocese. These are called Bishop's Transcripts (BTs), and they are not always exact copies of the registers. You will want to check the parish registers and the BTs if both are available.

Important Dates	
1538	Parish registers begin.
1597	Parchment books ordered. Copies of parish registers (Bishop's Transcripts) required to be sent yearly at Easter to the bishop of the diocese.
1642–1660	Commonwealth Period. Record keeping is irregular.
1733	Parish registers required to be in English (formerly in Latin).
1752	Calendar change. Beginning of year changes from March 25 (Lady Day) to January 1.
1754	Lord Hardwicke's Act: Marriages outside the Church of England are illegal (except Quakers and Jews).
1778	End of Penal Laws. Many Catholic registers date from this time.
1812	George Rose Act. Required separate standardized printed registers for baptisms, marriages, and burials.
1837	Civil registration begins.

WHAT DO THE PARISH REGISTERS CONTAIN?
Baptismal Registers

The amount of detail found in the registers can vary greatly. Baptismal registers from 1500 to 1700 often provide only the name of the child and the date of baptism. They may also be recorded in Latin. From the late 1600s the name of the father is usually stated. Sometimes his occupation is given as well. Until the mid-1700s, the mother's name was rarely given. From the mid to late 1700s the mother's given name will often appear, but her maiden surname will not be stated. In 1813 the parish registers were standardized. From that date, a record of baptism is on a preprinted form with columns for the following information:

Date of baptism

Child's Christian (given) name

Parents' Christian names and the surname of the couple (mother's maiden name is not given)

Abode (residence)

Quality, trade, or profession

By whom the ceremony was performed

Marriage Registers

Again, the early registers can vary greatly. Before 1754, only the consent of the parties was required to establish a legal marriage. The age of consent was fourteen for boys and twelve for girls. The marriage registers usually give only the names of the groom and bride and the date of marriage. Sometimes the parishes of the bride and groom are stated, especially if one came from a parish other than the one in which the marriage was performed. The marriage record may indicate whether the marriage was by banns or license. You will see why this is significant when we examine the marriage documents.

Marriages will usually be missing in the registers during the Commonwealth period because in 1653 the right to perform marriages was taken away from the clergy and given to Justices of the Peace. Between 1657 and 1660 both J.P.s and clergy could perform marriages. From the late seventeenth century, increasing numbers of nonconformists ignored the Church of England, thus many marriages are not recorded.

Hardwicke's Marriage Act of 1753 was designed to stop irregular marriages, including marriages without clergy, marriages performed without banns or license, minors marrying without parental consent, or couples marrying outside the parish in which they lived. The most famous place for these abuses was the area around the Fleet Prison in London. These are referred to as "Fleet marriages." Here a couple could get a quick marriage with almost no questions asked. Fleet marriages could even be backdated in cases of illegitimacy. Record keeping was irregular at best. Therefore, Hardwicke's Marriage Act required all marriages to be performed and recorded by the Church of England; the only exceptions were for Jews and Quakers. It also required consent of a parent or guardian for anyone under the age of twenty-one. From 1754 until the introduction of civil registration in 1837, the vast majority of our ancestors were recorded in the Church of England marriage registers.

From 1754 the information in the marriage record is standardized. Signatures or marks of the bride, groom, and witnesses appear on the parish register. They do not appear on the Bishop's Transcript, however, because the BT is a copy of the original. The marriage record will also tell you the parish of the bride and groom and whether the marriage was performed by banns or license. If one or both of the parties was married by consent of parents or guardians, this will be stated. The name of the minister will also be recorded.

After 1837 the marriage records contain the same information as the civil registration certificates. **If the post-1837 parish registers are available on microfilm, it can save you considerable money and greatly increase your knowledge of the family if you view all of the marriages of a parish on film rather than ordering individual civil registration certificates.**

Money Saver

Burial Registers

Burial records are the least informative. They will usually only give you the name of the person buried and the date of burial. Sometimes the register may include a man's occupation, the name of the father of a child, or the name of a woman's husband. You may even find the date of death.

Burials after 1813 are on preprinted forms with columns for the following information:

Name

Abode (residence)

When buried

By whom the ceremony was performed

What Do I Need to Know Before Searching This Record?

Warning

You will need to have some background on the history of your ancestor's parish. **Despite your urge to dive right into the parish registers, do not do this.** You need to know the environment in which your ancestor lived: the local geography, types of agriculture and industry in the area, health issues, religious forces, etc.

To find out more about the geography, you should locate the parish on a map and look in several gazetteers to find out more about the parish. You will want to know the names of nearby places and the routes by which your ancestor would have traveled to get to these places. You can determine possible migration routes by looking at the rivers, canals, roads, and railroads in the area. You will also need to know who had jurisdiction over the local records. Two good places to start are *The Phillimore Atlas and Index of Parish Registers* and *A Topographical Dictionary of England* (see page 25 for both sources).

A knowledge of local history is essential. For example, the parish history may tell you how your ancestor lived, what he likely would have done for a living, where he would likely have moved to obtain work, what the predominant religions were and when large numbers of people converted, when emigration agents were active in the area, when diseases were rampant, etc. You can waste a lot of time doing radial searches when a parish history may provide the answer you need. It is impossible to do an effective family history without knowing what was happening in the area where your ancestors lived.

Sources

Look for a history of your ancestor's parish or county. First check the GENUKI site on the Internet: Go to England, then to the name of the county. See the categories "Church History" and "History." For example, the GENUKI listing for the County of Northumberland indicates that volumes 1–15 of the *A History of Northumberland* are available on microfiche. After you have found the available county histories, look to see if there is a list of towns and parishes for that county. On the Northumberland page, there is a list of towns and parishes that includes the parish of Stamfordham. Under the category "History" we found the following entry: "The history of Stamfordham parish is included in: Northumberland County History Committee, *A History of Northumberland*, Volume 12. Newcastle, A. Reid, 1926." We had already seen that these volumes are available on microfiche, so we can purchase volume 12.

After checking listings on the Internet, you should go to local libraries to see what histories of your area of interest are available by interlibrary loan. *A History of Northumberland* mentioned above, is available in hardcover at major libraries. One very useful series is commonly called the Victoria County Histories (VCH). This multivolume series, begun in 1899, is still being written, but some counties have no volumes, including Northumberland. Look for the title, *The Victoria History of the County of* [name of your county], published by the Institute of Historical Research; University of London. Many of them are also available on microfilm through the Family History Library. You can also use the Family History Library Catalog to find other histories to view at your Family History Center. Look under England-[County]-History and under England-[County]-[Parish]-History. We found *A History of Northumberland*, volume 12, in the Family History Library Catalog. It is available on microfilm. Not only will you find essential historical details in a local history, but your family may be recorded. Look at Figure 10-1 to see what was mentioned about the Dixon family of the township of Ingoe in the parish of Stamfordham. We even found a great map of the townships within the parish and adjacent parishes (see Figure 10-2). You can see why you must always look for parish histories.

Figure 10-1
This page on the Dixon family from Ingoe, in the parish of Stamfordham, Northumberland, shows the wealth of information that can be found about many families in local and county histories. This is from *A History of Northumberland*, volume 12, by A. Reid.

INGOE TOWNSHIP   393

1687, who became a tinsmith in Newcastle and sold his property in Ingoe on 24th March, 1713/4.[1]

The family of Dixon was holding land in Ingoe as early as 1586, when Percival and Thomas Dixon occur in Stockdale's Survey. In 1622 as stated above William Dixon of Fenwick took a mortgage on the lands of William Shaftoe. In 1663 Percival Dixon of Fenwick was rated on lands in Ingoe.[2] He married Catherine Moor, widow, of Whalton, at Whalton on 19th April, 1664. She was buried at Whalton on 10th May, 1673, and he at Stamfordham on 29th September, 1674.[3] William Dixon of Fenwick purchased lands in Ingoe on 2nd December, 1724.[4] He made his will on 10th May, 1728 and was buried on 26th November, 1729. In his will he mentioned his wife Isabel, whom he advised to marry again for the good of her children.[5] He had a large family, of whom his son Robert Dixon, baptised 29th May, 1705, succeeded him. By his will dated 10th May, 1753, and proved 20th April, 1762, he made his brother Lionel his heir. Lionel Dixon's will was dated 21st May, 1793, and he was buried on 6th June, 1793, aged 80. He made William Dixon, a captain in the army, the son of his brother John Dixon of Newcastle, the heir to his property, with remainder to the family of another brother, William Dixon of Newcastle, who had died on 26th February, 1749/50, leaving children, of whom his daughter Margaret in 1770 became the wife of William Brown of Willington.

Captain William Dixon, the immediate heir of Lionel Dixon lived in Gower Street, Bedford Square, London. On 15th August, 1787, he married Britannia Hill at St. Andrews, Holborn. He made his will on 21st May, 1793, leaving his property to his wife for life, and then to his son William, with remainder to Dixon Brown of Long Benton, the eldest son of William Brown and Margaret Dixon. Captain Dixon's son William was the child of a previous marriage to that of 1787, as in 1798 he was a captain in the Royal Engineers serving at Woolwich. He died a colonel in 1825, childless, and was succeeded by his cousin Dixon Brown, who took the name of Dixon, and thus became Dixon Dixon. He died on 9th March, 1859,[6] without direct heirs, and the duke of Northumberland is now the only important landowner in Ingoe.

William and Isabell Dixon, the great-grandparents of Mary Dixon who married Robert Dixon (see Figures 10-11, 10-12, 10-13)

Dixon Dixon, whose will we examined in chapter nine

[1] Abstract of Title, Dixon property in Ingoe.   [2] Hodgson, pt. 3, vol. i. p. 297.
[3] *Par. Reg.* Whalton and Stamfordham.   [4] Abstract of Title, Dixon property in Ingoe.
[5] Raine MS., *Testa. Dun.*   [6] Monumental Inscriptions, Jesmond Cemetery.

Vol. XII.   50

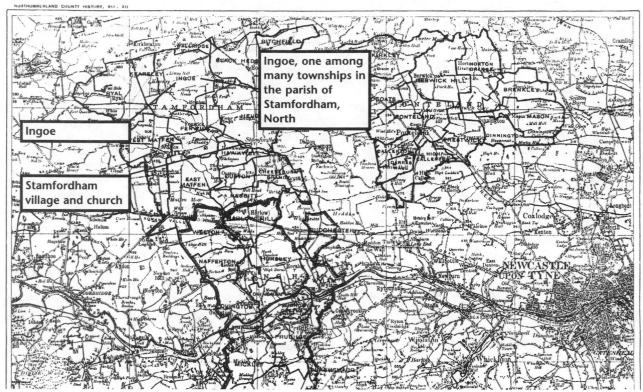

Figure 10-2
Map from the introduction to volume 12 of *A History of Northumberland* by A. Reid. The map shows all of the townships within the parishes of Stamfordham, Ovingham, and Ponteland covered in this volume. Useful detailed maps like this can be difficult to find anywhere else.

How Do I Know What Parish Registers Exist and If They Have Been Indexed?

Sources

Once you know the location of your ancestor's parish and some local history, you are ready to find out what parish registers exist, where they are located, and if they are indexed. **The best resource that will give you this information is** *The Phillimore Atlas and Index of Parish Registers* **(see page 25). You can purchase it from the Phillimore Web site at <http://www.phillimore.co.uk> or borrow it on interlibrary loan.** *The Phillimore Atlas* lists every parish in England and tells you what parish registers exist and where the registers are located. The book is divided into two sections:

- The atlas contains a topographical map and a parish boundary map for each county. (See example in Figure 11-1.)
- The index contains an alphabetical list of parishes for each county.

Using Phillimore's Index

Step By Step

We will look for the parish of Stamfordham, Northumberland. Turn to the index at the back of *The Phillimore Atlas and Index of Parish Registers*, and find the county of Northumberland (see Figure 10-3). The parish names are listed alphabetically.

219

NORTHUMBERLAND	deposited original registers	I.G.I.	local marriage indexes	copies of registers at Soc. Gen.	Boyd's marriage index	copies of regs. not at Soc.Gen.	Pallot's marriage index	non-conform. records at P.R.O.
Ramshope (ex.par.)								8H
Rennington	1765-1982	1768-1895	A 1813-1837	1768-1812	1769-1779			3I
Rock	1768-1981	1769-1896	A 1813-1837	1768-1812	1771-1780			3I
Rothbury	1653-1969	1653-1812	A 1813-1837	1653-1816	1653-1812		1769-1840	5G
St John Lee	1664-1961	1664-1896	A 1813-1837		1664-1812	1664-1812		6D
Shilbottle	1723-1986	1691-1815	A 1813-1837	1813-1837	1695-1851	1684-1812		3H
Shotley	1670-1971	1670-1837	A 1813-1837	1670-1837	1670-1818	1670-1812		5B
Simonburn	1681-1959	1681-1877	A 1813-1837	1681-1851				7D
Slaley	1703-1971	1703-1895	B 1722-1837	1703-1851	1725-1812	1703-1812		6C
Stamfordham	1662-1978	1662-1812	A 1813-1837		1662-1812	1662-1812		5D
Stannington	1658-1959	1658-1877	A 1813-1837					3E
Thockrington	1715-1936	1715-1886	A 1813-1837	1715-1851				6E
Thorneyburn	1819-1910		A 1813-1837					8F
Tweedmouth	1711-1952	1711-1812	A 1813-1837	1813-1837	1711-1812	1711-1812	1751-1785	5L
	1607-1981	1607-1884	A 1813-1837	1607-1734	1607-1733		1756-1840	2D
Stamfordham	1602-1962	1602-1875	A 1813-1837					3F
	1669-1970	1669-1812	A 1813-1837		1669-1812	1669-1812	1813-1837	2D
Warden	1695-1979	1695-1896	A 1813-1837	1695-1724	1695-1723			6D
Wark	1818-1979	1818-1877	A 1813-1837					7E
Warkworth	1676-1974	1677-1812	A 1813-1837	1667-1812	1677-1812		1790-1812	3G
West Allen or Ninebanks	1767-1959	1767-1877	A 1813-1837					7B
Whalton	1661-1900	1661-1896	A 1813-1837	1661-1812	1661-1812		1790-1812	4E
Whitfield	1600-1981	1606-1877	B 1600-1837	1600-1840	1606-1812	1606-1812		8B
Whitley	1764-1978	1764-1896	A 1813-1837	1764-1851				6B
Whittingham	1658-1962	1659-1876	A 1813-1837	1813-1837				5H
Whittonstall	1754-1960	1750-1877	A 1813-1837					5C
Widdrington	1698-1884	1698-1876	A 1813-1837		1698-1711	1698-1812		2G
Woodhorn	1605-1986	1605-1812	A 1813-1837		1606-1812	1605-1812		2F
Wooler	1692-1923	1692-1895	A 1813-1837	1813-1837	1693-1812	1692-1812		5J(B)

Northumberland and Durham Family History Society Marriage Index

Original registers deposited at:
Northumberland Record Office, Melton Park, North Gosforth, Newcastle upon Tyne NE3 5QX

Study adjacent parishes in counties of Scotland, Cumberland and Durham
Northumberland Record Office, Mellton Park, North Gosforth, Newcastle-upon-Tyne NE3 5QX
Berwick-upon-Tweed Record Office, Borough Council House, Wallace Green, Berwick-upon-Tweed TD15 1ED
Tyne and Wear Archive Service, Blandford House, Blandford Square, Newcastle-upon-Tyne NE14 4JA

The following indexes have been compiled - see Introduction
Census Indexes -
South East Northumberland 1851 (Northumberland and Durham Family History Society) - Mrs. C. Danson, 22 Ferndale Avenue, East Boldon, Tyne and Wear NE36 0TQ
1851 Census on M/F - Mr R. Dalkin, 12 St Aidans Crescent, Crossgate Moor, Durham DH1 4AP

Marriage Indexes -
A = Northumberland and Durham Family History Society - Mr. K. Dalkin, 12 St Aidan's Crescent, Crossgate Moor, Durham DHJ 4AP
B = Co. Durham Index - Mr. W.E. Rounce, 40 Salcombe Avenue, Jarrow, Tyne and Wear NE33 3SY
Mr J.A. Readdie, 38 Archery Rise, Neville's Cross, Durham DH1 4LA
Co. Durham Index - W.E. Rounce, 40 Salcombe Avenue, Jarrow, Tyne & Wear NE32 3SY

Northumberland is triangular in shape; its greatest length from north to south is almost 70 miles and its breadth at the southern extremity from east to west almost 48 miles. It is watered by five principal rivers: the Trent, North Tyne, South Tyne, Coquet and Read. The population in 1841 was 266,020; in 1851, 303,568; in 1861, 343,025; in 1871, 386,959; in 1881, 434,086.

The soils include clay, loam, sand and gravel. The produce were corn, cattle, sheep, lead and coal, the latter being of particular importance. The principal manufactures were glass, pottery and iron and the rivers were the source of considerable numbers of fish, especially trout and salmon.

The information in the Index is abbreviated, and may mislead the searcher if reference is not made to the details contained in the several publications listed in the Introduction. It is essential that users of this book check the appropriate works before making further enquiries.

Figure 10-3
Index page for Northumberland in *The Phillimore Atlas and Index of Parish Registers* tabulating much information from a variety of different resources, including original registers and major indexes.

The first column in the index is the name of the parish. The second column is labeled "deposited original registers." This column tells us that the registers for 1662 to 1978 have been sent to another repository. There may be missing entries or gaps in the registers, but in general the registers cover those years. At the end of the index for the county, we find that all original registers were deposited at the Northumberland Record Office. Therefore, we know that any search of the original registers must be made at the Northumberland Record Office, not at the church at Stamfordham.

The third column tells us whether the registers are indexed in the International Genealogical Index. It indicates that the IGI contains entries for the years 1662 to 1812. This is only a portion of the records. Use this column only as a rough guide to IGI coverage. You will use the Parish and Vital Records List (explained below) for a more accurate description.

The next column tells you whether the parish registers have been indexed in any local marriage indexes and where to locate such indexes. The years 1813 to 1837 have been indexed. "A" refers you to the bottom of the section, which says that the index is available from the Northumberland and Durham Family History Society.

Column 5 lets you know if a copy of the registers is available at the Society of Genealogists (SoG) in London. There are no copies of Stamfordham parish registers at the SoG.

Column 6 indicates whether marriages for the parish are indexed in Boyd's Marriage Index. We will show how to use this index later in the chapter.

Column 7 tells whether there are copies of the parish registers somewhere other than at The Society of Genealogists. If so, the dates of the registers held are included. However, you do not know where they are located by looking at this column. This doesn't appear to be very useful, but if you read the introduction you'll learn that the SoG has published a guide to parish register copies held at other repositories in England and Wales. You will need to refer to the guide to find out who holds the copies. The name of the SoG guide is *Parish Register Copies, Part Two, Other Than the Society of Genealogists' Collection*; it was published in 1974.

Column 8 lets you know if the parish registers are indexed in Pallot's Marriage Index. This index is held by the Institute of Heraldic and Genealogical Studies located at Canterbury, Kent, England. The staff will search the index for a fee. The registers of Stamfordham are not included in this index.

Column 9 will tell you if any nonconformist records for the parish have been deposited at the Public Record Office.

The last column is the grid reference for the Northumberland map in the atlas section of *The Phillimore Atlas*. Stamfordham is located at section 5D of the map. We have reproduced this parish boundary map in **chapter eleven, Figure 11-1**. Look at section 5D to find Stamfordham.

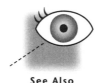

See Also

NATIONAL INDEX OF PARISH REGISTERS

You can obtain a more detailed listing of the availability of parish registers from the National Index of Parish Registers (NIPR). This multivolume set is a continuing series published by The Society of Genealogists. Not all volumes have been published. If the county you need is not available through your local library, check the online bookshop on the SoG Web site at <http://www.sog.org .uk> to find out about the most recently published volumes.

NIPR covers pre-1837 registers, but it sometimes mentions later dates. It tells us that the original registers for Stamfordham cover 1662–95 and 1733–1836 for christenings, 1662–1704 and 1727–1926 for marriages, 1754–92 and 1823– for banns, and 1667–96 and 1722–1865 for burials. All of the original registers are at the Northumberland County Record Office. It also says that copies of the registers are available at other named repositories and that the copies have more extensive coverage than the originals. Compare this information to that found in *The Phillimore Atlas*. Phillimore's tells us that the overall coverage of the original registers at the Northumberland County Record Office is 1662–1978, but it does not mention the gaps. NIPR also tells us that the years covered by the Bishop's Transcripts are 1769–1836 with gaps. You know that you will definitely want to check the original registers and the BTs to see if one fills in the gaps of the other. The National Index of Parish Registers does not mention local indexes and other items listed in Phillimore's. **It is best to use these two sources together to get a more complete picture of the availability of parish registers and indexes.**

Tip

PARISH AND VITAL RECORDS LIST

Notice that *The Phillimore Atlas and Index of Parish Registers* lists several marriage indexes, but no indexes specifically for baptisms or burials. However, there are two large indexes that include baptisms—the International Genealogical Index and the Vital Records Index: British Isles. They also include a very large number of marriages. As you know, the IGI is available on the Family-Search Web site, the FamilySearch program at Family History Centers, and an older edition on microfiche. The Vital Records Index: British Isles is available on compact disc. You can purchase it from the FamilySearch Web site or from the Salt Lake Distribution Center. To know the extent to which your ancestor's parish has been included in these indexes, use the Parish and Vital Records List (PVRL).

The PVRL contains a list of parishes showing what records have been extracted by the Genealogical Society of Utah. It tells us what we can expect to find in the International Genealogical Index and in the Vital Records Index: British Isles. Eventually all listings in the PVRL will appear on the IGI, but it may take several years from the time an entry is extracted to its appearance on the IGI. In the meantime, the entries that are not yet on the IGI are on the Vital Records Index: British Isles. We will need to check both sources.

The Parish and Vital Records List is available on microfiche at every Family History Center. You search the PVRL the same way you search the Family History Library Catalog. Look for the name of the country first, then the county, then the name of the parish. To find what records have been extracted for Stamfordham, we look for England, Northumberland, Stamfordham. See Figure 10-4; the example is from the July 1998 edition of the Parish and Vital Records List. This edition of the PVRL is ten years more current than the list in *The Phillimore Atlas and Index of Parish Registers*. The PVRL is also more specific. Phillimore's states that the IGI contains entries for the years 1662 to 1812. The PVRL tells us that christenings have been extracted for the years

```
███ 0 01 ███                                                                      ███ 0 01 ███
ENGLAND                        PARISH AND VITAL RECORDS LIST        JUL 1998
                                                                         PAGE 1,082
  1.           2.                              3.     4.   5.         6.        7.
COUNTY   TOWN AND/OR PARISH                   PERIOD  RECO PRINTOUT  NUM  PROJECT  SOURCE
                                             FROM - TO TYPE CALL NO. FCH           CALL NO.

NORTHU  ROCK                                 1769-1886 CHR  NONE          C  13-2 ██ 1068848
        ROCK                                 1771-1780 MAR  NONE          M  13-2 ██ 1068848
        ROCK                                 1771-1780 MAR  NONE          M  13-1 ██ 0094970
        ROCK                                 1861-1896 MAR  ■ 6905711  1|  M  13-3 ██ 1068875
        ROTHBURY                             1653-1812 CHR  ■ 6905680  2|  P 1524-1    0094975
                                                       CHR                             0094975
        ROTHBURY                             1653-1812 MAR  ■ 6905681  1|  M 1524-1    0094975
        ROTHBURY, THROPTON ROMAN CATHOLIC    1769-1840 CHR  ■ 6905791  1|  C10498-1   0825357 (RG4 1779)
        ROTHBURY, THROPTON ROMAN CATHOLIC    1772-1821 MAR  ■ 6905792  1|  M10498-1 ██ 0825357 (RG4 1779)
        RYTON, CHEESEBURN GRANGE AND STELLA ROMAN CATHOLIC  SEE: CHEESEBURN GRANGE AND STELLA, ROMAN CATHOLIC
        SCREMERSTON                          1843-1875 CHR  ■ 6900581  1|  P  431-1   0252561
                                                       CHR                            0252561
                                                       CHR                            0252561
                                                       CHR                            0252561
        SCREMERSTON                          1845-1885 MAR  ■ 6900582  1|  M  431-1   0252561
        SEATON-DELAVAL, PRIMITIVE METHODIST CIRCUIT  1886-1887 CHR  ■ 6905808  1|  C15601-1 ██ 1068978
        SHIELDS, BROOM'S CHAPEL ROMAN CATHOLIC  SEE: TYNEMOUTH, ROMAN CATHOLIC
        SHILBOTTLE                           1691-1725 CHR  ■ 6905617  1|  P  442-1   0094975
                                             1763-1815 CHR                            0094975
        SHILBOTTLE, BTS-98X                  1695-1812 MAR  ■ 6905618  1|  M  442-1   0094975
        SHILBOTTLE, ST. JAMES                1681-1885 CHR  NONE           C  442-2 ██ 0991788
        SHILBOTTLE, ST. JAMES                1695-1895 MAR  ■ 6905618  1|  M  442-2 ██ 0991788
        SHOTLEY                              1670-1812 MAR  ■ 6905612  1|  M  439-1   0095027
                                             1813-1876 MAR
        SHOTLEY                              1675-1861 PAS    6905611      M  438     71
        SIMONBURN                            1682-1861 CHR  ■ 6905607  2|                52
                                                       CHR                             52
        SIMONBURN                            1681-1762 MAR  ■ 6905608  1|
        SIMONBURN                            1763-1877 MAR  ■ 6905608  1|
        SLALEY                               1703-1812 CHR  ■ 6905733  1|
                                                       CHR
                                                       CHR
        SLALEY                               1703-1885 CHR  NONE           C  40-2 ██ 0991786
        SLALEY                               1722-1812 MAR  ■ 6902824  1|  M  40-1    0095030
        SLALEY                               1723-1895 MAR  NONE           M  40-2 ██ 0991786
        SPITTAL OR SPITTLE, UNITED PRESBY    1751-1853 CHR  ■ 6905776      C 8068-1   0825357 (RG4 4038)
        SPITTAL OR SPITTLE, UNITED PRESBY    1781-1784 MAR  NONE           M 8068-1 ██ 0825357 (RG4 4038)
                                             1787-1788 MAR  NONE                    ██ 0825357 (RG4 2684)
                                               -1803 MAR                           ██ 0825357 (RG4 4038)
        STAMFORDHAM                          1662-1812 CHR  ■ 6905625  2|  P  447-1   0095028
                                                       CHR                            0095028
        STAMFORDHAM                          1662-1715 MAR  ■ 6905626  1|  M  447-1   0095028
                                             1727-1792 MAR                            0095028
        STAMFORDHAM, PRESBYTERIAN CHURCH     1754-1860 CHR                            0087905
                                                       CHR                            0087905
        STANNINGTON                          1658-1861 CHR                            0252495, 0252496
                                                       CHR                            0252495, 0252496
        STANNINGTON                          1658-1760 MAR  ■ 6905610  1|  M  438-1   0252495
                                             1754-1812 MAR                            0252497
```

Notice gap 1715–1727 in marriage extractions, raising question Is the register missing or was that period just not extracted?

Index printouts available for christenings and marriage for this time period

Original registers on this film

█ THE PRINTOUT IS ON MICROFILM ONLY
█ THE PRINTOUT IS ON MICROFICHE ONLY

██ RECORDS IN THIS BATCH AND PERIOD ARE NOT IN THE 1988 EDITION OF THE IGI.

Figure 10-4

The Parish and Vital Records List, available at all local Family History Centers, lists which birth and marriage registers have been extracted and included in the International Genealogical Index (IGI) and the Vital Records Index: British Isles.

1662 to 1812, but marriages have only been extracted for the years 1662 to 1715 and 1727 to 1792. There are also extractions of christenings from 1754 to 1880 for the Presbyterian Church of Stamfordham.

Column 5 of the PVRL tells us if there was a computer printout made of the extracted entries. If there is one, you can order the referenced microfilm or fiche number. It can be very valuable because it will contain extracts of the parish registers neatly typed. Column seven tells us the call number of the original source. We see that the extracted Church of England christenings and marriages for Stamfordham were taken from FHL film 0095028.

We will refer to the PVRL when we search for Mary Dixon's family. We now know that we should not expect to find any christenings extracted for the parish of Stamfordham after 1812 or any marriages after 1792 or between 1715 and 1727. It is, however, possible to find some entries for these dates on the IGI (but not on the Vital Records Index: British Isles) if information was submitted by a descendant of the Dixons. With this information, we are ready to search the International Genealogical Index.

USING THE INTERNATIONAL GENEALOGICAL INDEX

As mentioned earlier, the Genealogical Society of Utah is actively microfilming and extracting original records. The IGI currently contains several million of these extractions of births, baptisms, and marriages. It also contains names submitted by members of the Church of Jesus Christ of Latter-day Saints. Deaths and burials are rarely recorded. The parish registers of some counties have almost total coverage in the IGI; other counties have limited representation.

We will see if we can find the christening record for Mary Isabel Dixon or for Dorothy Jane Dixon. We found them in the 1851 census, which indicated that both were born in the parish of Stamfordham. If the census ages are correct, Mary Isabel Dixon should have been born about 1813 and Dorothy Jane should have been born about 1810.

Searching the IGI for Baptisms

If you do an "Individual Search" on the IGI to look for the baptism of Mary Isabel Dixon, you will not find her name. Why not? Looking at the PVRL you will see that christenings have been extracted for the years 1662–1812. Therefore, if her year of birth (1813) is correct in the 1851 census and if her baptism occurred in Stamfordham, it will not be on the IGI. We will need to search the parish registers on microfilm to find her baptism. However, according to the 1851 census, Dorothy Jane should have been born around 1810. This means that her baptism is more likely to be on the IGI. We cannot tell from the census if her surname is Dixon, but let's see if we can find a Dorothy Jane Dixon on the IGI. **See the International Genealogical Index section in chapter five starting on page 40** to see what we found about her and about other possible family members.

See Also

After you have searched the IGI, the second index to check is the Vital Records Index: British Isles. It contains a list of entries that have been extracted from original records but may not yet be on the IGI. The first edition of this set of compact discs was released in 1998. The CDs contain approximately five million births, christenings, and marriages. As more names are extracted, the Church plans to release them first on the Vital Records Index: British Isles, and then on the IGI. You can do even better searches on the Vital Records Index: British Isles than you can on the compact disc of the IGI! The program is very easy to use.

Because of the ever growing number of names in these two indexes, it is becoming easier and easier to trace your family through the parish registers.

Finding Baptismal Records

The International Genealogical Index showed two children (Ann and Dorothy Jane) born to Robert and Mary Dixon in the parish of Stamfordham. It did not show Mary Isabel Dixon. We will search the records on microfilm to see if we can find her.

If you found your ancestor on the IGI, you should now have a copy of the PVRL listing your ancestor's parish and a copy of the IGI which lists your ancestor. The third thing you will need is a copy of the page from the Family History Library Catalog that contains the call numbers for the church records of your ancestor's parish.

Search the Family History Library Catalog under England-[County]-[Parish]-Church Records. If you don't find anything, try England-[County]-Church Records. A search for England-Northumberland-Stamfordham-Church Records returned the entries given in Figure 10-5. You will want to get all available listings for the parish registers, the Bishop's Transcripts, or any other transcripts. We will search the parish registers first to find the original baptismal entry of Dorothy Jane Dixon. Her baptism will be on FHL film 1468834, items 9 and 10.

Look at the record of baptism for Dorothy Jane in Figure 10-6. The baptisms

Figure 10-5
Family History Library Catalog listing for Stamfordham in Northumberland.

```
                    Family History Library Catalog 21 Sep 1999        Page 1
                              **Full Display**

       AUTHOR
       Church of England.  Parish Church of Stamfordham.

       TITLE
       Parish registers, 1662-1929.

       PUBLICATION INFORMATION
       Salt Lake City : Filmed by the Genealogical Society of Utah, 1986.

       FORMAT
       on 3 microfilm reels ; 35 mm.

       NOTES
       Microreproduction of original records housed at the Northumberland
       County Record Office, Gosforth.
                                                               BRITISH
       CONTENTS                                                FILM AREA
       Minute and account book, 1859-1926. ----------------------- 1068900
                                                                   item 3
       Tithe offering book, 1767-1789. -------------------------- 1068900
                                                                   item 4
       Baptisms, 1692-1695 -- Burials, 1662-1672, and one ---------- 1468834
          in 1678.  Includes index.  Original registers            item 4
          in poor condition.
       Marriages, 1662-1704 -- Burials, 1662-1695. ---------------- 1468834
          Register in very poor condition.                         item 5
       Baptisms and burials, 1695-1723.  Register in very --------- 1468834
          poor condition.                                          item 6
       Baptisms and burials, 1722-1737 -- Marriages, -------------- 1468834
          1727-1737.                                               item 7
       Baptisms and burials, 1737-1767 -- Marriages, -------------- 1468834
          1737-1766.                                               item 8
       Baptisms and burials, 1767-1812. -------------------------- 1468834
                                                                   item 9-10
       Baptisms, 1813-1907. -------------------------------------- 1468834
                                                                   item 11-12
       Marriages and banns, 1754-1792. -------------------------- 1468834
                                                                   item 13.
       Marriages and banns, 1792-1926 -- Burials, ---------------- 1468835
          1813-1870.                                               item 1-4, 6
       Baptisms, 1662-1723 -- Marriages, 1663-1703 (these --------- 1468835
          are 19th century transcripts of the originals)           item 5
          -- List of furniture, with various instructions
          -- Charity payments to the poor, 1836-1918.
       Vestry minutes and churchwardens' account books, ----------- 1468835
          1644-1929.                                               item 7-9
       Tithe offering book, 1767-1789. -------------------------- 1468835
                                                                   item 10.


       THIS RECORD FOUND UNDER
          1. England, Northumberland, Stamfordham - Church records
          2. England, Northumberland, Stamfordham - Poorhouses, poor law, etc.


       Family History Library Catalog Copyright © 1987, Mar 1997 by
       The Church of Jesus Christ of Latter-day Saints.  All Rights Reserved.
```

of Northumberland in this time period contain much more detail than you can expect elsewhere. The record tells us not only her date of baptism, but also her date of birth. Notice that she was baptized almost seven months after she was born. The record also tells us that she is the second daughter of Robert Dixon of Ingoe, Gentleman, and his wife Mary Dixon. The other baptismal entries give the maiden name of the wife. We now know Robert's wife's maiden name—Dixon! However, we must consider the possibility that the minister made a recording error and wrote down her married name.

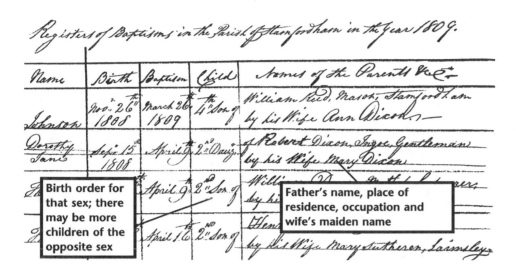

Figure 10-6
Baptismal register from 1809 for the parish of Stamfordham, Northumberland. This register also includes birth dates and the child's birth order in the family.

We saw in our IGI search (see pages 41-45 in chapter five) that there was a child named Ann born to Robert and Mary Dixon in the same parish. We will also look for the baptism of Ann on 4 May 1806 to see if she was born to the same Robert and Mary Dixon, or if there was another couple by this name in the parish. See Figure 10-7. You can see that this record is very difficult to read. However, there is a nineteenth-century transcript of this register on FHL film 95028 (Figure 10-8). This is much more legible and confirms how we read the example shown. Ann is the first child listed on the page. It appears to say that

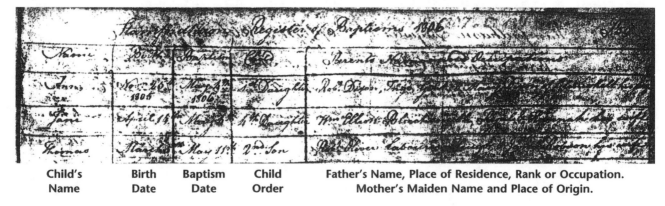

Child's Name	Birth Date	Baptism Date	Child Order	Father's Name, Place of Residence, Rank or Occupation. Mother's Maiden Name and Place of Origin.

Figure 10-7
Baptismal register from 1806 for the parish of Stamfordham illustrates that not all registers have survived in good condition. In this case, however, a nineteenth-century transcript has been made. See Figure 10-8.

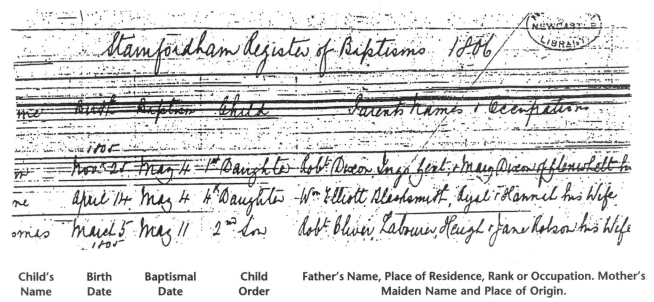

Child's Name	Birth Date	Baptismal Date	Child Order	Father's Name, Place of Residence, Rank or Occupation. Mother's Maiden Name and Place of Origin.

Figure 10-8
Nineteenth-century transcript of the baptismal register for the Parish of Stamfordham. Compare with the original in Figure 10-7. The names are partially covered because of tight binding on the original.

Sources

Ann was born 25 November 1805, was baptized 4 May 1806, and is the first daughter of Robt. Dixon, Ingo, Gent. & Mary Dixon of Glenwhelt his wife. The father's occupation and residence are the same as those on Dorothy Jane's baptismal record. Ann's baptism contains the first clue that Mary came from another town. **We will need to look in a gazetteer to find the location of Glenwhelt so that we can trace her in the records.**

We still do not know if our Mary belongs to this family, so we will now search the Stamfordham parish registers after 1812 for other children that are not included in the IGI. They will be found on FHL film 1468834, items 11 and 12. Look at Figure 10-9. Here you see the baptism of three children of Robert and Mary Dixon. They were all baptized the same day. We are first tempted to believe that they were triplets, but fortunately, the Stamfordham parish register gives the date of birth for the first two children. Mary, daughter of Robert and Mary Dixon and born 26 January 1811, was baptized 2 May 1817! This looks like she may be the person we want. The baptism occurred more than six years after her birth. William, born 29 June 1813, was also baptized 2 May 1817. Robert Maughan Dixon was baptized the same day, but no date of birth is given for him. Why would someone baptize children so long after birth? You can probably think of several reasons for this. For example, the family may have been traveling for an extended period or living elsewhere. Robert is a gentleman, so this is a possibility. Another very likely possibility is that the family was nonconformist. When you find marriages in the Church of England but no baptisms of children, it is a strong indication of nonconformity. Delayed baptisms are another indication. These

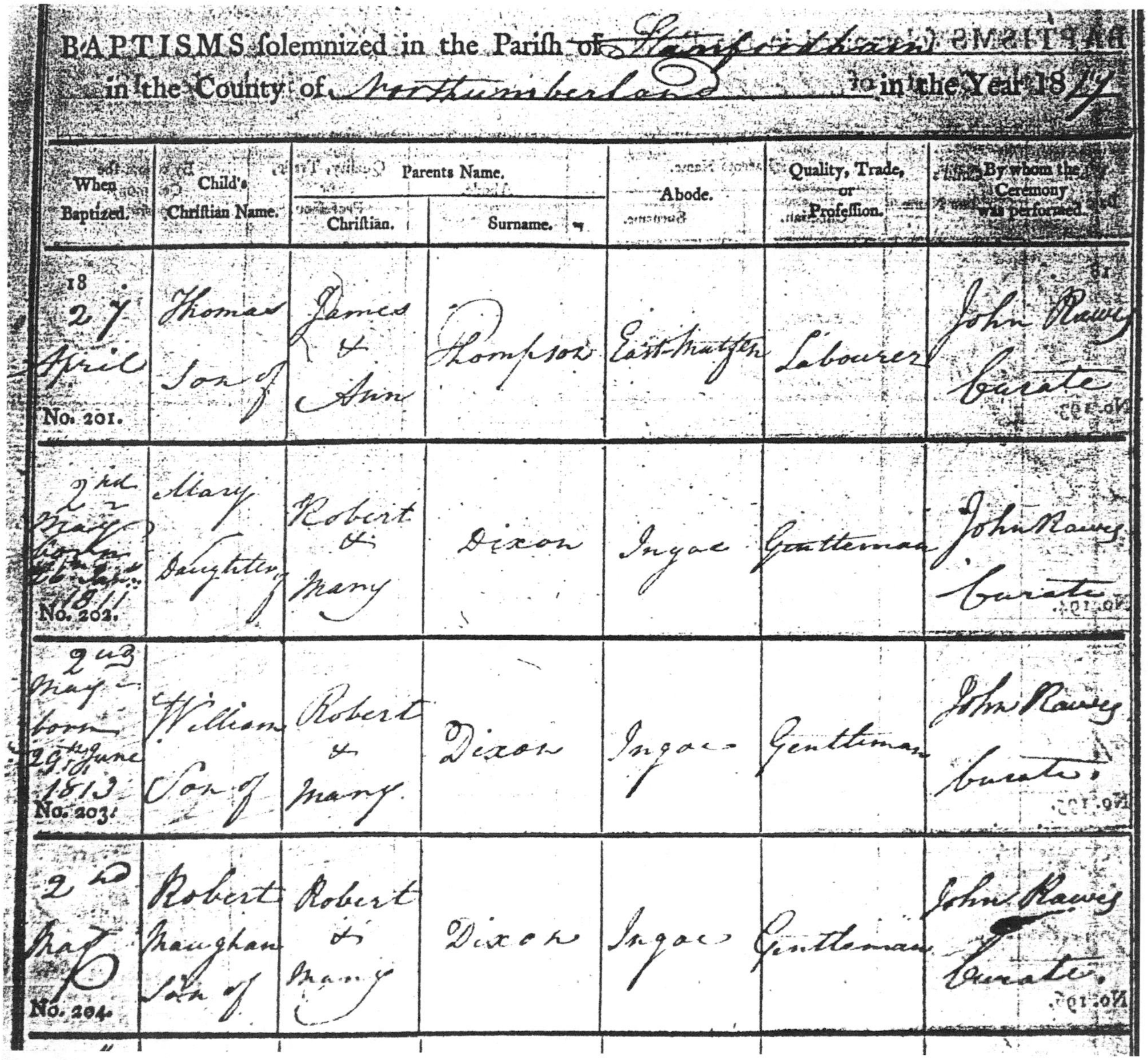

BAPTISMS solemnized in the Parish of Stamfordham in the County of Northumberland in the Year 1817

When Baptized.	Child's Christian Name.	Parents Name. Christian.	Parents Name. Surname.	Abode.	Quality, Trade, or Profession.	By whom the Ceremony was performed.
18 27 April No. 201.	Thomas Son of	James & Ann	Thompson	East Matfen	Labourer	John Rawes Curate
2nd May born [illegible] 1811 No. 202.	Mary Daughter of	Robert & Mary	Dixon	Ingoe	Gentleman	John Rawes Curate
2nd May born 29th June 1813 No. 203.	William Son of	Robert & Mary	Dixon	Ingoe	Gentleman	John Rawes Curate
2nd May No. 204.	Robert Maughan Son of	Robert & Mary	Dixon	Ingoe	Gentleman	John Rawes Curate

Figure 10-9
Preprinted baptismal forms were introduced by law in 1813. This 1817 page from the parish of Stamfordham shows three Dixon children being baptized on the same day. They are not triplets, nor all infants. Luckily birth dates for two of them were added to the register.

children may have been baptized in the Catholic church, for example, and later rebaptized in the Church of England so that their records are recorded there. We will certainly want to look at nonconformist records to see if we can find any mention of this family.

There are more children of Robert and Mary Dixon in this parish. If we check the parish records of the other children that we found on the IGI parent search, Figures 5-4 and 5-5, we will see that they were not members of this family. They were not the children of Robert Dixon, Gentleman, but of other Robert Dixons.

Research Tip

Notes

There is one more search you should always do: Go back to the IGI and conduct a parent search including the maiden name of the wife. The results of the search are illustrated in Figure 5-6. You can see that there is an Ann Dixon, born or baptized in 1805 to a Robert Dixon and Mary Dix*. The full entry said that Ann Dixon, daughter of Robert Dixon and Mary Dixon was baptized 6 December 1805 in the parish of Haltwhistle. Is there another Robert Dixon who married another Mary Dixon? Is this the same family with another daughter named Ann? The answer may surprise you. Look at Figures 5-7 and 10-10 noting the additional information in the actual registers. Ann Dixon, born 25 November 1805, was baptized 6 December 1805. She was the first daughter of "Robt. Dixon, Gentleman, Native of Stamfordham, by his Wife, Mary Dixon Native of Stamfordham." This is the same daughter who was baptized 4 May 1806 in the parish of Stamfordham. Ann was baptized twice.

What Did We Discover in These Baptismal Records?

Although it should be fairly straightforward to search indexes and then parish registers, it almost never is quite that easy. We learned that

1. The IGI does not index all baptisms. You must use it with the Parish and Vital Records List to see what has actually been extracted.

2. You should do a parent search in the computerized version of the IGI. Although the parent search feature of the IGI can be very useful for locating the children of a couple, not all of the children are guaranteed to be those of your ancestors. The result of a parent search is only a list of possibilities. We saw that there were more than one Robert and Mary Dixon, but the children of all of them were listed together. For example, Margaret Dixon, John Dixon, Elizabeth Dixon, and Thomas Dixon were not the children of our Robert and Mary Dixon. You must check the source for each child to make sure that all of them have the same parents.

3. The parent search may not include all children of a family. For example,

REGISTER of BAPTISMS in the Parish of HALTWHISTLE, in the Year 1805

NAME.	BIRTH.	BAPTISM.	CHILD.	NAMES OF THE PARENTS.
Ann. Nattrass	April 30	Dec.r 6	5 Daughter of	Thos. Nattrass, Mason, Native of Stanhope, by his Wife, Ann Glendenning, Native of this Parish
Ann Dixon	Nov.r 25	Dec.r 6	1 Daughter of	Robt. Dixon, Gentleman, Native of Stamfordham, by his Wife, Mary Dixon Native of Stamfordham
Ann Thompson	Nov.r 29	Dec.r 9	1 Daughter of	Michael Thompson, Farmer, Native of this Parish, By his Wife Eliz: Surtees, Native of Bywell Saint Andrew.

Figure 10-10
1805 baptismal register for the parish of Haltwhistle, Northumberland, showing an earlier baptism for Ann Dixon. Compare with the information given for Ann Dixon in Figures 10-7 and 10-8.

ours does not show Mary Dixon, William Dixon, and Robert Maughan Dixon. Records of the parish of Stamfordham were not extracted after 1812, and all of these children were baptized after that date.

4. You will need to do more than one parent search. Some baptismal records will include only the father's name. Others will include the mother's given name but not her maiden name, and still others will include the mother's maiden name. Furthermore, sometimes a parent may be listed with his or her first given name and other times with a middle name. For example, to find the children of Walter Telford and Mary Isabella Dixon, we would want to search for children of Walter Telford and Mary, Walter Telford and Isabella, Walter Telford and Mary Dixon, Walter Telford and Isabella Dixon, Walter Telford with no wife's name, etc. You also need to consider nicknames. Do not try only one parent search and think that you have all of the children!

5. A child may be baptized more than once. He or she may be baptized in a nonconformist church and again in the Church of England. The child may even have two recorded baptisms in the Church of England.

6. A child may be baptized long after birth. If you find two or more children of the same parents baptized on the same day, it is not necessarily an indication of twins, triplets, etc. We are lucky that the dates of birth were recorded for the first two Dixon children who were baptized 2 May 1817. This is more than you can expect in a parish register.

FINDING MARRIAGE RECORDS

Marriage records are much easier to locate than records for baptisms or burials. There are two reasons for this: (1) The marriage record is more likely to be recorded in the parish registers than the baptism or burial, and (2) the marriage record is much more likely to be indexed. **We will now look for the marriage record of Robert Dixon and Mary Dixon.**

A marriage search on the IGI revealed that Robert Dixon married Mary Dixon in the parish of Haltwhistle, Northumberland. Once you know the name of the parish, look at the Family History Library Catalog to find the film number for the marriage and also the film numbers for christenings and burials to potentially find more records about the family.

The Haltwhistle marriages for 1754 to 1882 are on FHL film 0252514. They continue from 1882 to 1959 on film 0252515. Notice that this is long after the beginning of civil registration records in 1837, so you can find post-1837 records in the parish registers. The marriage of Robert and Mary is on the first film. As shown in Figure 10-11, "Robert Dixon of the Parish of Stamfordham and Mary Dixon of this Parish [Haltwhistle] were Married in this Church by Licence by consent of Parent." Notice that the ages of the bride and groom are not given. Their parents are not mentioned either.

At first glance, it would appear that this record doesn't tell us anything we didn't already know. But you will see that it contains significant clues. We know that Robert Dixon is from Stamfordham, so we will look for his earlier records there. We know that Mary Dixon is from Haltwhistle, so we

Step By Step

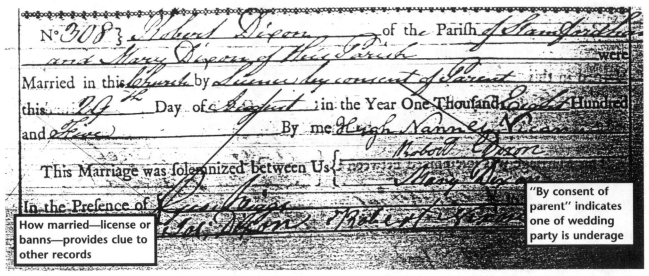

Figure 10-11
Preprinted marriage forms were used starting in 1754. This is the 1805 marriage entry for Robert Dixon and Mary Dixon in the Parish of Haltwhistle, Northumberland.

will search there for her. However, this does not mean that these were their birthplaces. It only means that they were living there at the time of marriage. We also know that either the bride or groom was under twenty-one years of age, because at least one of them had the consent of a parent to marry. We know that they could sign their names because their signatures appear on the record. You will not always see copies of the original signatures, especially if you are looking at Bishop's Transcripts. But all of the signatures here are in different handwriting, indicating that they were signed by the parties themselves. The names of the witnesses may be very important. The names are Geo. Biggs, Jos. Dixon, and Robert Nixon. Joseph Dixon is likely to be related. George Biggs signed the marriage above and several other marriages, so he is likely to be someone connected with the parish rather than a relative. We don't know anything about Robert Nixon. Always investigate the names of witnesses on marriage records, because they are often close relatives of the couple. The most significant item on this certificate, however, is that Robert and Mary were married by license.

Marriage Banns, Licenses, Allegations, and Bonds

A couple marrying in the Church of England had to be married either by banns or by license. Licenses were more expensive, but they were also more prestigious. Some people married by license in order to avoid the waiting period required for the calling of banns. If a woman was pregnant, for example, the couple may have obtained a license to marry more quickly. They also may have wanted to avoid the publicity of the banns, which many considered embarrassing. A license may also be an indication that the bride or groom was not a member of the Church of England.

Marriage by license

Applications for licenses generated three pieces of documentation. The first, which you are not likely to find, is the marriage license itself, which was given to the local minister to show that the couple was approved for marriage within that parish. The other two are the marriage bond and the marriage allegation, which often survived and are found in the County or Diocesan Record Offices. Most marriage licenses are common licenses issued by the archdeacon or bishop of the diocese. The name is given of the parish where the marriage is to take place. The couple could also have obtained a Special License, issued by the Archbishop of Canterbury, which allowed the marriage to take place anywhere, but these are very rare.

The best source for locating marriage license records is Jeremy Gibson's, *Bishops' Transcripts and Marriage Licences, Bonds and Allegations: A Guide to Their Location and Indexes* (4th ed. Baltimore, Md.: Genealogical Pub. Co., 1998). The ones that are available on microfilm are usually cataloged in the Family History Library Catalog under England-[County]-Church Records.

Sources

Let's look at the allegation and bond for the marriage of Robert and Mary Dixon. The allegation is shown in Figure 10-12. Here Robert Dixon alleges the reasons that the couple are entitled to get married. He says that he is from the parish of Stamfordham and that he is the age of "Twenty One years and upwards," a bachelor, and intends to marry Mary Dixon of the parish of Haltwhistle who is "aged Twenty years and upwards, and a spinster." He does not know of any reason they should not be married. For example, they are not precontracted to any other person and are not too closely related by blood or marriage. He intends to marry Mary Dixon in the Parish Church of Haltwhistle. It has been Mary's usual place of abode for at least the past four weeks. The bottom of the allegation contains very important information, "Upon the said Day appeared personally Ann Nixon the Natural and lawful Mother of the said Minor and made Oath that she is consenting to the above said intended Marriage." The signature of Ann Nixon is also on the document.

We now know that Ann Nixon is the mother of Mary Dixon, because Mary is the one under the age of twenty-one. Why do mother and daughter have different surnames? Mary is listed as a spinster, so she has never been married. Is Ann Nixon the mother's maiden name? Is it her married name? Remember that someone named Robert Nixon was a witness on the marriage record. We now have two people with the surname of Nixon. We can follow those clues to find out why Mary's surname is not the same as her mother's. If we do, we will find that Ann Dixon, a widow, married Robert Nixon. Robert Nixon is Mary Dixon's stepfather.

The bond (Figure 10-13) is the other document required to obtain a license. It begins, "Know all Men, by these Presents, that we Robert Dixon of the Parish of Stamfordham Gentleman, George Biggs of Haltwhistle Parish Clerk are bound. . . ." These people are posting a bond in the sum of £200, which they will be obliged to pay if there is any reason why this couple should not be married. If there is no impediment to the marriage, the obligation will be void. We found from this document that George Biggs is the parish clerk

Figure 10-12
Marriage license allegation for Robert Dixon, who intends to marry Mary Dixon. This record came from the Durham Diocesan Record Office. At the bottom of the allegation you will find a handwritten parental consent statement made by Mary's mother, Ann Nixon.

Age of Groom

Age of Bride

Consent statement by mother: "Upon the same day appeared personally Ann Nixon the natural and lawful mother of the said minor and made oath that she is consenting to the above said intended marriage.—Ann Nixon"

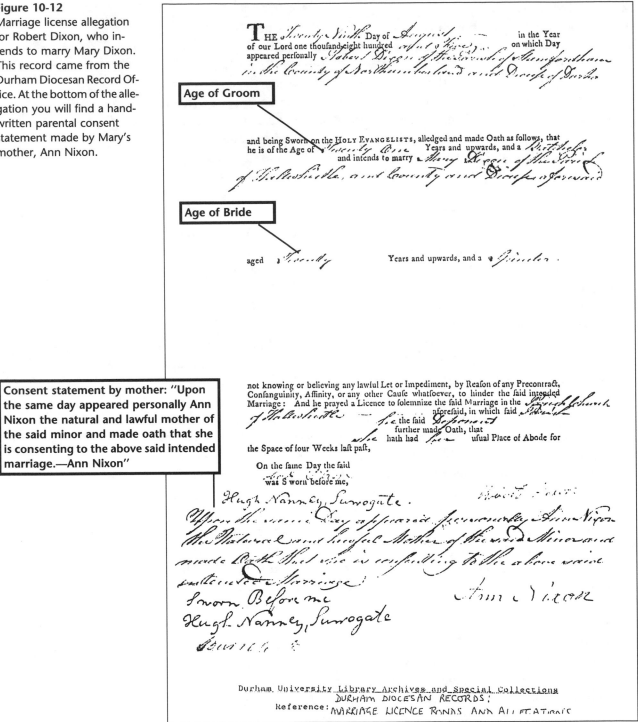

of Haltwhistle. This is the reason he was a witness on the marriage record. The signatures of Robert Dixon and George Biggs appear at the bottom of the bond.

You will notice that the marriage allegation, bond, and marriage certificate are all dated the same day (29 August 1805). Robert and Mary did not want to wait for the publication of the banns. You will also notice that their first

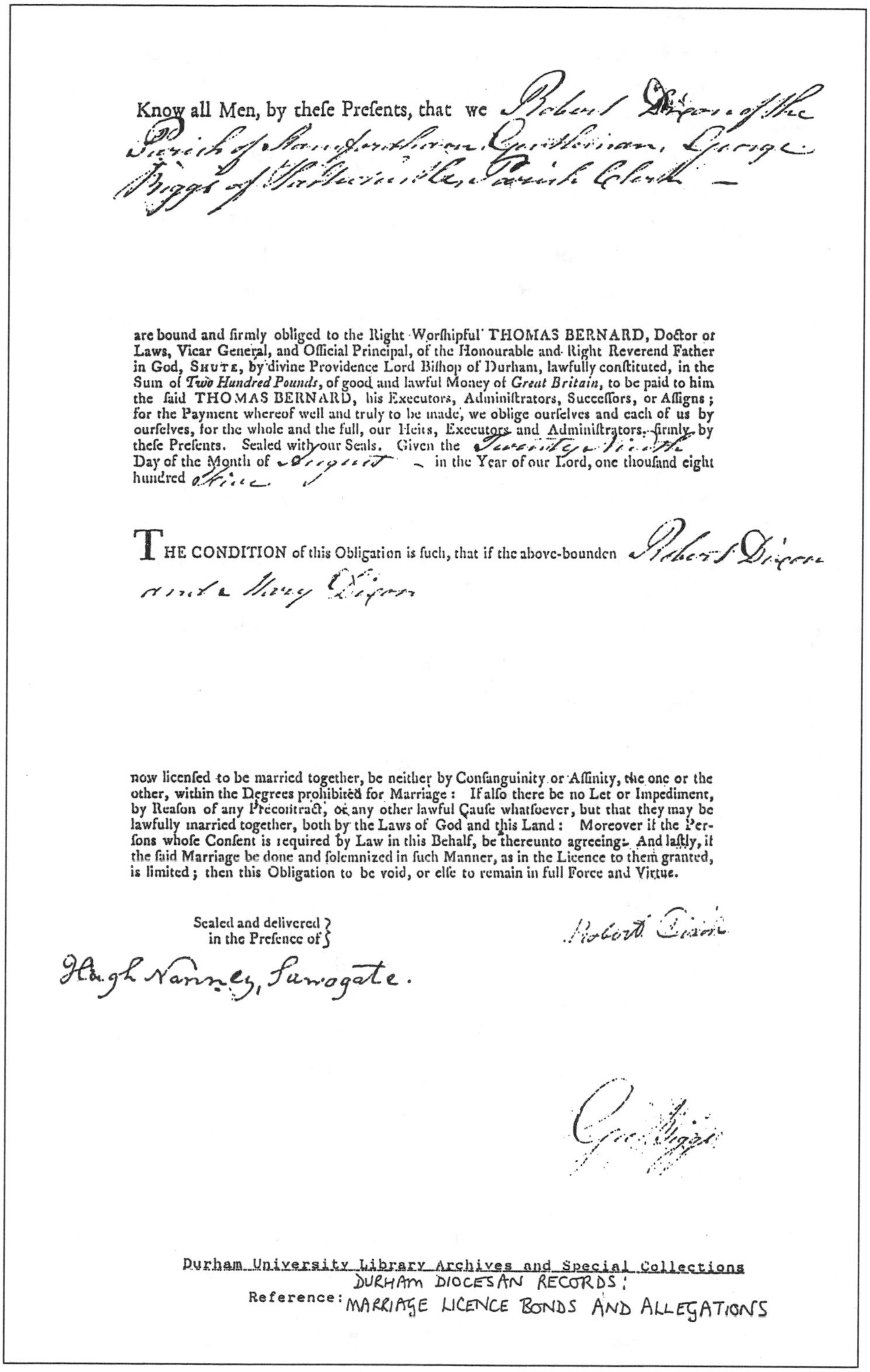

Know all Men, by these Presents, that we *Robert Dixon of the Parish of Hamsterley Gentleman, George Triggs of Wolsingham, Parish Clerk* —

are bound and firmly obliged to the Right Worshipful THOMAS BERNARD, Doctor of Laws, Vicar General, and Official Principal, of the Honourable and Right Reverend Father in God, SHUTE, by divine Providence Lord Bishop of Durham, lawfully constituted, in the Sum of *Two Hundred Pounds*, of good and lawful Money of *Great Britain*, to be paid to him the said THOMAS BERNARD, his Executors, Administrators, Successors, or Assigns; for the Payment whereof well and truly to be made, we oblige ourselves and each of us by ourselves, for the whole and the full, our Heirs, Executors and Administrators, firmly by these Presents. Sealed with our Seals. Given the *Twenty Ninth* Day of the Month of *August* — in the Year of our Lord, one thousand eight hundred *Nine.*

THE CONDITION of this Obligation is such, that if the above-bounden *Robert Dixon and Mary Dixon*

now licensed to be married together, be neither by Consanguinity or Affinity, the one or the other, within the Degrees prohibited for Marriage: If also there be no Let or Impediment, by Reason of any Precontract, or any other lawful Cause whatsoever, but that they may be lawfully married together, both by the Laws of God and this Land: Moreover if the Persons whose Consent is required by Law in this Behalf, be thereunto agreeing: And lastly, if the said Marriage be done and solemnized in such Manner, as in the Licence to them granted, is limited; then this Obligation to be void, or else to remain in full Force and Virtue.

Sealed and delivered
in the Presence of }

Robert Dixon

Hugh Nanney, Surrogate.

Geo Triggs

Figure 10-13
Marriage license bond for Robert Dixon states that he does not know any legal reasons why he should not marry Mary Dixon. If it is later found that the couple should not have been married, there is a £200 fine to pay.

child was born 25 November 1805. This is very common. Do not assume that the marriage occurred a year or more before the birth of the first child. The ability to have children was important, so many couples made sure that they could have children before getting married.

\di'fin\ *vb*

Definitions

Warning

Marriage by banns

When a couple married by banns, an announcement of the impending marriage was made in church for three consecutive Sundays prior to the wedding. This announcement also requested that if anyone knew of any just reason why the couple should not be married, he was to come forward. This process was a very public ceremony, and the announcements were recorded, often in a separate banns register. If the groom and bride were from different parishes, the announcement was made in both parishes. The record of the banns will state in which parishes the parties reside. This means that if you have a male whose marriage record does not appear in his parish, check the banns register. If he was married by banns, the banns register in his parish will tell you the name of the bride and where to look for the marriage. Most couples were married in the parish of the bride. **Warning: The existence of banns does not mean that the couple actually married; it means only that they intended to marry.** Most, however, went through the ceremony shortly after the publication of banns.

What If the Marriage Is Not Indexed in the IGI?

The marriage of Robert and Mary Dixon was easy to find because it was indexed in the IGI. If the marriage you are seeking is not indexed in the IGI, you can go to *The Phillimore Atlas and Index of Parish Registers* to find out about other indexes. You will first want to check Boyd's Marriage Index. If the marriage is not in Boyd's, you will want to search all other available indexes, especially those compiled by the local family history society. The marriage of William Dixon and Dorothy Robson is not on the IGI. They are believed to be the parents of Robert Dixon who married Mary Dixon. The marriage of William and Dorothy is a great example of English marriage law.

After 1754, marriages in England were only legal if they were conducted in the Church of England or by Quakers or Jews. There were few ways to avoid this law. People in Northern England could easily avoid the strict English marriage law by crossing the border and marrying in Scotland. Tradition has it that William Dixon did so, marrying Dorothy Robson in Gretna Green, Scotland. However, when William Dixon and Dorothy Robson got married (again?) many years later in the parish of Stamfordham, they are listed as bachelor and spinster. We want to find documents of this marriage, but there is no record of it in the IGI. We can see from the Parish and Vital Records List that marriages for Stamfordham have not been extracted after 1792, so if the marriage occurred there, it probably occurred after that date. *The Phillimore Atlas and Index of Parish Registers* and the National Index of Parish Registers both indicate that marriages for Stamfordham are included in Boyd's Marriage Index from 1662 to 1812. **Boyd's Marriage Index is the second largest marriage index for England (the largest is the IGI).** Let's see how to use it.

Boyd's Marriage Indexes contain over seven million marriage entries. They were compiled by Percival Boyd from printed and transcribed parish registers, bishops' transcripts, marriage licenses, and other miscellaneous sources. They are arranged in three series which are available from the Family History Library in both microfilm and microfiche formats. The first series is arranged by county, but not every

Sources

English county is included. It is known as the "Main Series." The second and third series are known as the "Miscellaneous Series" and are alphabetized by grooms and brides rather than by county. The second and third series are combined into one sequence on the microfilm version, but they are separate on the microfiche.

A Key to the Parishes Included in Boyd's Marriage Indexes is on FHL fiche 6035667. It contains full instructions and includes the FHL microfilm and microfiche numbers for all three series. It is important to read the introduction on fiche 6035667 or film 0472000 before using the indexes.

A Key to the Parishes Included in Boyd's Marriage Indexes told us that the County of Northumberland was included in the first series. The Northumberland page is shown in Figure 10-14 below. The years 1776 to 1800 have separate brides and grooms indexes. The grooms index for surnames beginning with A through K is on microfiche 6054242. Turning to that fiche we find the marriage on page 120 (see Figure 10-15). The Church of England marriage between William Dixon and Dorothy Robson occurred at Stamfordham in 1798, just seven years before their son Robert was married! We would certainly have discounted this couple as the parents of Robert Dixon if we did not have other evidence.

The actual marriage record reads:

> William Dixon and Dorothy Robson both of this Parish were married in this church by Licence this twelfth day of November in the year one thousand seven

Boyd's Marriage Index

Co. Northumberland — Call # 942.82 K22b

Year	Groom/Bride	Surname	Volume #	Film #	Fiche #
1538–1600	Groom/Bride	A–Z	1	472084	6054224
1601–1625	Groom/Bride	A–Z	2	472084	6054225
1626–1650	Groom/Bride	A–Z	3	472084	6054226
1651–1675	Groom/Bride	A–K	4	472084	6054227
1651–1675	Groom/Bride	L–Z	5	472084	6054228
1676–1700	Groom/Bride	A–K	6	472085	6054229
1676–1700	Groom/Bride	L–Z	7	472085	6054230
1701–1725	Groom/Bride	A–G	8	472085	6054231
1701–1725	Groom/Bride	H–Q	9	472085	6054232
1701–1725	Groom/Bride	R–Z	10	472086	6054233
1726–1750	Grooms	A–K	11	472086	6054234
1726–1750	Grooms	L–Z	12	472086	6054235
1726–1750	Brides	A–K	13	472086	6054236
1726–1750	Brides	L–Z	14	472087	6054237
1751–1775	Grooms	A–K	15	472087	6054238
1751–1775	Grooms	L–Z	16	472087	6054239
1751–1775	Brides	A–K	17	472087	6054240
1751–1775	Brides	L–Z	18	472088	6054241
1776–1800	Grooms	A–K	19	472088	6054242
1776–1800	Grooms	L–Z	20	472088	6054243
1776–1800	Brides	A–K	21	472088	6054244
1776–1800	Brides	L–Z	22	472089	6054245
1801–1824	Grooms	A–Z	23	472089	6054246
1801–1824	Brides	A–Z	24	472089	6054247

Figure 10-14
Key to finding film or fiche copies of Boyd's Marriage Index for Northumberland.

Figure 10-15
Dixon entries in Boyd's Marriage Index for Northumberland give the year of the marriage, the names of bride and groom with abbreviated forenames, and the parish in which the marriage occurred.

Marriage of William Dixon and Dorothy Robson

		120	**DIX**
1797	DIXON **cont**	Tho & Mary Richardson	Hexham
1797		Jn & An Milburn	do
1797		Jn & Jane Armstrong	do
1798		Rob & Tamer Wilson	Haydon Bridge
1798		Pat & Dy Alder	Holy Island
1798		Job & Grace Marshall	Warkworth
1798		Cris & Isb Grame	Earsdon
1798		Wm & Dy Robson	Stamfordham
1798		Tho & Sara Dinnin	Hexham
1798		Thos & Ann Moffat	Warkworth
1798		Benj & Isb Readhed	do
1798		Wm & Isb Shotton	Rothbury
1798		Tho & Isb Carbreath	Newcastle A.S
1799		Hen & An Delap	do do
1799		Rob & Ann Black	Eglingham banns
1799		Pet & Fran Blackburn	Hexham
1799		Wm & Mgt Smart	Kirk Whelpington
1799		Wm & Ada Hedly	Morpeth
1799		Wm & Ada Hedly	Whalton banns
1799		Jn & Jane Hudson	Rothbury
1799		Geo & Barb Curry	Long Benton
1800		Tho & Agn Miller	Alwinton banns
1800		Jn & Mgt Midlemas	Alnwick
1800		Roland & Jane Cook	Newcastle S.Jn
1800		Tho & An Milburn	do A.S
1800		Jas & Mgt Solsby	do do
1800		Jn & Elnr Wite	Edlingham
1800		Jn & Isb Sandilands	Ilderton banns
1800		Rob & An Singleton	Morpeth
1800		Wm & Mgt Foster	Hexham
1800		Jn & Mary Waugh	Earsdon
1800		Tho & Ruth Hall	Hartburn
1779	D'NEVILLES	Jn & Jane Laiton	Newcastle S.Nic
1777	DOBY	Jn & Mary Cook	do S.And
1784		Jas & Sara Stuart	Wallsend
1784	DOBINSON	Tho & An Storer	Rothbury
1789		Fran & Eliz Bredworth	Newcastle S.And ba

hundred and ninety eight by me Ri. Baxter Curate. This marriage was solemnized between us [signed] William Dixon, Dorothy Robson now Dixon in the presence of us [signed] William Bewick, Matthew Coulson.

Notice that no ages, occupations, or parents' names are given in the marriage record. The marriage allegation (Figure 10-16), however, contains William's age (forty) and status (Gentleman). It also contains Dorothy's age (thirty-five).

The marriage of William Dixon and Dorothy Robson is in Boyd's Marriage Index but not in the IGI. The marriage of Robert Dixon and Mary Dixon is in the IGI; but it is not in Boyd's, because the parish of Haltwhistle is not included in Boyd's Marriage Index. You can see why you will need to use both marriage indexes.

The best source for locating other marriage indexes is *Marriage, Census, and Other Indexes for Family Historians* (see page 159). This is an inexpensive, but very comprehensive, book that shows the availability and location of known marriage indexes.

Sources

FINDING BURIAL RECORDS

Burial records can be very difficult to find because they are not indexed in the IGI and there is no other large index to them. However, the family history

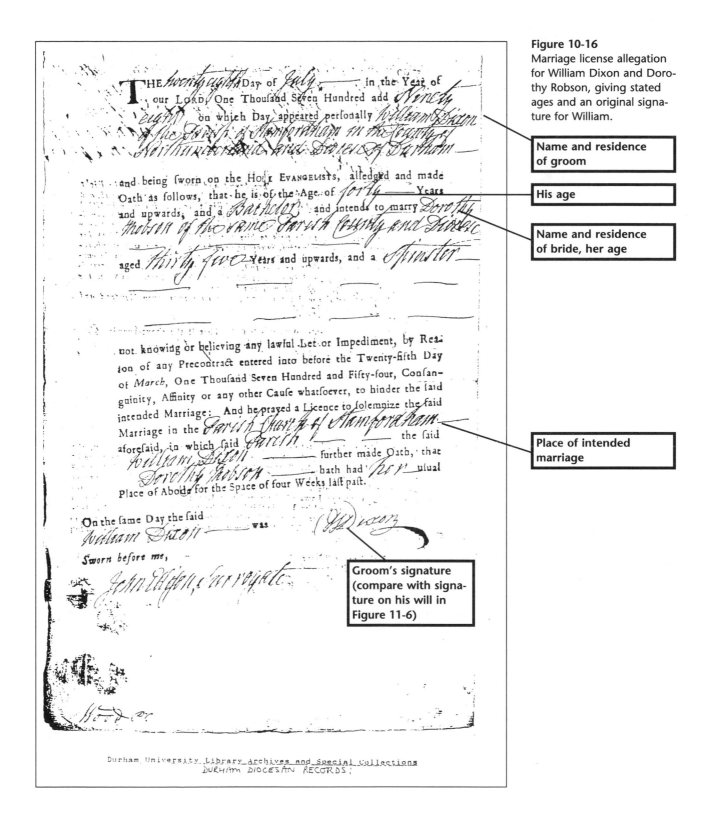

Figure 10-16
Marriage license allegation for William Dixon and Dorothy Robson, giving stated ages and an original signature for William.

Name and residence of groom

His age

Name and residence of bride, her age

Place of intended marriage

Groom's signature (compare with signature on his will in Figure 11-6)

Tip

societies in England are working on a national burial index to remedy this problem. **Therefore, the best way to find an index is to contact the family history society in the area where your ancestor lived.**

Because you are working backward in time, you will often have a general idea of when your ancestor died from other documents. But sometimes, you'll just have to resort to searching page by page. Although burial records usually contain scanty information, you should always search for them. The records generated at your ancestor's death and afterward can often tell you more about him than documents generated in his lifetime. Burial records are a good place to start.

Look at the burial entry of William Dixon (Figure 10-17). He is the one who married Dorothy Robson. The marriage record did not give us his age or tell us that he was a gentleman, but the burial record does. Although the burial almost never indicates the names of parents of adults, it will often give the name of the father of a child. Burial records may also identify the husband of a woman. Women are listed by their married surname, not by the maiden name. You can see that Isabel Young's entry states the name of her husband who predeceased her. Margaret Mitchell's husband is named. He is still alive.

Starting in 1813, burial records are standardized. The standardization of the information worked against us because the post-1812 registers often contain less information than the prior registers. Look at the burial record of Robert Dixon (Figure 10-18). His occupation is not mentioned. Look also at the burials of Edward and Elizabeth Green. They were both only one day old when they died, and the name of the father is not given. We cannot tell from the burial

Figure 10-17
1809-1810 Burial register for the parish of Stamfordham just prior to the introduction of preprinted registers. It lists the name and abode of the deceased, profession or trade, date of death, date of burial, and age. Remember that the reported age is only as good as the informant's knowledge.

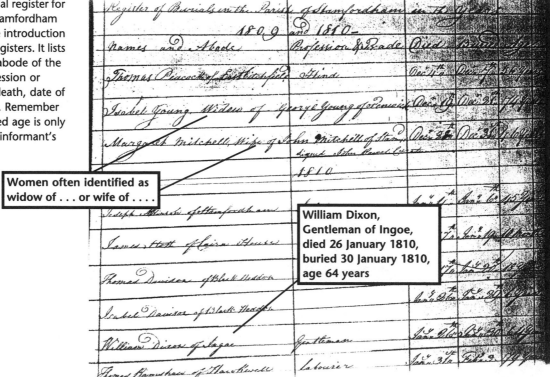

Women often identified as widow of . . . or wife of . . . .

William Dixon, Gentleman of Ingoe, died 26 January 1810, buried 30 January 1810, age 64 years

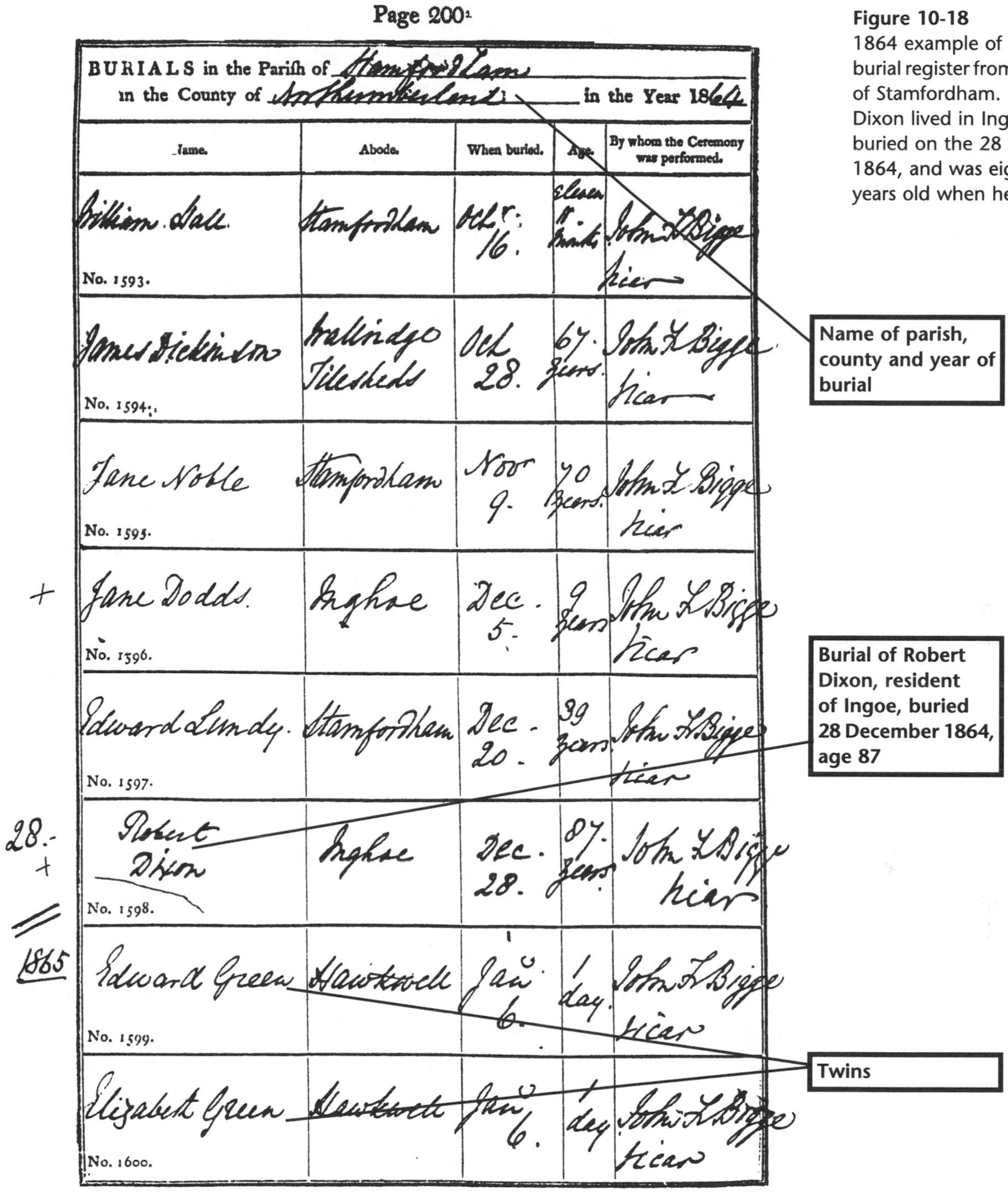

Page 200[1]

Figure 10-18
1864 example of preprinted burial register from the parish of Stamfordham. Robert Dixon lived in Inghoe, was buried on the 28 December 1864, and was eighty-seven years old when he died.

Name of parish, county and year of burial

Burial of Robert Dixon, resident of Ingoe, buried 28 December 1864, age 87

Twins

record of Jane Noble if she was a spinster, a married woman, or a widow. No husband's name is mentioned. After 1837, of course, you should go from the burial register to the civil registration index. The death certificates are far more informative than the burial registers. See chapter seven for more information about civil registration certificates.

Burial records lead to monumental inscriptions (MIs) which include tombstone inscriptions and other monuments to the deceased. Many monumental inscriptions have been published, often by the local county family history society. You should look for them because they can contain very detailed information.

Burial records also lead you to probate records, which can be the most genealogically valuable records of all. We will examine the will of William Dixon in chapter eleven on pre-1858 probate records.

WHY CAN'T I FIND MY ANCESTOR IN THE PARISH REGISTERS?

Technique

You are looking in the wrong place. If an event was not located in a major index and not in the parish where you expected to find it, then it might have occurred somewhere else. It could have occurred in the neighboring parish or even on the other side of the world. You may not find a baptism because the mother of the child went to her parent's parish to have the child baptized. A marriage may not have occurred where you expect because the couple married in the big city away from the country home. Your ancestor may have died while traveling or serving in the military. Be creative about why your ancestor may not be in the place you expect. Learn more about the family. Obtain other clues by tracing your ancestor's siblings. Check the local histories again to see if they might provide clues. If you think the event occurred nearby, doing a radial search around the parish may produce results.

Your ancestors were nonconformists. Depending upon the time period and the county, this can have a big impact, especially toward the end of the eighteenth and into the nineteenth centuries. In the sixteenth and seventeenth centuries, it is more likely the family will be recorded in the Church of England records, even if they were practicing another religion. If you find a marriage but no christenings of the children, this may indicate nonconformity. If you can't find a burial record, it may be because the nonconformists increasingly used the municipal cemeteries. In major urban areas, there is generally at least one cemetery noted for the high number of nonconformists buried there. You will need to research the community to identify the cemetery.

There are too many people with the same name. This problem is more common than we assume at first. Even in small communities, similar names can multiply rapidly because families might have followed the same naming patterns. Therefore, within a couple of generations, lots of people with the same names might have been living in an area. You may need to reconstruct the community, extracting the records of everyone with the surname you are looking for plus any of the families that you have allied with yours, such as the in-laws. This may be the only way to determine who belongs to whom.

The marriage was not recorded. Before 1754, marriages did not have to be performed by any official. A couple could even marry themselves with no witnesses present. The Church of England frowned on this and often punished couples for marrying outside the Church, but under English common law these marriages were still legal. Therefore, it is possible that a pre-1754 marriage is not recorded.

Misleading clues. Maybe you are looking under the wrong name. You are looking for the death of a woman who remarried, but you are looking under her previous married name. Maybe the person had changed his name to inherit; this is rare, but certainly not unheard of. There is one of these on the Dixon tree. Maybe the place of birth given on the census return was totally wrong and has lead you to the wrong part of the country.

WHERE DO I FIND OUT MORE ABOUT THIS TOPIC?

A List of Parishes in Boyd's Marriage Index. Library Sources Number 3. London: Society of Genealogists. Reprinted with minor corrections, 1994.

Gibson, Jeremy, and Elizabeth Hampson. *Marriage, Census, and Other Indexes for Family Historians.* 6th ed. Federation of Family History Societies, 1996.

Herber, Mark D. *Ancestral Trails: The Complete Guide to British Genealogy and Family History.* Baltimore, Md.: Genealogical Publishing Company. 1998.

McLaughlin, Eve. *Parish Registers.* 3rd ed. Aylesbury, Bucks: Eve McLaughlin, 1994.

Rogers, Colin D. *The Family Tree Detective: Tracing Your Ancestors in England and Wales.* 3rd ed. Manchester: Manchester University Press, 1997.

Sources

AFTER SEARCHING PARISH REGISTERS, WHAT SHOULD I DO NEXT?

Because the parish registers cover such a large time span, you will use them, go to other sources, and come back again. Rarely will you be able use parish registers alone to document and fully prove a complete family structure over multiple generations. You will need other documents, such as marriage licenses and bonds or probate records, to support your hypothesis. **See chapter eleven to learn how to find pre-1858 probate records.**

You will also get into other classes of records to support the family structure as your experience increases. There are many more records that were created by the parish that can put flesh onto the bones of a baptism, marriage, and burial. **When you have used the basic sources from this book, see chapter twelve, What's Next?**

For More Info

ELEVEN

Pre-1858 Probate Records

P re-1858 wills and inventories are records that will really take you beyond compiling names, dates, and places. You can find out how your ancestor lived, what possessions he held, and even how he felt about his family, church, and community.

Who Could Make a Will?

Before 1837, boys fourteen or older and girls twelve or older could make wills. After 1837, anyone making a will had to be twenty-one or older. Until 1882, a married woman could not make a will without her husband's consent unless she was able to do so under the conditions of a marriage settlement created before her marriage. A woman and all her possessions were by law her husband's property. Single women and widows could make their own wills.

What Could My Ancestor Leave in a Will?

We first need to understand the distinction between wills and testaments. You have seen the term *last will and testament*. Originally a will and a testament were two separate documents. A will was the document by which your ancestor devised (transferred) real property, which includes land and buildings. A testament was used to bequeath personal property, all moveable property such as money, furniture, tools, clothing and other personal items, and livestock.

Before 1540, your ancestor could only make a testament. This means he could only dispose of his personal (moveable) property. One-third of his personal property had to go to his wife, one-third went to his children, and the rest to whomever he wished. He could not devise his real estate by will; the inheritance of land and buildings was determined by law. In most of the country, real property was automatically inherited by the eldest surviving son. This is called *primogeniture*. However, in the County of Kent and a few other areas of the country all sons inherited equally. This system was called *gavelkind*. There was even a third system, called *borough English*, in some ancient boroughs and manors in southern England where the youngest son inherited the

\di'fin\ *vb*

Definitions

property. Under any of these systems, your ancestor could not cause the land to descend to someone other than the legal heir.

In 1540 the Statute of Wills made it possible for your ancestor to distribute most land by will to anyone he wished. He could also continue to bequeath his personal property by testament. It was then possible to combine both documents into a Last Will and Testament, which we now call simply a will. After 1661 all land could be distributed by will. Therefore, if you don't see land mentioned in the testaments of your early ancestors, it doesn't mean they didn't have any. The law determined who inherited your ancestor's land.

What Did the Will Include, and Who Was Mentioned?

Most of your ancestors decided not only what was to be done with their property upon death, but also what was to be done with their body and soul. Many wills began by bequeathing the soul to God and giving instructions about the disposal of the body. Your ancestor often mentioned the place where he wanted to be buried. Many left specific instructions for memorials. In early Catholic wills especially, provisions were made for masses to be said for the deceased, bells to be tolled, etc. Your ancestor also left money to the church and included a legacy for the poor people of the parish. After this he began to distribute his personal property to family and friends. He did not need to mention those who had already received their legacies. For example, it was the custom to provide for a child upon marriage, so many wills only mention children who had not yet married. Furthermore, it was not necessary to mention the eldest son (or other heir at law) who would automatically get the land according to law. Children who were already deceased may have also gone unmentioned. Previous spouses were not usually mentioned, so the wife named in the will may not have been the mother of the children.

Where Was the Will Probated?

Prior to 1858, probate was the responsibility of the Church of England. There were over three hundred ecclesiastical, peculiar, and manorial courts proving wills and administering estates.

The location of a probate record depends on where the deceased held property. The will could be probated in a number of courts. The easiest way to explain the court structure is to first review the organizational structure of the Church of England.

1. **A parish** is a township or group of townships under the administration of a vicar, rector, or perpetual curate.
2. **A peculiar** is a parish or group of parishes within an archdeaconry which are exempt from the authority of the archdeacon and often the bishop. Peculiars could have been overseen by a bishop, dean and chapter, lord of a manor, or other official.
3. **A rural deanery** is a collection of parishes overseen by a rural dean. The rural dean is often a parish minister. The Diocese of York was divided into rural deaneries.

Notes

161

4. **An archdeaconry** is a group of rural deaneries overseen by an archdeacon.

5. **A diocese** consists of a group of archdeaconries overseen by a bishop.

6. **A province** is group of dioceses overseen by an archbishop. There are only two provinces in England: Canterbury and York.

Your ancestor's will would have been probated in one of the following courts depending on where his property was held:

1. **Peculiar Court:** Probate was granted here when all property existed within the peculiar.

2. **Rural Deans** often had probate jurisdiction in the Province of York, but not in the Province of Canterbury.

3. **Archdeacon's Court:** If your ancestor held all of his property within one archdeaconry, his will would usually have been probated here. The archdeacon's court usually had probate jurisdiction in the Province of Canterbury, but rarely operated in the Province of York (except the large Archdeaconry of Richmond).

4. **Bishop's Court:** This court can also be called a **Diocesan, Episcopal, Consistory** or **Commissary Court.** Probate was granted here when property existed in more than one archdeaconry but within one diocese.

5. **Court of Dean and Chapter** or **Court of the Cathedral** often acted on the bishop's behalf. Probate could be granted here instead of the Bishop's Court.

6. **Archbishop's Court:** Probate was granted in this court when property existed in more than one diocese. There were two archbishop's courts: the Prerogative Court of York (PCY) and the Prerogative Court of Canterbury (PCC). The PCY covered Cheshire, Cumberland, Durham, Isle of Man, Lancashire, Northumberland, Nottinghamshire, Westmorland and Yorkshire. The Prerogative Court of Canterbury (PCC) had jurisdiction over the rest of England. If property was held in both the Province of York and the Province of Canterbury, the estate was probated in the Prerogative Court of Canterbury. The PCC had superior jurisdiction over all probate courts of England, Wales, and Ireland.

In theory, when a person died, the executor would take the will to the lowest court with jurisdiction to probate the estate. Property valued at more than five pound sterling in multiple jurisdictions was needed before going to a higher court. In reality, however, there was nothing to stop the executor from going to a higher court; he often did and paid the greater expense. This was especially true for the upper social classes who wanted the additional status and privacy of a higher and more distant court.

What Records Were Created?

Prior to 1858, many of the records are the same as the ones after 1858. These include probated wills, administrations with will annexed, and letters of administration.

When a will was first taken to the court and probate granted, it was recorded

Sources

in the Act Book, which is a diary of the daily court actions. The recording in the Act Book would include the name of the deceased; his address and occupation; names of the executors with notations on any relationships; and dates of the will, death, and probate. The date of death and value of the moveable goods were noted on the original will, which is preserved by the court. A copy of the will was given to the executors giving them the power to execute the terms of the will. If no will was available, a letter of administration was granted, and a bond was taken out by the administrators stating that they would fulfill their duties.

At the same time that a record was made in the Act book, a recording was made in the court calendar. For most courts this is a listing by first letter of the surname, with the names in chronological order as they came to the court. Sometimes a place would be added to help distinguish individuals. In the PCC, the number of probates granted was greater, so the calendar is by the first letter and the first vowel, thus Telford will be grouped with Theobald, Thresher, Tremayne, Tweddle, etc.

Inventories were almost always required by the courts between the years 1529 and 1750. They provide a fascinating look into the lives of our ancestors because they give a list of moveable goods of the deceased. Two reputable neighbors were appointed to take the inventory by going from room to room and listing all goods and their value. You will find the number of beds, dishes, and books in your ancestor's house. If you do not know the occupation or interests of your ancestor, the inventory can often provide clues. For example, you may find your ancestor's tools listed in the inventory, and you can often tell an occupation by the tools used. Debts, credits, and leases were also listed, but the laws on what should be included changed over time.

Contested wills generated additional court records. There may also be guardianship papers. Unfortunately, these and other rarer papers have often not been microfilmed and are only available for examination in England. You are beyond the stage of beginner if you are getting into these records.

Where Are the Records Now?

Pre-1858 probate records are now in the Public Record Office or at county or diocesan archives. You can find exactly where they are by checking *A Simplified Guide to Probate Jurisdictions: Where to Look for Wills* (see page 164).

The majority of the probate records have been microfilmed. Check the Family History Library Catalog under England—[County]—Probate Records.

HOW TO SEARCH FOR PROBATE RECORDS
What Do I Need to Know Before Searching for Pre-1858 Probate Records?

Prior to 1858, there were more than three hundred courts in which estates could be probated. The good news is that for your ancestor there are generally only four or five courts to search. What you need to do is determine which four or five courts are most likely to contain the probate records of your ancestor.

Research Tip

To get started, you need to know the name of your ancestor, an approximate date of death, and a place where you think your ancestor held property. You then determine the probate jurisdiction for the area.

Date of Death: You can get an approximate date of death from burial dates in the parish registers. After 1837, you can get the date of death from a death certificate. You can also estimate a probable date from your ancestor's disappearance from other records. The more you can narrow down the date of death, the easier your search will be.

Place of Property: Unless you have other evidence to the location of property held by your ancestor, start with the parish in which your ancestor lived. Determine the probate jurisdiction for this locality. **You can do so using any of the following resources:**

Sources

> Gibson, J.S.W. *A Simplified Guide to Probate Jurisdictions: Where to Look for Wills.* (4th edition). Federation of Family History Societies. 1997.
>
> Gibson, J.S.W., comp. *Wills and Where to Find Them.* Chichester, West Sussex: Phillimore. 1974.
>
> Humphery-Smith, Cecil. *The Phillimore Atlas and Index of Parish Registers.* (2nd edition). Chichester, West Sussex: Phillimore. 1995.
>
> Lewis, Samuel. *A Topographical Dictionary of England.* [1831] 4 volumes. Baltimore, Md.: Genealogical Publishing Company. Reprinted 1996.
>
> Smith, Frank. *A Genealogical Gazetteer of England.* Baltimore, Md.: Genealogical Publishing Company. 1982. Reprinted 1995.

One benefit of *The Phillimore Atlas* is its ease of use; you just look at the map to determine the probate jurisdiction. Another benefit is that you can see how close your ancestor's parish is to other jurisdictional boundaries. Furthermore, you should have already located this book when you started your parish register research.

Exceptions to the Process: Probate records are usually found in the Prerogative Court of Canterbury for soldiers, sailors, employees of the East India Company, clergy, and those dying overseas or owning property there.

What If I Don't Find My Ancestor's Probate in the Lowest Court?

There is a set of booklets for each county called *Pre-1858 English Probate Jurisdictions.* The booklets were compiled by the Genealogical Department of the Family History Library. Each has an introduction to probate records of the area. Most importantly, they contain colored maps of the county showing the probate jurisdictions, and they include a table showing in priority order the courts to search. The booklets are called "Research Papers" and have been available individually from the Family History Library in series A, numbers 7–46. These guides are currently out of print. Some Family History Centers may have them, and you can use them in the Family History Library in Salt Lake City. Until they are reissued, you will usually need two resources:

1. *The Phillimore Atlas and Index of Parish Registers.*
2. *Hand List of English Probate Jurisdictions, of Filmed and Printed Probate*

Technique

Records. This series is usually called the "probate keys." The probate keys contain microfilmed copies of the Research Papers mentioned above. They also include the appropriate FHL film numbers for the probate records. However, you should still check the Family History Library Catalog for a complete up-to-date listing of probate film numbers. The probate keys are available on FHL fiche 6026312. It is a set of ninety microfiche arranged alphabetically by county. They are also available on FHL films 0599217–222. The microfiche version is missing the county of Lancashire, so if you need that county you should order FHL film 0599219.

The colors on the maps are tied to the adjoining probate jurisdiction tables. However, the microfilmed version of the probate keys does not show the maps in color. Use the county maps arranged alphabetically in the atlas section of *The Phillimore Atlas* to find the original probate jurisdiction. There are two maps—the topographical map and the parish boundary map, which is outlined in color. Find your ancestor's parish in the parish boundary map. The date below the name of the county is the date of commencement of the parish registers. The areas outlined in color are the probate jurisdictions. On the county map of Northumberland, Figure 11-1, the parish of Stamfordham is within the area outlined in red. There is a key labeled "Ecclesiastical Jurisdictions" that shows each color and the name of the corresponding probate court. The table shows that red is for the Consistory Court of Durham.

Once you know the name of the probate jurisdiction for the area where your ancestor lived, you will use the *Hand List of English Probate Jurisdictions* (probate keys) at your nearest Family History Center. It will tell you the order in which to search the higher courts. The probate keys are in several volumes, organized by county. You can obtain a list of counties and their volume numbers in the Family History Library Catalog. Search by film/fiche number using fiche 6026312.

The Family History Library Catalog tells us that the County of Northumberland is in volume 26 of the probate keys and gives us both microfilm and microfiche numbers for that volume. We will obtain that volume to find a probate jurisdiction table for the county. The table for Northumberland is shown in Figure 11-2. We know from *The Phillimore Atlas* that our ancestor lived in the jurisdiction of the Consistory Court of Durham. The table tells us that we should look for probate records in the following order:
1. Court of the Bishop of Durham
2. Court of the Archbishop of York
3. Court of the Dean and Chapter of York
4. Court of the Archbishop of Canterbury

Notice that if your ancestor lived within the Peculiar of Hexham, you would need to search six courts. These probate keys take all of the guesswork out of pre-1858 probate research. Simply search the courts in order.

Figure 11-1
Map of Northumberland, from *The Phillimore Atlas and Index of Parish Registers* (see page 164), showing the location of all parishes, the years in which the parish registers began, and the probate court boundaries.

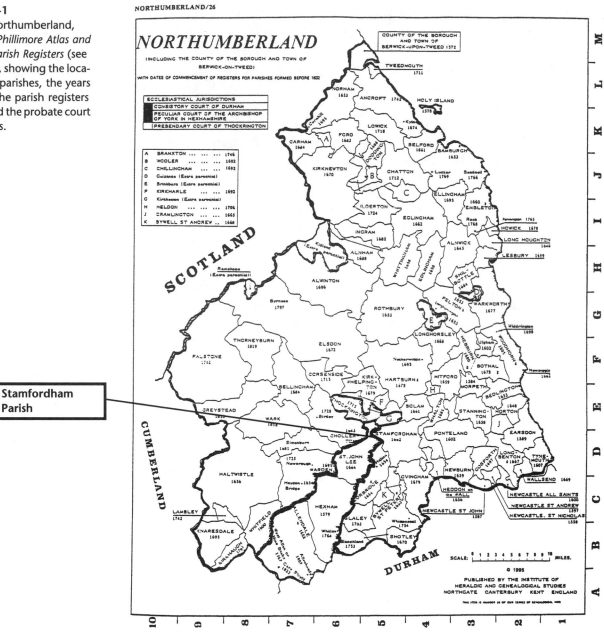

Stamfordham Parish

Sources

USING INDEXES TO DEATH DUTY REGISTERS

If your ancestor died between 1796 and 1857, you may be able to easily find where your ancestor's will was probated. **Even though there is no national probate index prior to 1858, the nationwide indexes to Death Duty Registers serve as a partial substitute.**

After a will or administration was proved in probate court, the amount of tax payable on the estate was determined. The taxes are recorded in the Death Duty Registers. The indexes to the registers are valuable because the index tells the name of the court where your ancestor's estate was probated. The indexes for 1812 to 1903 are available on microfilm. Search the Family History Library

If your ancestor lived in one of these jurisdictions . . . Search the probate records of these courts in the order shown . . .	Peculiar of Hexham and Hexhamshire (1593-1602; 1694-1706)	Peculiar of Hexham and Hexhamshire (before 1858)	Peculiar of Thockrington, Tockerington, or Tockerton	Episcopal Consistory of Durham	Anywhere in the County 1653-1660
			●	●	
Court of the Peculiar of Archbishop in Hexham and Hexhamshire	1				
Court of the Peculiar of Thockrington or Tockerington or Tockerton			1		
Court of the Bishop of Durham	3*	3*	3*	1	
Chancery Court of the Archbishop of York	2		4		
Court of the Archbishop of York (P.C.Y.)	4	1	5	2	
Court of the Dean and Chapter of York (Cathedral)	5	2	2	3	
Court of the Archbishop of Canterbury (P.C.C.)	6	4	6	4	1

*Technically, the Court of the Bishop of Durham did not have superior jurisdiction of these courts, but as the largest court of original jurisdiction in the county, it will often contain probate records of persons who resided in the other jurisdictions.

Figure 11-2
Probate key for the County of Northumberland. The parish of Stamfordham is in the area covered by the Episcopal Consistory of Durham. The column for that court shows the order in which to search courts for probate records of a person living in that area. Similar probate keys exist for all counties.

Catalog by fiche/film number 1419473 to get the entire series of film numbers. Once you have obtained the name of the court from the index, you will be able to find your ancestor's will.

After checking the indexes to find the court you need, you may want to also look at the complete Death Duty Register. The registers are even more very valuable than the indexes because they often provide significant genealogical information not found in other records. They are all on microfilm at the Family History Library. You can find them in the FHLC under England-Probate Records.

IDENTIFYING AND USING PROBATE INDEXES

You can use the *Guide to Probate Jurisdictions* to identify any available indexes whether printed, manuscript, or computerized. You can also check the Internet to find the Web site of family history societies in the county where your ancestor lived and look for new indexes for the courts within the county or diocese.

Examine the Family History Library Catalog under England-[County]-Probate Records-Indexes to see if any of these indexes are available from the Family History Library.

You may be able to find indexes that cover a large geographical area or a long time period. For example, the Kent Family History Society has produced surname and locality indexes for the Archdeaconry Court of Canterbury, so you can search for everyone with a particular surname or for all people in a specific locality. The Northumberland and Durham Family History Society is producing in segments an every-name index to the wills of the Diocese of Durham, so you can not only find the will of your ancestor, but you can find out if your ancestor is mentioned in the will of someone else. The Society of Genealogists has produced an index to the wills of the PCC for 1750 to 1800. This means that you don't have to know the exact year of death; you can search an entire fifty-year time span at once. It is important to learn what indexes are available for the courts you need.

What Do I Do If I Can't Find Any Printed Indexes?

Technique

If printed indexes are not available, check for the availability of the court's own calendars or indexes on microfilm. These take longer to search, but the advantage is you are looking at the original handwriting, not someone else's interpretation of the handwriting. Since searching these indexes can be difficult, we will show you how to do this.

Let's see if there is a probate record for William Dixon. We saw his burial record in the chapter on parish registers; he died in 1810. The probate keys told us to start with the Court of the Bishop of Durham. Search the Family History Library Catalog under England-Northumberland-Probate Records to find records of this court.

See the listing from the FHLC in Figure 11-3. Nowhere does the title say the "Court of the Bishop of Durham." It does, however, use three words that indicate a bishop's court: "Diocese," "Episcopal," and "Consistory." The "Episcopal Consistory Court" is the same as the "Court of the Bishop," so these are the films we need. The index that includes the year 1810 is on film number 0090804.

The index on the film is arranged chronologically. Wills are separated from administrations. In 1810, William Dixon is listed under the section for wills (see

Figure 11-3
Family History Library Catalog entry for the probate records at the diocese of Durham. It shows the film numbers on which you will find the indexes and the wills or administrations.

```
              Family History Library Catalog 21 Sep 1999      Page 1
                            **Full Display**

AUTHOR
Church of England.  Diocese of Durham.  Palatine and Episcopal Consistory
Court with the Peculiar of Craike.

TITLE
Wills and administrations, 1526-1858.

PUBLICATION INFORMATION
Salt Lake City : Filmed by the Genealogical Society of Utah, 1975.

FORMAT
182 microfilm reels ; 35 mm.

NOTES
Microfilm of originals.
For additional index to these materials, see Calendar to
the Episcopal Consistory Court of the Bishop of Durham,
1650-1786.

CONTENTS
Jusisdiction of court:  Durham and Northumberland counties and parts
   of Cumberland and Yorkshire.
                                                            BRITISH
                                                            FILM AREA
       Index to wills and admons.          1540-1660 ——————0090802
       Index to wills and admons.          1661-1786 ---------------- 0090803
       Index to wills and admons.          1787-1858 --------------- 0090804
       Original wills and admons.          1526, 1534, --------------- 0090982
                   1546, 1550-1553, 1557-1560, 1574
       Original wills and admons.          1565-1566, 1569 ----------0090983
       Original wills and admons. A-Y      1540-1557 ---------------- 0090805
       Original wills and admons. A-Y      1558-1567 ---------------- 0090806
       Original wills and admons. A-Y      1567-1571 ---------------- 0090807
       Original wills and admons. A-Y      1571-1576 ---------------- 0090808
       Original wills and admons. A-Y      1577-1582 ---------------- 0090809
       Original wills and admons. A-Y      1582-1614 ----------------> 0090810
       Original wills and admons. A-Y      1586 -------------------- 0090811
```

Diocese of Durham Wills and Administrations with description of geographic area covered

Film numbers for indexes

Film numbers for wills and admons for specific years

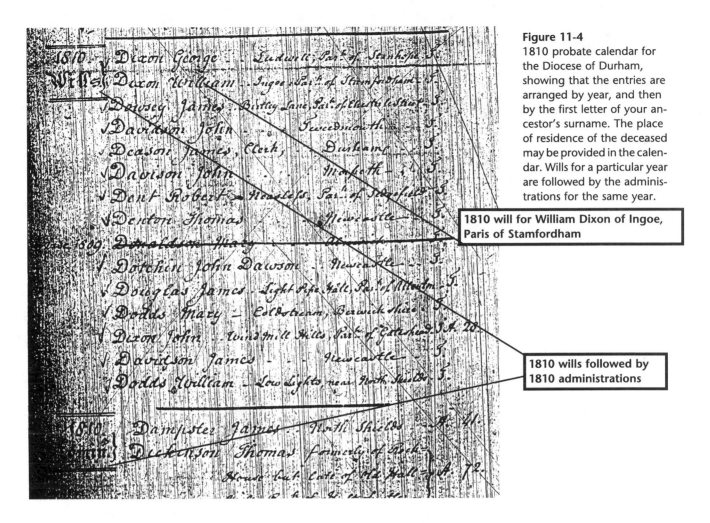

Figure 11-4
1810 probate calendar for the Diocese of Durham, showing that the entries are arranged by year, and then by the first letter of your ancestor's surname. The place of residence of the deceased may be provided in the calendar. Wills for a particular year are followed by the administrations for the same year.

1810 will for William Dixon of Ingoe, Paris of Stamfordham

1810 wills followed by 1810 administrations

Figure 11-4). The index reads, "Dixon William Ingoe, Parh. of Stamfordham." "Parh" is the abbreviation for "Parish." Since his name is listed, we know that we will find a will for William Dixon in the Episcopal Consistory Court of Durham in 1810. We need to locate those wills on microfilm.

FINDING THE PROBATE RECORDS

Your index searching has now produced one or more possibilities. **The nice thing is that the wills for most courts have been microfilmed and can be ordered at your nearest Family History Center.**

To find your ancestor's will, search the Family History Library Catalog under England-[County]-Probate Records. If the records are on microfilm, order the appropriate film and carefully search for the wills you need. Make photocopies and cite your source. You can read the details at your leisure later.

If the calendar shows that an administration exists or if you suspect an inventory should exist, but neither one is on microfilm, write to the repository where the records are currently stored and request copies. Check the current edition of *A Simplified Guide to Probate Jurisdictions: Where to Look for Wills* to determine the current repository.

Library/Archive Source

Case Study

Let's get William Dixon's will. Since he is in the index, we know that we will find his will in 1810. Look again at the example from the Family History Library Catalog in Figure 11-3. This page includes original wills and administrations for years up to 1587, but we continue through the listing until we find the year 1810. The "Original wills and admons. D-P 1810" are on FHL film 0090940. We order the film and wait for it to arrive. The wait is the hardest part of the process!

When the film arrives, we notice that the pages of the film are not numbered, so we have to search page by page to find the will. See the beginning of the will at Figure 11-5. It reads:

> I William Dixon of Ingoe in the Parish of Stamfordham in the County of Northumberland Gentleman do make my last Will and Testament in manner following, that is to say, I Give devise and bequeath unto my natural son Robert Dixon and to his Heirs and Assigns for ever all and singular any Real and personal Estate and Effects whatsoever and wheresoever and of what nature kind or quality the same doth or may consist subject and chargeable nevertheless with the payment of my just debts and the annuities and Legacies hereinafter mentioned, that is to say, an annuity or yearly payment of Forty Pounds to my wife for and during the Term of her natural life in lieu of bar and full satisfaction of all Dower, Widow right or thirds at Law . . .

Notice that William does not give the name of his wife. He just says, "my wife."

The end of the will has William's signature (see Figure 11-6). He signs "W Dixon." Most wills that you find are from will books. They are copies of the original wills, so the signature you will see is not your ancestor's signature. This particular filming is of original wills! The description in the Family History Library

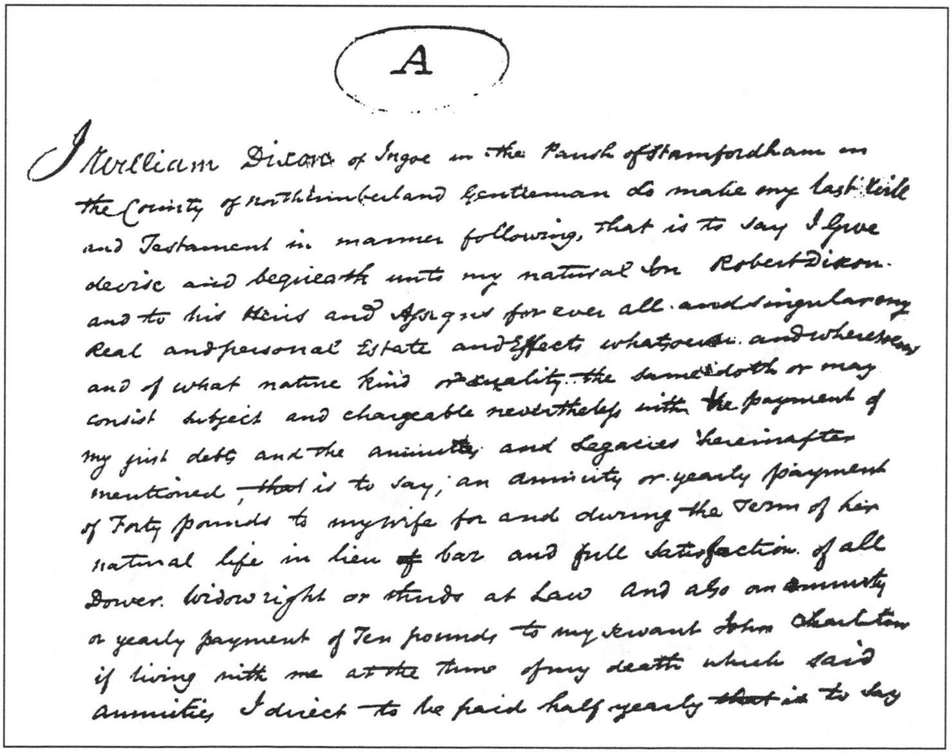
A

I William Dixon of Ingoe in the Parish of Stamfordham in
the County of Northumberland Gentleman do make my last Will
and Testament in manner following, that is to say I Give
devise and bequeath unto my natural Son Robert Dixon
and to his Heirs and Assigns for ever all and singular any
Real and personal Estate and Effects whatsoever and wheresoever
and of what nature Kind or quality the same doth or may
consist subject and chargeable nevertheless with the payment of
my just debts and the annuities and Legacies hereinafter
mentioned, that is to say; an annuity or yearly payment
of Forty pounds to my wife for and during the Term of her
natural life in lieu of bar and full satisfaction of all
Dower, Widowright or thirds at Law And also an annuity
or yearly payment of Ten pounds to my Servant John Charlton
if living with me at the time of my death which said
annuities I direct to be paid half yearly that is to say

Figure 11-5
William Dixon's original will, written in 1809. See also Figures 11-6 and 11-7.

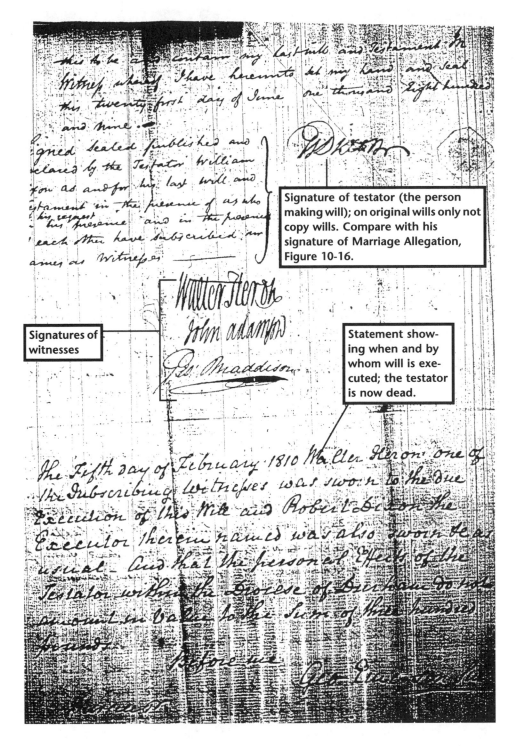

Signature of testator (the person making will); on original wills only not copy wills. Compare with his signature of Marriage Allegation, Figure 10-16.

Signatures of witnesses

Statement showing when and by whom will is executed; the testator is now dead.

Catalog will usually tell you if the filming is of original wills or copy wills.

After the will we find an extraordinary notation shown in Figure 11-7. It reads:

> In Chancery between Dorothy Dixon—Plaintiff
> and
> William Charlton—Robert Dixon—John Rewcastle and Jane his wife. Richard Craster Askew and Thomas Charlton—Defendants

Figure 11-7
Statement added to the will nineteen years after William Dixon's death stating that the will is being used as an exhibit in a court case. Obviously, you will want to find the court case. See also Figures 11-5 and 11-6.

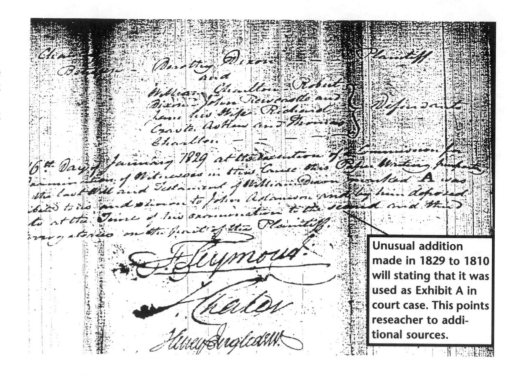

Unusual addition made in 1829 to 1810 will stating that it was used as Exhibit A in court case. This points reseacher to additional sources.

The 16th Day of January 1829 at the execution of a Commission for the Examination of Witnesses in this Cause this Paper Writing purporting to be the last Will and Testament of William Dixon marked A was exhibited to us and shown to John Adamson and by him deposed unto at the Time of his examination to the second and third Interrogatories on the part of this Plaintiff

What does this mean? It means that Dorothy Dixon took a case to Chancery against Robert Dixon and the others. Of course, we have to find the Chancery case, which unfortunately has not been filmed and can only be found at the Public Record Office at Kew, England. When we do, we find that Dorothy was complaining because Robert had not fulfilled the provisions of his father's will. Dorothy had not been paid the annuities to which she was entitled. The case contains many interesting details about their lives. Contested cases are great; they contain a lot of scandal!

Technique

WHY CAN'T I FIND MY ANCESTOR'S WILL?

Your ancestor did not make a will. Most people did not make wills, because they had little property. If your ancestor was from the middle and upper classes, you are more likely to find a will. Although most of our ancestors were from the lower classes, this does not mean they did not make a will. Look for both wills and administrations. Even if your ancestor did not make one of his own, he may have been named in a will of another person. Check for other wills in the area for people with the same surname and also for the surnames of relatives by marriage.

You're looking in the wrong court. Go through the probate keys mentioned earlier in this chapter and make sure that you have examined all courts in the probate hierarchy. You will need to look in the Prerogative Court of Canterbury for all wills between 1653 and 1660.

Your ancestor is not mentioned in a potential will. Not all children are mentioned in the wills of the parents. They might have already received their inheritance or dowry and thus did not need to be mentioned again. The child could have already died, or she was not born until after the will was written. Carefully check the date the will was written as opposed to when it went through probate. Look in other records, such as parish registers, for evidence of the relationship.

The will was not proven. Before 1750 many heirs did not prove wills in court because they wanted to avoid the probate costs. Until the Court of Probate Act of 1857, wills that disposed only of land and contained no moveable goods were not subject to probate. These wills may survive in family papers, in solicitors' archives, and other archives.

The will was proven many years after the death of your ancestor. Many families did not feel the need to probate wills, but they kept the wills among the family papers in case someone later objected to the distribution of the property. In case of an objection or lawsuit, the will may have been proven many years after the fact. If you are fairly certain that your ancestor had a will, check the probate indexes for several years after the date of death.

Wills are poorly indexed. Spellings were not standardized before the beginning of the nineteenth century. Check the index to see if it is arranged in strict alphabetical order as written (in which case you have to think of all possible spelling variants) or by phonetic spelling, pulling together all variants. Some indexes contain cross-references to surname variations, but be sure that all variations for your name are included.

You are looking in the wrong section of the index. This is easy to do when the wills and administrations are listed separately. Recheck the film to see if wills and administrations are listed in different sections of the film or if they are on different microfilms altogether.

The will has been lost. Wills, like many documents, have disappeared over time. Many wills are known to be missing, such as early Exeter wills due to enemy bombing in 1942. Some have been improperly stored, have had poor caretakers, and have often been repeatedly moved and abused. Do not use this as an excuse to give up too soon. You can sometimes determine if a will ever existed by looking in the Probate Act Books for the particular court. This may even provide an abstract.

You haven't read what you found correctly. All the related documents produced by the courts prior to 1733 were in Latin, except for the Commonwealth period between 1653 and 1660. Often the documents contain legal abbreviations complicating the translation process even further. If you find yourself in this situation, obtain a book that will help you with the handwriting, language or abbreviations. Some of these are listed in chapter three.

Review the section Why Can't I Find My Ancestor in the Calendar? in chapter nine. It contains more suggestions for helping you find probate records.

Probate searching is rarely a quick and easy process, but the results can be make it very worthwhile. You can reconstruct whole families across multiple generations. As you progress in your research, use the guides listed in the following section for additional assistance.

Sources

WHERE TO FIND MORE ABOUT THIS TOPIC

Cox, Jane. *Affection Defying the Power of Death: Wills, Probate & Death Duty Records*. Federation of Family History Societies, 1993.

Cox, Jane. *Hatred Pursued Beyond the Grave*. London: HMSO, 1993.

Gibson, J.S.W. *A Simplified Guide to Probate Jurisdictions: Where to Look for Wills*. 4th ed. Federation of Family History Societies, 1997.

Herber, Mark D. *Ancestral Trails: The Complete Guide to British Genealogy and Family History*. Baltimore, Md.: Genealogical Publishing Company, 1998.

Milward, R. *A Glossary of Household, Farming, and Trade Terms: From Probate Inventories*. 3rd ed. Chesterfield: Derbyshire Record Society, 1991.

Pratt, David H. *Researching British Probates, 1354–1858: A Guide to the Microfilm Collection of the Family History Library*. Vol. 1, *Northern England/Province of York*. Wilmington, Del.: Scholarly Resources Inc., 1992.

Scott, Miriam. *Prerogative Court of Canterbury Wills and Other Probate Records*. Public Record Office Readers Guide No. 15. PRO Publications, 1997.

Smith, Frank and David E. Gardner. *Genealogical Research in England and Wales*. Vol. 2. Salt Lake City, Utah: Bookcraft Publishers, 1959.

West, John. *Village Records*. Chichester, West Sussex: Phillimore, 1982.

For More Info

AFTER SEARCHING THE PROBATE RECORDS, WHAT SHOULD I DO NEXT?

If your ancestor made bequests to people who were born, married, or died during the period July 1837 to 1857, return to the chapters on civil registration (chapters six and seven) and census records (chapter eight). Obtain the necessary certificates for additional family members you have found. Use any addresses given to locate the families in the census records.

See also suggestions in chapter nine, Post-1857 Probate Records.

If your ancestor named people who were born, married, or died between 1538 and 1837, see chapter ten on parish registers to locate these people in birth, marriage, and burial records. Once you have located their church and probate records, see chapter twelve.

If the probate record pertains to people who lived before 1538, then first consider yourself very lucky. You are already further back than most English researchers will ever get. See chapter twelve for more advanced research.

TWELVE

What's Next?

C ivil registration, census records, parish registers, and probate records are the basic resources for English family history, but they are only the beginning. Sources for English family history are some of the richest in the world. You have now successfully gathered lots of information about your ancestors, and you're ready to find out what else exists.

THERE'S MORE AT THE FAMILY HISTORY LIBRARY

You have not even begun to exhaust the resources of the Family History Library. You are now probably very adept at locating the resources you need by using the Family History Library Catalog, but it still helps to have a guide to the vast collections of the FHL. If you haven't done so already, get the *Research Outline: England*. It lists by subject category the most important records for English family history. The subject categories in the Research Outline are the same as those used in the Family History Library Catalog. Go through the Research Outline and experiment with the various records. You can purchase *Research Outline: England* at a Family History Center, order a copy from the Salt Lake Distribution Center (see address and phone number in chapter five), or download one free from the FamilySearch Web site at <http://www.familysearch .org/sg/> (click on "England Research Outline"). If you bought the SourceGuide CD-ROM (which we highly recommend), you can also obtain the Research Outline there.

The *Research Outline: England* **describes so many resources that you may wish to visit the Family History Library in Salt Lake City (see address below) to immerse yourself in them.** The majority of the records described in the Research Outline will be instantly accessible in the FHL. Most genealogists agree that a week in the Family History Library is equivalent to a year or more of research anywhere else. Many genealogical societies conduct annual research tours to Salt Lake City, and you may be more comfortable going with a group the first time. However, even if it's your first trip, you will quickly learn to get around the library all by yourself. Consultants are always available to assist you.

Library/Archive Source

Family History Library
35 North West Temple Street
Salt Lake City, Utah 84150

Sources

THE PUBLIC RECORD OFFICE

The largest repository of original English documents is the Public Record Office located in Kew, Surrey, England. You can find out about the records held there and how to use them by reading *Tracing Your Ancestors in the Public Record Office* (5th ed.) Amanda Bevan, ed. Richmond: Public Record Office, 1999. You should also visit the PRO Web site at <http://www.pro.gov.uk>. The PRO helps researchers with more than a hundred valuable Family Fact Sheets at <http://www.pro.gov.uk/genealogy/familyfacts.htm> and Research Information Leaflets at <http://www.pro.gov.uk/leaflets/riindex.htm>. These tools will tell you about the many records at the PRO and how to use them.

When *Tracing Your Ancestors in the Public Record Office* or a Research Information Leaflet refers you to a specific record class, you can look it up in the catalog of the Public Record Office, containing more than eight million document descriptions. The catalog is online and located at <http://www.pro.gov.uk/finding/catalogue/>. Let's use an example. Suppose you want to find more about Death Duty Registers to see if you can find any mention of William Dixon whose will was probated in the court of Durham in 1810. You locate the Research Information Leaflet called "Death Duty Registers from 1796." It tells you that indexes to the registers for country courts, 1796–1811, are in PRO class IR 27, pieces 67–93. To find the precise piece number you want, you can then go to the online catalog. There you will find that the index for the court of Durham, 1796–1811 is on IR 27/83. You now know the exact piece number you want to consult. What a gold mine this is when you can search from your own home! The Web site of the Public Record Office even has a list of researchers for hire. If you look through the catalog yourself, you can save money by giving a researcher the call numbers of records you want searched.

COUNTY RECORD OFFICES

Original documents for English counties are often found in a County Record Office. A list of all counties with links to information about each is available at <http://www.genuki.org.uk/big/eng/#Counties>. Click on the county of interest to find information and addresses of the important record offices for the county. Many County Record Offices have Web sites. You can see a list of them with links to their Web sites at <http://www.oz.net/~markhow/englishros.htm>.

Money Saver

Sometimes you can access the catalog of a County Record Office without traveling there. Many of them have been published by Chadwyck-Healey in a microfiche series called the National Inventory of Documentary Sources in the United Kingdom and Ireland (NIDS). NIDS may be available at large public or university libraries. The Family History Library also has it, so you can order the microfiche that pertains to your area of interest. A listing of repositories included in NIDS with Family History Library Catalog computer numbers is on the Internet at <http://www.rootsweb.com/~bifhsusa/nids/nids.html>.

FAMILY HISTORY SOCIETIES

Since you now know where your English ancestors lived, you should join the family history societies in the area. We talked about this in chapter three, but it is even more vital now that you want to go beyond the basics into more advanced research. You need to know who is doing what and what records and indexes are available in your ancestor's locality. **The local family history society is the best way to stay on top of the advances in local research.**

Research Tip

It will also be very helpful to join a society in North America that specializes in helping its members find their British ancestry. The biggest is the British Isles Family History Society–U.S.A. This society publishes a quarterly journal and six newsletters per year; sells books at member discounts; conducts research tours to England, Ireland, Scotland, and Wales; holds several seminars per year with internationally renowned speakers; and more. You can find out more about the society from its Web site at <http://www.rootsweb.com/~bifhsusa> or by writing to

British Isles Family History Society-U.S.A.
2531 Sawtelle Blvd. PMB 134
Los Angeles, California 90064-3124

You might also wish to join a regional society, such as the British Interest Group of Wisconsin and Illinois (BIGWILL; P.O. Box 192, Richmond, Illinois 60071), the British Isles Family History Society of Greater Ottawa (BIFHSGO; P.O. Box 38026, Ottawa, Ontario K2C 1N0), or the British Isles Genealogical Research Association (BIGRA; P.O. Box 19775, San Diego, California 92159-0775). These and other societies hold monthly meetings, conduct annual conferences, and offer many other services that can help you further your research. The most important aspect is that you will regularly get together with others who share your passion for family history.

Internet Source

The best place to find addresses of family history societies is from the Web site of the Federation of Family History Societies at <http://www.ffhs.org.uk/members/index.htm>. Your local librarian can also help you find one.

GENEALOGICAL PUBLICATIONS

You may want to subscribe to a genealogical publication that has articles that will help in your research. One of the best is *Family Tree Magazine*. It is published in England and is not to be confused with *Family Tree Magazine* produced in the United States. You can find out more about *Family Tree Magazine* at <http://www.family-tree.co.uk> or by writing to the publisher at

Printed Source

Family Tree Magazine
61 Great Whyte
Ramsey, Huntingdon, Cambridgeshire PE17 1HL
England

The International Society for British Genealogy and Family History publishes a quarterly newsletter that will keep you up-to-date on the latest developments in English research and will also tell you about recent acquisitions in the Family History Library.

International Society for British Genealogy and Family History
P. O. Box 3115
Salt Lake City, Utah 84110-3115

Printed Source

A REFERENCE BOOK

A good single-volume source for finding information about more advanced English records is *Ancestral Trails: The Complete Guide to British Genealogy and Family History* (see page 174). Despite its title, the primary focus of the book is English records. It describes in detail the content and use of most sources for English research. It will not always tell you if the records are held by the Family History Library, and thus available to you outside of England, so you should check the FHLC for any record that interests you. If the Family History Library does not have it, Herber will tell you where to find the record in England. *Ancestral Trails* is a resource that all English researchers should consult.

For More Info

WHERE DO I GO FROM HERE?

The information you have gathered in your many hours of research will now lead to a wonderful benefit for you. Having found the town or village of your ancestors, you are ready to walk in your ancestors' footsteps. You have accomplished a marvelous feat in finding your ancestral homeland, and you richly deserve a treat. The fourth step of the research process is a trip to England.

England is a superb place for American visitors, indeed for all visitors. The language is almost (but not quite) the same, but the customs sometimes vary greatly. Many of these are the customs your ancestors would have followed centuries ago. Accents may be local and indicative of the way your ancestors spoke. The same streets, pub, poorhouse, cemetery, and perhaps even your ancestor's original house may still be there. If you are lucky, you will be able to experience the timelessness of the church where the baptisms and marriages of your ancestors took place. Consider attending a Church of England service. You may be sitting in the same seat that your ancestor once did. Include a visit to the cemetery and spend a few quiet moments.

For many, taking a tour is the way to go for the very first time. While not designed for you to have time available in the particular locations you need, a tour is good for a general introduction to England.

However, England is one of the countries easiest for most Americans to access.

There are some wonderful systems in place that can make your trip delightful. One is the Book a Bed Ahead (BBA). Simply speaking, you book your first two nights and your last two nights from your home. Once in England, you can avail yourself of the BBA and book your rooms one day in advance for wherever you wish to go. This allows you great flexibility. In terms of getting around, you have the option of renting a car or using public transportation. The latter is highly recommended in cities. With a rental car, remember that driving on the "wrong" side of the road can make you (and your passenger) nervous. Think about how comfortable you will be with narrow lanes and different traffic laws. You may want to consider traveling by train; you will enjoy it and meet lots of locals in the process. Purchase a BritRail Pass before you leave for England. They must be purchased here, not in England. A BritRail Pass allows you unlimited train access. There is also a very good bus system in England. Even if you take a train, you will often take a bus into the village of your ancestors. If no bus goes there, consider asking a local taxi driver how much it would cost to have him take you there, wait for you, and bring you back. Some of the drivers are very accommodating; they will show you your village and tell you much more about the area than you would learn in two or more days on your own. Be sure to tell the driver that you will pay waiting time and get a price before you go. Schedule a trip to your ancestors' hometowns at the beginning of your vacation, not at the end. That way if you hit a gold mine in the village, you can spend an extra day or two there and skip some of the other sightseeing.

Here are a few suggestions to make your trip more enjoyable. Take very little luggage with you. Also, bring comfortable walking shoes. The English countryside is beautiful, and you will want to be able to walk around and enjoy it. When you have explored the countryside and marveled at how many sheep there are everywhere, try to schedule at least two or three days in London. The sights, history, and culture of the city are fascinating. Furthermore, many of your ancestors were in London at one time or another. Find out what the attraction was.

FINALLY, WRITE YOUR FAMILY HISTORY

We know that you have been doing a lot of this research for the pure joy of it, but why keep it to yourself? Submit your genealogy to Ancestral File and to various sites on the Internet. Create a Web site about your family. But most of all, write your family history. Don't just publish a list of names and dates; nobody will read it. Tell how your ancestors lived in England. Illustrate with documents that you have found about your family. Include pictures from your trip to England that show some of the original buildings. Talk about how your ancestors worked, played, loved, and suffered. Relate the experiences of your immigrant ancestor. **For advice on how to write a good family history, read Patricia Law Hatcher's *Producing a Quality Family History*,** (Salt Lake City, Utah: Ancestry Inc., 1996).

Printed Source

Remember these words from chapter one: "Your English ancestors have beautiful and often heart-wrenching stories to tell. It is up to you to tell them." You, your family members, and researchers who will come many generations later will be glad you did.

Index

A

Abbreviations
  census, 88
  county codes, 15
  for ditto ("do"), 105
  Latin, 23
  occupations, 86
Act Book, 163
Administrations with
  will annexed, 162
Adoption, 63
Age
  in census records,
    87-88
  on death certificate,
    81-82
  on marriage
    certificate, 75-76
Alan Godfrey Maps, 15
Ancestors
  immigrant, 2-3, 5-7
  not found. See
    Ancestors not found
Ancestors not found
  in census records,
    115-116
  in civil registration
    index, 61-64
  in parish registers,
    158-159
  in probate records,
    129, 172-174
Ancestral File, 27-28,
  44
Anglican Church. See
  Church of England
Archdeaconry, 20, 162
Aristocracy, 21

B

Baptism records, 6, 63
  indexes for, 139
  in International
    Genealogical Index,
    41-42, 141-147
  in parish registers, 132

Birth certificate
  analyzing, 69-74
  birth place on, 70-71
  father's name on,
    71-72
  informant for, 73
  mother's name on, 72
  name on, 71, 74
  occupation of father
    on, 72
  registration date on,
    73
  sex on, 71
  time on, 70
  See also Birth records
Birth place
  on birth certificate,
    70-71
  in 1841 census, 112
  in 1881 census, 98
  indexes, 98
Birth records, 21
  civil registration, 51,
    53, 55-57
  See also Birth
    certificate
Borough town, 18
Boyd's Marriage
  Indexes, 152-154
British Isles, 13
British Isles Family
  History Society—
  U.S.A., 32-33
Burial records,
  133-134, 154-158

C

Catholic Church, dates
  recorded by, 24
Catholics
  baptism records, 145
  marriage records, 52,
    78
  wills of, 161
  See also
    Nonconformists

"Census as
  enumerated," 92, 98
Census records, 21,
  85-117
  ancestors not found
    in, 115-116
  available years, 86,
    114
  background, 85-89
  cautions about using,
    116-117
  confidentiality of, 88
  Enumeration Books,
    110-112
  enumerators, 85-86
  lettercodes and class
    numbers on, 88
  place indexes, 98
  searching, 89-90
  street indexes,
    100-107
  surname indexes,
    107-109
Census records, 1841,
  87, 110-113
Census records, 1851,
  107-109
Census records, 1871,
  103-107
Census records, 1881,
  9-10
  birthplace index, 96
  on CD-ROM, 90-92
  census place index, 97
  as enumerated, 98
  on microfiche, 10,
    92-113
  microfiche numbers,
    93-94
  as starting point, 89
  by surname, 90, 95
Channel Islands, 13-14
Census records, 1891,
  101-102
Chapel, 18
Chapelry, 18

Chapman County
  Codes, 15
Children
  adopted, 63
  baptism records,
    41-42, 63, 132, 139,
    141-147
  birth certificates. See
    Birth certificate
  illegitimate, 63,
    71-72, 130
  kidnapped, 2
  parent search, 41-43
  probate records,
    129-130
Christening records, 6.
  See also Baptism
  records
Church, 18
Church of England, 20
  archdeaconry, 20, 162
  dates recorded by, 24
  diocese, 18, 20, 162
  marriage certificate
    information, 77
  marriage registers, 52
  marriages in, 148-149
  parishes in, 14-15,
    161
  parish registers,
    131-159
  peculiar, 161
  pre-19th century
    records, 50
  probate records, 119,
    161
  province, 162
  rural deanery, 161
Church in Wales, 77
City, 18
Civil registration
  certificate, 52-53
  analyzing, 69-84
  birth certificates,
    69-74
  changes in 2000, 69

marriage certificate, 74-80
ordering, 65-67
See also Civil registration records
Civil registration indexes, 50-69
birth indexes, 53, 55-57
codes for areas and volumes, 58
death indexes, 54, 60-61
at Family History Center, 55-61
marriage indexes, 53-54, 57-60
not finding ancestors in, 61-64
registration district, 54-55
using, 54
Civil registration records, 21
administration of, 85
birth certificates, 51, 69-74. *See also* Birth certificate
creation of, 50-52
death certificates, 51, 80-84
marriage certificates, 52, 57-60, 74-80
See also Civil registration certificate
Codicil, 119
County
codes, 15
defined, 18
guides, 37
record offices, 176-177
County Record Office, 8
Court records, 6
Courts, probate, 162
Cyndi's List, 33

D
Dates
on birth certificate, 73
calendars and, 23-25
on death certificate, 81, 84, 164
of marriage, 74-75
Death, unregistered, 63-64
Death certificate
Death Duty Registers, 166-167
Death records, 6, 21, 51
civil registration index, 54, 60-61
See also Death certificate
Deathbed marriage, 78
age on, 81-82
cause of death on, 82-83
date on, 81
name and surname on, 81
occupation on, 82
place on, 81
register entry number, 80-81
sex on, 81
signature on, 83-84
See also Death records
Dewey decimal system, 37
Diocese, 18, 20, 162
District court, probate records in, 124-125

E
England
the country, 13
record keeping in, 21-22
trip to, 8-9, 178-179
English research
modern process, 7-9
uniqueness of, 13-26
Enumeration Books, 110-112
Established Church. *See*

Church of England, 20
Executor/Executrix, 119
Extra-parochial, 18

F
Family history
health, 82-83
writing, 179
Family History Centers (FHC), 4, 8
Ancestral File, 44
birth indexes, 53, 55-57
civil registration indexes at, 55-61
death indexes, 54, 60-61
1881 census index at, 92-113
Family History Library Catalog. *See* Family History Library Catalog
getting started at, 40-49
International Genealogical Index (IGI), 40-44, 141-158
location of, 39
marriage indexes, 53-54, 57-60
in research process, 8
See also Family History Library
Family History Library (FHL), 4, 8
additional information at, 175
Latin word list, 23
materials not listed in catalog, 48-49
types of records, 38
what is, 38
See also Family History Centers
Family History Library

Catalog (FHLC), 44-45
call numbers, 45
1851 census in, 108
fiche/film numbers, 46
probate calendar, 122-123
probate keys in, 164-165
probate records, 169-172
street indexes, 100-102
subject headings in, 47
using, 45-48
Web site, 28
Family History Societies, 17-19, 177
probate indexes from, 167
Family Records Centre (London), 65, 88
Father
name on birth certificate, 71-72
name on marriage certificate, 77
occupation of, 72, 77
Federation of Family History Societies (FFHS), 19, 107, 177
FHLC. *See* Family History Library Catalog (FHLC), 44-45

G
Gazetteers, 14-18
Genealogical publications, 177-178
Genealogical Society of Utah (GSU), 3-4, 38
Genealogy, in reverse, 6
General Register Office (GRO), 50-51, 53, 65, 79

Gentry, 21
GENUKI Web site, 29-32, 107, 134
Great Britain, 13
GRO. *See* General Register Office

H
Hamlet, 18
Handwriting
misreading, 62
styles of, 22-23
Hide, 18
Holograph will, 119
Hundred, 18

I
IGI. *See* International Genealogical Index (IGI)
Illegitimate children, 63, 71-72, 130
Immigrant ancestors, 2
identifying, 5-7
indexes for, 7
Indexes
alternative, 64
baptism, 139
birth, 55-57
birth place, 98
census place, 98
civil registration, 50-69
death, 60-61
death duty registers, 166-167
1881 census, 98
immigrant, 7
marriage, 57, 59-60, 152-154
Office for National Statistics, 65
parish registers, 136-139
periodical source, 37
Phillimore's, 136-138
probate, 167-169
street, 100-107

surname, 33, 98, 107-109
Informant
for birth certificate, 51, 71, 73
for death certificate, 51, 83-84
International Genealogical Index (IGI), 40-44, 141-158
baptism records, 141-147
burial records, 154-158
marriage records in, 147-154
parent search, 41-43
Web site, 27-28, 40
Internet resources, 27-34
familysearch, 27-29
See also Web sites
Intestate, 119
Ireland, 13
Isle of Man, 13-14

J
Jews, 20, 78, 133

K
Kidnapped ancestor, 2

L
Land records, 6
Landranger Map Series, 15
Last Will and Testament, 119
Latin terms and abbreviations, 23
Legatee, 119
Letter of Administration, 119, 128, 162
Library of Congress catalog system, 37
Library research, 8, 35-38

Location. *See* Place
Lower middle class, 21

M
Maps, 14-17, 55
Marriage
legal, 152
valid (1754-1812), 20
unregistered, 63
Marriage certificate
age on, 75-76
analyzing, 74-80
church information on, 77-78
date of marriage, 74-75
entry number, 74
father's name on, 77
footer of, 77-79
header on, 74
marital status on, 76
names on, 75
occupation on, 76
process information on, 78-79
residence on, 76-77
signatures on, 79
Marriage records, 6, 21
civil registration, 52
civil registration indexes, 53, 57-60
in International Genealogical Index, 147-154
legal marriages, 152
marriage by banns, 152
marriage by license, 148-151
in parish registers, 132
See also Marriage certificate
Middle class, 21
Military records, 6
Money references, 19-20
Monumental inscriptions (MI), 157-158

Mother
consent on marriage license allegation, 150
name on birth certificate, 72

N
Name
on birth certificate, 71, 74
Christian, 22, 62
on death certificate, 81
father's, on marriage certificate, 77
on marriage certificate, 75
of mother, 72
spelling of, 62
surnames, 33, 45. *See also* Surname
National index
civil registration records, 53
for 1881 census, on CD-ROM, 90-92
National Index of Parish Registers (NIPR), 138-139
National Inventory of Documentary Sources in the United Kingdom and Ireland (NIDS), 176
Naturalization records, 6
NIDS. *See* National Inventory of Documentary Sources in the United Kingdom and Ireland
NIPR. *See* National Index of Parish Registers
Nonconformists
baptism records, 144

marriage records, 52, 77-78

parish records and, 158

See also Catholics; Jews; Quakers; Religion

Notice book, 52

Nuncupative will, 119

O

Obituaries, 6

Occupation, 2, 11

abbreviations, 86

on death certificate, 82

of father, 72, 77

on marriage certificate, 76

Office for National Statistics (ONS), 65-66

ONS. *See* Office for National Statistics

Original records, 6, 9

P

Parent search, 41-43

Parish

Church of England, 14-15, 20

defined, 18, 161

history of, 134

Parish records, 20

ancestors not found in, 158-159

See also Parish registers

Parish registers, 131-159

baptismal registers, 132

burial registers, 133-134

early origins of, 131-132

indexes for, 136-139

in International Genealogical Index, 141-158

marriage registers, 132-133

National Index of Parish Registers (NIPR), 138-139

Parish and Vital Records List (PVRL), 139-141

searching, 134-135

See also Parish records

Parish and Vital Records List (PVRL), 139-141

Passenger lists, 6

Peculiar, 161

Pedigrees of peerage, 21

PERSI (*Periodical Source Index*), 37

Phillimore's Index, 136-138

Place

birth, 70-71. *See also* Birth place

codes, in Civil Registration Index, 58

on death certificate, 81

FHLC records arranged by, 45-47

hard-to-find, 16-17

importance of, 14-17

incorrect, 62-63

on probate records, 164

Prison

census records for, 115

marriage in, 78

Probate

terms, 119

definition, 118-122

Probate calendar, 122-124

ancestors not found in, 129

Probate indexes, 167-169

Probate records, 21

Act Book, 163

finding, 169-172

nonfamily bequests, 130

not found in lowest court, 164-165

starting with, 6

wills as, 160-161. *See also* Wills

Probate records, post-1857, 118-130

availability of, 120-121

creation of, 119-120

district court, 124-125

information from, 120

location of, 120-121

principal registry, 124, 126

probate calendar, 122-124

who kept, 119

Probate records, pre-1858, 160-174

creation of, 162-163

searching for, 163-165

Province, 18, 20, 162

Public documents, 4. *See also* Civil registration records

Public Record Office (PRO), 8, 22

1881 census, 96

Family Fact Sheets, 176

Web site, 108

Puritans, 2

PVRL. *See* Parish and Vital Records List

Q

Quakers, 20, 78, 133

R

Records

Christian names in, 22

Church of England, 20

civil registration. *See* Civil registration records

dates in, 23-25

English, 21-22. *See also* Public Record Office

evaluating, 10-11

Family History Library, 38

handwriting styles in, 22-23

Latin terms in, 23

national government, 21-22

original, 6, 9

verifying, 9-10

See also entries for specific types of records

Registrar General, 51, 85, 88

Registration district, 18, 51, 54-55

Religion

importance of, 20

as reason for immigration, 2

See also Catholics; Church of England; Nonconformists

Research process

Family History Centers, 8

identifying immigrant ancestors, 5-7

Internet search, 7-8

library search, 8

starting, 5

trip to England, 8-9, 178-179

Residence

at death, 81

on marriage certificate, 76-77

unknown, 90

Roman Catholics. *See*

Catholic Church; Catholics
Rural deanery, 20, 161

S
Scotland, 13
Shire, 18
Signature, informant's
  on birth certificate, 73
  on death certificate, 83-84
Signature, registrar's
  on birth certificate, 73
  on death certificate, 84
Signatures on marriage certificate, 79
Social class, 2, 20-21
Society of Genealogists (SoG), 138
  probate indexes, 168
SoG. *See* Society of Genealogists
Source Guide Web site, 28
Street indexes, 100-107, 110
Superintendent Registrar, 51, 53-54, 85
  marriage records, 52, 79
  signature on birth certificate, 73
  signature on death certificate, 84
Surname
  books on, 46
  on death certificate, 81
  1881 census indexed by, 90, 95
  of father, 71-72, 77
  on marriage certificate, 75
  of mother, 72
  multiple entries for, 61

  previous research on, 45
  probate calendar by, 122
Surname index
  1851 census, 107-109
  1881 census, 98
  not available, 109-110

T
Testator, 119
Town
  defined, 18
  indexed by streets, 102-107
Trip to England
  in research process, 8-9, 178-179
  visit to Family Records Centre, 65
Twins, 70
Tything, 18

U
United Kingdom (U.K.)
  countries in, 13
  size and population, 14

V
Verifying evidence, 9-10
Village, 18
Vital Records Index: British Isles, 141

W
Wales, 13
Wapentake, 18
Ward, 18
Web sites
  Ancestral File, 27-28
  British Isles Family History Society—U.S.A., 32
  Cassell's Gazetters, 16
  census information, 89

county record offices, 176-177
Cyndi's list, 33
family, 7-8
Family History Centers, 39
Family History Library, 5, 27-29
Family History Library Catalog, 28, 44-45
Family Records Centre (London), 65
Family Tree Magazine, 177
familysearch, 5, 27-29, 39
Federation of Family History Societies, 19, 107, 177
GENUKI, 29-32, 107, 134
International Genealogical index, 27-28
Latin word list, 23
Office for National Statistics, 65
Ordnance Survey Gazetteer, 15
Periodical Source Index, 37
place index, 54-55
Public Record Office, 108, 176
Society of Genealogists, 138
Source Guide, 28
See also Internet resources
Will
  contested, 163
  holograph, 119
  inability to find, 172-174
  nuncupative, 119
  obtaining copy of, 123-125
  pre-1858, 160-161

  probated, 162-163
  who could make (post-1857), 118
  See also Probate records
Workhouse
  census records and, 115
  illegitimate birth in, 71
Working class, 21